Silenced Voices

Dear Andy & Carol,

Great you could
make it!

Inez Hollander

Ohio University Research in International Studies

This series of publications on Africa, Latin America, Southeast Asia, and Global and Comparative Studies is designed to present significant research, translation, and opinion to area specialists and to a wide community of persons interested in world affairs. The editor seeks manuscripts of quality on any subject and can usually make a decision regarding publication within three months of receipt of the original work. Production methods generally permit a work to appear within one year of acceptance. The editor works closely with authors to produce a high-quality book. The series appears in a paperback format and is distributed worldwide. For more information, contact the executive editor at Ohio University Press, 19 Circle Drive, The Ridges, Athens, Ohio 45701.

Executive editor: Gillian Berchowitz
AREA CONSULTANTS
Africa: Diane M. Ciekawy
Latin America: Brad Jokisch, Patrick Barr-Melej, and Rafael Obregon
Southeast Asia: William H. Frederick

The Ohio University Research in International Studies series is published for the Center for International Studies by Ohio University Press. The views expressed in individual volumes are those of the authors and should not be considered to represent the policies or beliefs of the Center for International Studies, Ohio University Press, or Ohio University.

Silenced Voices

*Uncovering a Family's
Colonial History in Indonesia*

Inez Hollander

Ohio University Research in International Studies
Southeast Asia Series No. 119
Ohio University Press
Athens

To obtain permission to quote, reprint, or otherwise reproduce or distribute material from Ohio University Press publications, please contact our rights and permissions department at (740) 593-1154 or (740) 593-4536 (fax).
www.ohioswallow.com

Printed in the United States of America
The books in the Ohio University Research in International Studies Series
are printed on acid-free paper ♾ ™

18 17 16 15 14 13 12 11 10 09 08   5 4 3 2 1

Library of Congress Cataloging-in-Publication Data

Hollander, Inez, 1965–
  Silenced voices : uncovering a family's colonial history in Indonesia / Inez Hollander.
      p. cm. — (Ohio University research in international studies. Southeast Asia series ; no. 119)
  Includes bibliographical references and index.
  ISBN 978-0-89680-269-8 (pb : alk. paper)
  1. Dutch—Indonesia. 2. Hollander, Inez, 1965—Family. 3. Indonesia—History—1798–1942. 4. Indonesia—History—20th century. I. Title.

DS632.3.D88H65 2008
929'.209598—dc22
                                                            2008038418

This book is dedicated to Peddy Francken,
  who was killed in Sukamiskin Prison in Bandung.

This book is also to honor the memory of his two daughters Joke and Willy,
  who were ambushed during the Gubeng transport in Surabaya.

And this book is for his son Harry,
  for having the courage to speak up and speak out:
  silence is never golden.

To articulate the past historically does not mean to recognize it "the way it really was." It means to seize hold of a memory as it flashes up at a moment of danger.

—*Walter Benjamin*

Contents

Illustrations

Acknowledgments

This book could not have been properly documented if my family had not provided me with their letters, e-mails, and interviews. I would especially like to thank the children of Jacques Francken, notably my own mother, Laurine Francken-Hollander, and aunts and uncles, Tineke Francken-Everard (and her husband, Ab Everard), Enny Francken-Harm, and Jack Francken. Henri Francken's son (another) Harry Francken, was also very helpful, providing details about my great-grandmother. Mannes's daughter, Marjolein, was especially supportive in writing me letters with facts, stories, photos, and details about Mannes, his wife Kitty, and their life at Kali Jompo. The memories of Huib Wiedenhoff, who, with his brother, played at Kali Jompo as a child, were very important for recreating the childhood and plantation milieu of the Francken children.

Harry Francken, Peddy's son and only survivor in my family of the Gubeng transport, was an invaluable and candid source and has become, in the process, a close friend. As he was a witness to a silenced event in our colonial history, his testimony and remembrances, however difficult at times, are important and have made this book into what it is. He and my mother were also readers of the book as it was still in manuscript form, and I am thankful for their interest and encouragement. Harry, who, before I met him, did not want to have anything to do with his colonial past, became a research buddy and was also instrumental in finding and scanning the pictures for this book.

Nienke Lels-Hohmann proofread an earlier version of the manuscript carefully and found typos no one else had managed to find. Other readers of the early manuscript include my good friends and fellow scholars Marian Janssen and Ger Janssens. I also want to thank Maria Nieuwenhuys-Lindner for sharing her unpublished memoir with me. Upik Djalins, one of my Southeast Asian graduate students, helped me out with some of the translations of Malay words. Sylvia Tiwon, a UC Berkeley colleague in the Southeast Asian Department, helped me finalize the glossary of Malay terms.

Since my employment at the Dutch Studies Program at UC Berkeley, I have been extremely grateful not only for my exposure to one of the greatest research libraries and collections of Dutch-language books in the United States, but also for my conversations with my Indonesian students, who have been so gracious in answering some of my questions and listening to my stories. While I had been afraid that these students would look harshly upon Holland or anything or anyone, like myself, that they might associate with the colonial experience, they have all assured me that, aside from the dark history we share, the two countries are still in a strange way connected. Evidence of this is that there are still many Malay words in Dutch and many Dutch words or derivatives thereof in Indonesian. Some of the more hilarious moments with these students were when we discovered these words by accident. Edward Said calls this strange marriage a "legacy of connections," and rather than condemning this legacy, we should use it as a bridge and foundation for a new and healthy postcolonial relationship.

A number of historians have been extremely helpful in sharing their knowledge and thoughts with me. Jeroen Kemperman of NIOD in Amsterdam was one. Winnie Rinzema-Admiraal was always helpful and informative. She is an unusual historian because she is also a witness: she was interned at the Japanese camps and survived the turbulent postwar period in Java. Willy Meelhuijsen was just as helpful. I cherished his gracious letters and encouragement. William Frederick was of critical importance to this project not only because of his knowledge of the revolution, which far exceeds mine, but also because he encouraged and supported me in my research and urged me that this was a story worth telling. I believe this book would not have seen the light of day without his continued support and devotion.

My friend Karel Berkhout of NRC Handelsblad was pivotal in getting access to the appropriate archives at the Ministerie van Buitenlandse Zaken (Ministry of Foreign Affairs). Hans den Hollander at

Buitenlandse Zaken was very helpful in finding the dossiers on the planters' conspiracy and sending me copies in the mail.

Gillian Berchowitz, Senior Editor at Ohio University Press, as well as Bill Frederick, worked on the last few versions of this manuscript with a tremendous amount of patience, spot-on comments, suggestions, and editorial advice. The craft of writing is really rewriting, and without their help, interest, and insights, this manuscript would not have been rewritten and would still be sitting in a box under my bed.

Lastly, I want to thank some dear friends and family with whom I have shared this story: These are my mother, Laurine Francken-Hollander, my father, Ton Hollander, who died in 2006, Alfred Birney, Christy Blackie-Taylor, Laurine Boelaars, Tim Boelaars, Geert Buelens, Betty Chandra, Megan Cohen, Upik Djalins, Karen Englund, Ageeth Heising, Dani and John Hoenemier, Sally Hogarty, Ellen Hollander, Marc and Minke Hollander, Regine Schade, Cornelia IJssel de Schepper, Sue and Tom Imperiale, Marian Janssen, Ger Janssens, Rafal Klopotowski, Dorothy and Bud Lake, Nienke Lels-Hohmann, Gerard Lemmens, Melanie Light, Geert and Mietsie Mak, Lynn Ruth Miller, Mia Mochizuki, Che Mott, Claire Petitt, Maria Roden, Maureen de Rooy, Pauline Schrooyen, Xenia Soster-Olmer, Willem ten Wolde, Brian and Denise Tuemmler, Albert-Jan and Marlène van Creveld, Martine van der Laan, Mary Waltermire, Karel Woltering, Kitty Zijlmans, and doubtless others whom I have forgotten to mention here. I also want to thank my students who participated in the Indonesian Connection (Colonial Literature) course that I taught at Berkeley in the fall of 2006. Some students in this class had Eurasian roots themselves, and their stories of their families reinforced my belief that postcolonial Indies families share a hidden pain that is a continuing source of intrigue to their children, grandchildren, and great-grandchildren.

Finally, I want to mention my darling children, William and Caroline, for being so patient when mommy could not tear herself away from the computer or a book. I am hugely indebted to my loving husband, Jonathan Lake, who is always there when I have lost all faith in myself. Life is humbling, but never as humbling as what Harry, Fré, Peddy, Joke, and Willy Francken went through.

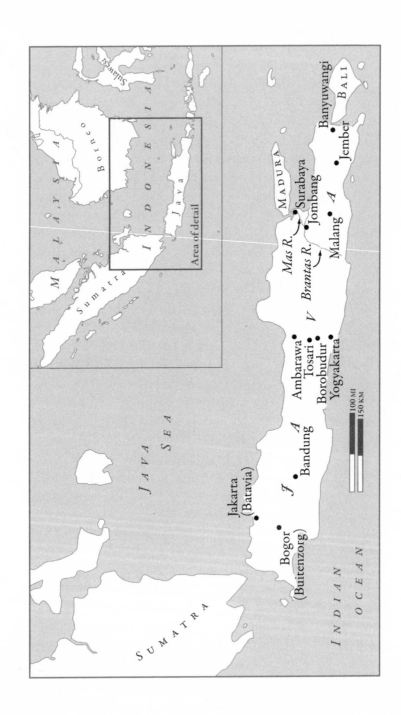

Introduction

I am the family face;
Flesh perishes, I live on.
—*Thomas Hardy*

As soon as the leaves were forming piles in the woods and the wind and rain left marks on the windowpanes, my mother would take me to my grandfather's grave in Bloemendaal, the Netherlands. I never knew my grandfather, Jacques Francken. In the black-and-white picture that sat on my mother's antique desk, he was a bald man with a stern expression on his face, and I felt no curiosity whatsoever about this paterfamilias.

At the graveyard, I would wade through piles of leaves. I remember enjoying the earthy smell that came from the wet and rotting leaves, dead branches, and black soil. It was the smell that went into new life, a life that was oblivious of everything that went before it. Like the dead leaves, my dead grandfather and our shared family history were too much things of the past, and I was too busy growing up.

When I was small, I was dwarfed by the big headstone of my grandfather's grave. As I grew up and learned to read, I tried to decipher the eroded letters on my grandfather's enormous, mossy tombstone. When I was about eleven years old, I noticed my grandfather's unusual place of birth for the first time: it was not Amsterdam, Rotterdam, or The Hague but Jombang. Jombang is in Java, but no one in my family ever talked about Java or Indonesia. It was a hidden past and, as I found out much later, taboo even to remember. Bad things had happened, people had suffered, the family had lost something it could never recover . . . and so it was better to be silent and move on.

When I started asking my mother about my grandfather's colonial past, I met with resistance and denial: "Why do you want to know? My father never talked about it . . . I know very little" and "None of us talked about those Indies dealings, it was like a closed chapter, a finished book that you put away and never bothered to open again."

But once I was older and had children of my own, I wanted to know more. The fact that the whole subject seemed shrouded in silence made me all the more curious. Was this a family cover-up, a conspiracy of silence or, at its most innocent, a muted agreement to pay no attention to the subject so it might fade away and be forgotten over time?

I have come to see this denial on my family's part as a form of self-censorship, which to some extent plays out in Dutch society as well. The average Dutch person will be able to tell you all about the Second World War, the German occupation, the Holocaust, Anne Frank, and the hunger winter of 1945, but when you ask him when the Dutch East Indies were liberated, what exactly happened during the police actions, and when Indonesia gained independence, that person may well draw a blank.[1]

Colonial history is no longer a standard part of the Dutch school curriculum, and yet most everyone is familiar with the greatest Dutch novel, *Max Havelaar* (1860), by Multatuli. This book, which exposed the exploitative cultivation system of the colonial class and the corruption of the Javanese aristocracy, has left such a mark on the Dutch psyche that the consensus seems to be that most everything the Dutch did in Indonesia was evil, coercive, and politically incorrect.

The climax of the story I am about to tell occurred at the height of the Indonesian Revolution in 1945, yet the event is difficult to retrace in Dutch and Indonesian history books. English-language sources describe this story, but Dutch sources scarcely mention it.[2]

When my great-aunt, Fré Francken, was one of the first war widows to return from the Indies in January of 1946, she sat down in my grandparents' living room and said, "I'm going to tell you my story, but I will tell it to you only once."

While my grandmother was pouring tea, Fré told a troubling story that she would repeat only twice, shortly before her death, to an aunt and to a close friend. But since she first told the story in 1946, there have been mostly whispers and rumors that gradually vanished as Fré and my grandparents' generation died.

There were gaps in Fré's tale, some of which I have managed to fill by writing this book. In short the story is this: Fré was married to

Peddy, the youngest brother of my grandfather Jacques. In the 1930s Peddy and Fré were running Kali Jompo, the Francken coffee and rubber estate in the eastern part of Java, outside of Jember. They had two daughters, Willy and Joke, and one son, Harry.

When the Japanese invaded Java in 1942, Peddy was arrested by Japanese troops, interned separately from his family, and finally imprisoned. Fré and her children were interned soon thereafter but survived Banyubiru, one of the worst camps in Central Java. After the Allied liberation in August of 1945, they found out that Peddy had died in Bandung on March 15, 1945. They did not know and would never know anything about the circumstances of his death or where he was buried.

In October 1945, Fré and her three children were evacuated to the eastern port of Surabaya. During another evacuation within Surabaya (which, due to bad timing and bad luck, coincided with the Indonesian Revolution), Fré's transport was attacked by Indonesian independence fighters and her two daughters were killed. Harry was injured but survived.

Fré and Harry never talked to each other about the transport again; they were classic cases of severe posttraumatic stress disorder. The critical reader might think this is a typical (albeit tragic) story that happens in wars and revolutions. What is atypical about it is that neither Indonesian nor Dutch historians have given it the kind of weight it deserves. The extreme forms of violence against non-Indonesians (besides the Dutch and other Europeans, the Chinese, the Japanese, Eurasians, and the Arab population in Java were just as much a target) have not been properly documented, as there has been a tendency to downplay or ignore the excesses as being largely committed in the name of a good cause, Indonesian independence.

What needs to be highlighted here is that unlike the misinformed and misguided Dutch government of the time, many Dutch colonials, like my great-aunt Fré, had come to see the Indies as a lost cause. They were determined to leave anyway, and thus were no threat to the independence of the emerging Indonesian Republic.

This book is not an attempt to vilify Indonesian independence fighters or to diminish the importance of the revolution. On the contrary, the fact that Harry's sisters were killed by Indonesians but that Harry himself was saved by one shows rather pertinently that times of war and revolution are never black and white or fights between pure good and pure evil—it is the gray area that reveals elements of salvation that we need to cling to and share in order to carry on with dignity and respect.

Nonetheless, because the violence of these events has not been fully acknowledged, I have felt compelled to write this book and give the violence a face, rather than allow it to be a statistic that does not bleed. The exploitation and hardships of nameless Javanese peasants in Multatuli's *Max Havelaar* do not have the desired effect on the reader until the author inserts the moving story of Saïdjah and Adinda. Willy and Joke are the Dutch Saïdjah and Adinda and although this is a provocative statement to make, I believe provocation is sometimes necessary in order to be heard and thus have this story gain its place in Dutch colonial history.[3]

As for the documentation of the violence during the revolution, one of my Chinese Indonesian students urged me to tell my family's story here, for in more recent outbreaks of Indonesian violence, especially against the Chinese population, identical atrocities have been committed. Freek Colombijn commended historian William Frederick for showing "that rogue violence during the Indonesian Revolution (1945–1949) was not merely tolerated, but probably consciously exploited by the military and political leaders of the Indonesian Republic. The use of violence as a legitimate means to solve problems was thus already institutionalized at the birth of the independent Indonesian state."[4] My book can serve as a reminder that a diligent documentation of these incidents can bring both perspective and healing. Even before publication, this manuscript has worked as a salve for the wounds in my own family. It came more than sixty years too late, but it is healing nonetheless.

Because the last generation of Dutch children who grew up in the Indonesian archipelago is now beginning to share its stories with relatives and friends, I should say something about how I compiled this family memoir, as a guideline for people who want to lay down their own family histories. Because family archives and documents regarding my forebears' times in the Indies had been lost in the war, I was confronted with huge gaps in the narrative. I was afraid that I had come too late and my grandparents' and great-grandparents' generations had taken all the information with them into their graves. Thus in my imagination and dreams, my grandfather's tombstone became a high, impenetrable wall.

My first "living archive" consisted of my relatives in my mother's generation, the cousins of Willy and Joke, who were the nieces and nephews of my grandfather, Fré and Peddy. Through interviews I did in the Netherlands with several of them, and thanks to the ease with which one can communicate via e-mail these days, I gathered little bits of information, memories, and sometimes actual breakthroughs in stories where I thought I had nothing but loose ends. Apart from interviewing, it is important to go back to the interviewees and verify information as well as ask new questions. Revisiting the information and mulling over the bits and pieces is an exercise well worth the effort in resurrecting and framing the story.

But it was a difficult process, and there was too much missing information. One of my biggest challenges was a geographic one. I live in California, and in order to write a story about colonial times in the Indies, the two best places to be are Indonesia and the Netherlands. I could combine my research in the Netherlands with family visits. But while I was yearning to go to Java and see some of the places, smell the air, and visit the archives, I was skeptical whether the family story could be reconstructed in full, even if I went there in person. To make up for this, I relied on novelists and journalists who were contemporaries of my great-grandparents and grandparents. How did they write about the stifling heat, the mold-forming humidity, the extraordinary food, the strange but intriguing superstitions of the Indonesians, and the many exoticisms of their surroundings? E. M. Beekman has argued that this kind of literature "will always remain an important part of the total colonial experience" as it is first-hand experience rather than the second-hand reflection of historical analysis.[5] Colonial texts are some of the more interesting Dutch texts on record, exactly because they are so far removed from life in the polder and on the farm. Much of this literature has not been translated into English until now, and I hope my translations will make this book all the more interesting for an English-speaking audience.

Although my knowledge of Malay vocabulary has significantly increased during the writing of this book, I cannot speak or read Indonesian, and therefore Indonesian sources and experiences have been completely closed off to me. No doubt this has given the book a Eurocentric bias, and regrettably, it has been impossible for me to penetrate and represent the Indonesian side of this story in full. The only opportunity I have had to mitigate this is through my contact with Indonesian students in Southeast Asian Studies who came to me to learn Dutch.

Access to the archives in the Netherlands, such as Nationaal Archief and Koninklijke Bibliotheek in The Hague and Koninklijk Instituut van de Tropen and Nederlands Instituut voor Oorlogsdocumentatie in Amsterdam, is not straightforward.[6] Access to some of the Indies archives relating to the war is restricted, and permission to see them needs to be obtained in writing. The Netherlands does not have a Freedom of Information Act but does have an *Archiefwet* (Archive Law) since 1995. Besides unrestricted-access archives, there are A-archives (restricted access) and B-archives (very restricted access). The term for opening these archives to the public is seventy-five years.

In a 2000 report, a government official, R. van der Ploeg, charged that the archives had too few means (financial, technical, and staff) to present material to the public and online. As a result, too many archives are not used in their proper capacity.[7] While large public archives like NIOD and NA have finally digitized a list of their collections, in order to browse the collections themselves, one has to travel there in person and request the material for perusal in the various reading rooms. For the A and B archives permission is required in advance, so it is wise to ask for and obtain permission before traveling to Amsterdam and The Hague.

While many people after the war were notified about a death in the family by the Red Cross, due to the chaos in Java after the liberation and the difficulties of collecting and disseminating information, there were many others who did not even get that notification and thus may have been kept in limbo for the rest of their lives. Still others, like my great-aunt Fré, received a date and place of death and a formal letter from Queen Wilhelmina, but no further details at all. One needs to know this kind of specific information to recover from trauma. I advise the reader who wants to do a similar search to be prepared before contacting and/or making the trip to the archives, as my experience with the archives was frustrating.

As a literary historian and biographer I have tried to write a biography of a place, our family estate, Kali Jompo (1884–1957), and the members of my family who lived there. My Indies relatives finally spiraled down from being colonizers to being colonized by the Japanese. They ended up as exiles in the Netherlands, a country that has never fully acknowledged their contribution, their status, or their suffering. This is their story, but in the telling, it has become mine as well.

Family Tree

Jacobus (Koos) Johannes Hubertus Kervel (1828–95)
X **Laurina F. T. van Roessing van Iterson** (1824–91)
(Widow of Albertus Gerrit van Krieken)

Eight children:
1. Maria Laurina Suzanna Kervel
2. Laurina (Laura) Catherina Arnoldine Kervel
3. **Antonius (Anton) Jacobus Kervel**
4. Hermanus (Herman) Leonardus Kervel
5. **Jacoba (Coba) Johanna Huberta Kervel** (great-grandmother of the author)
6. Adrienne Albertina Petronella Kervel
7. Jacobus Kervel
8. Lucia Jeanne Kervel

Ad. 5. **Jacoba (Coba) Johanna Huberta Kervel** (1863–1949)
X **Jacques Marinus Wilhelmus Francken** (1850–1929)
(great-grandfather of the author)

Six children:
1. **Laurina (Laurine) Jacoba Maria Frederica Theresia** (1885–1942)
2. Henri (Herman) Maria Mathieu (1886–1937)
3. **Herman (Mannes) Jean Marie** (1888–1948)
4. **Jacques (Jacques) Willem Eugene Ferdinand Marie** (1891–1949) (grandfather of the author)
5. **André Marie** (1895–99)
6. **Ferdinand (Peddy) Adriaan Marie Francken** (1897–1945)

Ad. 1. **Laurine** married twice:

(1) **Josephus (Jos) Antonius Hermanus Everard**

(2) Thomas Maria Alphonsus Bonnike

Ad. 3. **Mannes** married **Catharina (Kitty) Diest Lorgion**

Ad. 4. The author's grandfather married Johanna (Anny) Maria Augustina Josepha Huijsser

They had five children: Jack, Tineke, **Laurine** (the author's mother), Enny, and André

Ad. 5. **André** died in Tosari (see chapter 3)

Ad. 6. **Peddy** married **Frederika (Fré) Klazina Zuidstra** and they had two daughters and one son:

(1) **Wilhelmina (Willy) Jacoba Louise** (1930–45)

(2) **Johanna (Joke) Laurina Maria** (1932–45)

(3) **Henri (Harry) Jacques Marie** (1937–)

The names of people discussed in the book are given in bold print.

Chapter 1

FROM POLDER TO EMPIRE

> Don't denigrate Indonesian spices. . . . Remember that
> they turned hordes of Calvinists into determined bandits.
> It's unbelievable what those shopkeepers did in their search
> for new wares. They became seafarers and then found out
> that they could also change into robber barons, with their
> fortified warehouses.
>
> Edgar du Perron, *Country of Origin* (1935)

Americans will say that they like and know spicy food: do they not
have Mexican cuisine with its fiery jalapeño peppers? So when I was
about to bring over my American husband-to-be to my sister's house
in The Hague, I told my sister Ellen it was no problem to get some
take-out from Toko Frederik, one of the many Indonesian restaurants you can still find there. To impress Jonathan, Ellen asked for
the "extra spicy."

"Have you tried Indonesian food before?" Ellen asked as she
handed Jonathan a Heineken. Jonathan said he had, but during our
appetizers I saw that he was already in trouble. His eyes were
welling up with tears, and beads of perspiration were forming on
his forehead. At dinner, the perspiration became so dramatic that
Jonathan finally said, "A bit spicy, huh?" which did not prevent my
sister from dumping some more beef rendang onto his plate. At this
point poor Jon had rolled up his shirtsleeves and pants legs and the
sweat was gushing from his head. Because paper napkins would no
longer do, I handed him a dish towel, which he held under the
kitchen tap, wrung out, and put on the top of his head. Ellen and I

had not shed a single drop of perspiration. Indies food was in our blood, and well, the hotter, the better.

Ten years later, when I ate at an Indonesian restaurant in San Francisco with Jon and my children, Caroline and William, my son started asking me all sorts of questions about the gamelan music, the shadow puppets that were hanging from the walls, and the map of the Indonesian archipelago that was mounted above the hostess's head. I was well aware that people have kids to be humbled by the Socratic maxim that the only thing we know is that we know nothing, but it threw me off because I felt I was supposed to know *more*. After all, the Dutch had been in Indonesia for three and a half centuries.

Out of frustration and with a hint of snobbery, I then sputtered, "We once had a farm in Java," which was a shabby echo of "I had a farm in Africa," the unforgettable opening line of Isak Dinesen's *Out of Africa* (1937). I realized that I knew nothing of this "farm," my family who lived there, or the Indonesians who worked the land. Why did I know so little?

Spurred on by William, I decided to find out more, in a process that felt like following the concentric circles on a lake after you drop a stone in it. The stone had been dropped by my ancestors in Java more than a century ago, and I found myself on one of the outer circles, trying to get in. This meant reading around some of the key events rather than immediately shooting for the center. I needed context—how come my fellow countrymen started their empire in the East Indies in the first place? Why did those seventeenth-century burghers board those rickety wooden ships to explore and conquer?

Long before my own ancestors ventured out to the Indies, and even before they were pulling their potatoes out of the soggy land, the English called the Dutch Republic mere "vomit of the sea." Throughout history, Holland has been challenged by its waterlogged environment. Whereas in other European countries royalty and aristocracies waxed and waned depending on how much land they possessed, in Holland there was not much land to go around, and if one owned any at all, it was not very useful as there was a high chance of losing it again to the sea. By the end of the sixteenth century the Dutch did not accumulate land at home but focused on other lands where resources could be traded and lands could be conquered and plundered.

The Dutch Empire actually started with Holland's Flemish neighbors to the south. When the successful port city of Antwerp in Flanders fell to the Spanish in 1585, many of the affluent Protestant merchants of Antwerp moved their business to Amsterdam harbor, which became a boom town for shipping bulk. Entrepôt trade, meaning the trade based on the transit of goods between Europe and the rest of the world, still represents more than half of the country's national income today.[1] Back in the 1600s the city by the Zuiderzee already formed the perfect midway point between the Baltic and the Mediterranean. Due to what Jonathan Israel has called the "Dutch blend of political intervention and business efficiency," in 1602 regents, citizens, and merchants worked together to set up one of the most successful trading companies of all time, the Verenigde Oostindische Compagnie (VOC), or Dutch East Indies Trading Company. "In the first half of the seventeenth century," historian Mike Dash writes, "the VOC was not only the most important organization, and one of the largest employers in the United Provinces of the Netherlands; it was also the wealthiest and most powerful company on earth. It had become powerful and wealthy by putting trade and profit ahead of every other consideration."[2]

By the middle of the seventeenth century, the Dutch did not merely transport bulk goods across Europe, but had emerged

> as the uncontested masters of the spice trade. They had achieved what the Portuguese had sought in vain: dominance in the trade in pepper and cinnamon and a near-total monopoly in cloves, nutmeg, and mace. . . . Whereas the finances of Portugal's Estado da India had never made the leap out of medievalism, hamstrung by the clumsy royal monopolies and endemic corruption, the annual fleets setting off from the *Zuiderzee* were backed by the full panoply of joint-stock companies, shareholders, and boards of directors. In time the East India companies of the Dutch and their English rivals grew into the armies and administrators of imperialism.[3]

For me personally, teaching a lesser-taught language like Dutch at UC Berkeley, it is hard to believe that the first foreign language the Iroquois Indians in the seventeenth century spoke was Dutch and that this language was heard in most harbors around the globe.[4] Fernández-Armesto writes that "although Spain's empire was far bigger and more populous, it stretched neither so far north nor so far east. Dutch trading factories, sovereign forts, plantations, and whaling stations were scattered, north-south, from the White Sea to the southernmost tip of Africa and east-west, from Nagasaki to Pernambuco and the Hudson."[5] The Dutch florin went as far as the U.S. dollar goes today. "The name of Amsterdam," Charles Boxer writes, was "known in remote regions round the world that had never heard of London, Paris, and Venice."[6] The wealth that poured into Holland should not be underestimated. Some voyages had returns of more than a thousand percent, and according to Dash, "the fortunes that the merchant princes of Amsterdam and Middelburg accumulated exceeded in some cases those of European royalty."[7]

It is easy to get caught up in the velvet, lace, and ruddy complexions of Amsterdam burghers showing off their newfound wealth and the parties that went with it in portraits and scenes by Dutch masters such as Frans Hals and Jan Steen. Growing up in Holland, I had seen these paintings that portrayed the sudden wealth of Holland's citizenry in the Golden Age, but did I ever, as a child roaming the halls of the Rijksmuseum and the Mauritshuis, ask myself from what or from whom this wealth had been extracted? What had been happening in precolonial Indonesia?

Although Indonesia's early history is much less documented than that of the Netherlands, before the Portuguese touched down in the Indonesian archipelago, Muslim traders arrived, and in some cases stayed, converted the population, and intermarried. In the fourteenth and the fifteenth centuries, there were two major states, Majapahit (East Java) and Malacca (Malaya). The latter was the greatest of the Muslim trading empires.

Many islands of the Indonesian archipelago, like Java, consist of volcanic mountain ranges with dense, impenetrable rainforest. Volcanic soil and the many rivers give Java enormous agricultural potential, but because the landscape was so hard to penetrate, with rivers forming the only infrastructure between the coasts and its interior, precolonial Java was sparsely populated until the nineteenth century.[8]

Due to Malacca's trading routes, which reached via Venice into Europe, the Dutch had been exposed to pepper, clove, nutmeg, mace, and gold. The first Dutch expedition (1595–97) to Java was led by the ineffectual Cornelis de Houtman. Everywhere he touched down, he fired his cannons and slaughtered members of the local population, yet in 1597 De Houtman returned with "enough spices on board to show a profit: it had been demonstrated that even an incompetent voyage could make money."[9] Did any of my forebears stand on the Amsterdam quays to witness De Houtman's return? Did any of them work in the warehouses where these spices were stored? Did the thriving Amsterdam trade enter my ancestors' minds at all? Probably not, as my family, based in the old cities of Heusden and Leiden, seemed merely to have been preoccupied with owning some land and weaving the famous Leiden broadcloth.

As the Dutch were crossing the seas in their ships, they were mapping the world: "The world unfolded in the pages of Blaeu's Atlas. In engravings and tympana, Holland hoisted the globe onto his back."[10] As lens crafters, diamond cutters, and mapmakers, the Dutch displayed an extraordinary optical finesse that would extend to the invention of the microscope and reveal itself in the world of painting. In the seventeenth century there seemed to be a visionary urge to capture the world by recording it from all angles. In the domestic interiors of the painter Johannes Vermeer, maps on walls dominate the rooms to remind the viewer that the Dutch were engaged witnesses to world exploration.[11]

The Dutch fascination with the possibilities of an empire, which was always envisioned as more of a trading empire than a colonial one, did not necessarily amount to an overriding interest in power, religion, or exploration. The fire in the belly of the average seventeenth-century Dutch burgher was greed, as Joseph Conrad said, and the desire for spice burned in his chest "like a flame of love."

In the seventeenth century, nutmeg and pepper had become important and expensive commodities. While pepper was extensively used to mask the rank odor and flavor of rotting beef in a time when refrigeration did not exist, nutmeg was rumored to be the cure for the "bloody flux," the common cold, and the "sweating sickness" (better known as the plague). Nutmeg had other benefits too, all of which were exaggerated except for the fact that the fragrant spice does have a preservative effect when it is rubbed into meat.[12]

In the eighteenth century, when spices had become less important and prices had stabilized, trade with the Far East continued, the focus now being on coffee, tea, sugar, cotton, and silk. Holland had lost its edge as an empire, and the eighteenth century in Holland was, compared to the action and toil of the seventeenth century, an uneventful age. Conrad Busken Huet writes that the seventeenth-century riots had turned into civilized get-togethers, the "pamphlets were benevolent without pepper or salt," and "after 1713 it was no longer possible to make a career in the navy." The patricians, whose ancestors had accumulated fortunes through their association with the VOC, "lived peacefully in their elegant homes on the *Heren-* or *Keizersgracht* or at their country estates in the *Gooi* area or along the river *Vecht*."[13]

Dutch colonialism in Southeast Asia really began with the unfailing and ruthless leadership of Jan Pieterszoon Coen (1587–1629), whose austere portrait with long fingers, a pointy nose, and a manicured beard sitting on top of a big white collar as big as a Gouda cheese I still remember from elementary school. Coen became the fourth governor-general (the highest colonial post in the Indies), monopolized the nutmeg and mace trade, and founded Batavia (present-day Jakarta) in 1619 by building a big fortress on the remains of the city of Jayakĕrta, which two thousand VOC troops had managed to conquer and burn down.[14]

Coen's cold-blooded reign of terror, especially against the Bandanese people of the Spice Islands, was criticized by the VOC directors, the Heeren XVII, in Amsterdam. "We had wished that it could have been accomplished by more moderate means," they reported back to Coen, who was indignant since it was the directors themselves who had originally recommended that "the Bandanese should be overpowered, the chiefs exterminated and chased away, and the land repopulated." Coen protested by voicing a familiar racist stereotype: "They are indolent people of whom little good can be expected."[15]

The Oriental, as explicated by Edward Said in his influential book *Orientalism* (1978), was hereby established as the inverted mirror image of the hard-working Calvinist Dutchman. The easy stereotyping of the Indonesians apparently had not changed by the time my mother overheard her father saying that Indonesians could not be trusted: "If they want to steal something from you," he told her one day, "they put it in a different place in the house, and if you do not seem to notice its disappearance, they take it home." Even though I think it is funny that my mother used the same strategy when getting rid of my father's old clothes, which he would not throw away himself, I am embarrassed by the level of distrust and racism in my family and have wondered whether the stories of faithful and loving indigenous nannies in the literary works of Rob Nieuwenhuys, Jeroen Brouwers, and others are expressions of a misplaced nostalgia and mutual devotion that never existed. Were my ancestors ruthless imperialists, or was there more to it than the earning of an easy guilder?

Long before my ancestors disembarked in the harbor of Batavia, the tall homes and warehouses of old Batavia were made out of brick, brought over from Holland; the streets looked like those in Amsterdam, lined with trees and running "in dead straight lines, [with] churches, schools and even canals built in the European style. The whole town indeed made few concessions to the tropics."[16]

In the eighteenth century the Secretary of the British Admiralty, John Barrow, visited Batavia and described it as one of "the neatest and handsomest cities in the world": "The streets are laid out in straight lines, and cross each other at right angles. Each street has its canal in the middle, cased with stone walls, which rise into a low parapet on the two margins. At the distance of six feet from this parapet wall is a row of evergreen trees, under the shade of which, on this intermediate space, are erected little open pavilions of wood, surrounded with seats where the Dutch smoke their pipes and drink their beers in the cool of the evening."[17] There is not much left of old Batavia in present-day Jakarta, but in the oldest part of town, amidst the gloomy slums, the canals still exist, drained and filled with garbage, or so my Indonesian students tell me.

Although Jan Pieterszoon Coen was not the first governor-general in Java, he is probably the only governor-general Dutch people remember. He had an iron will and dogged determination, and he was callous and cruel. His motto said it all: "Don't despair, don't spare your enemies, for God is with us." While it is amazing to realize that an area slightly bigger than Amsterdam could be the launching pad for an empire fifty-two times the size of the Netherlands, one should realize that this empire was created through aggression and cruelty that would be completely unacceptable by today's standards: "By the 1620s, the VOC had worked to death or expelled practically the entire indigenous population of the Bandas. The company imported slaves to work the plantations; Javanese convicts and Japanese mercenaries were called in to mop up any local resistance."[18] At the same time, Ricklefs reminds us that "these were cruel times, and [that] Indonesians showed no greater gentleness"; but because the Europeans had the more advanced weaponry, they came to dominate and thus subdued and killed more Indonesians than vice versa.[19]

The English East India Company (1600) was the VOC's fiercest competitor. The rivalry between the two nations culminated in the 1623 Amboyna massacre, of which Giles Milton gives a lurid account: twelve English trading agents in Ambon were arrested and extensively tortured on charges of espionage. Ten of the men were executed, which caused a diplomatic quarrel in Europe as well as much anti-Dutch sentiment. The massacre, which was still remembered fifty years later, when it was dramatized by the English poet John Dryden in his tragedy *Amboyna, or The Cruelties of the Dutch to the English Merchants,* marked the end of the English presence in the

Indies. Instead, the English began concentrating on the Indian subcontinent, where they built their own empire.[20]

Meanwhile, the spice monopoly was carefully protected and maintained by controlling supply and demand in Holland: "To maintain the price at an artificially high level, the Dutch regularly staged spiced bonfires. . . . In 1735, 1,250,000 pounds of nutmeg were burned in Amsterdam alone. One witness saw a bonfire of nutmeg so great that the oil flowed out and wet the spectators' feet. An onlooker was hanged for taking a handful of nutmegs from the flames." A similar bonfire was lit in 1760. This time it was cinnamon, which caused a "fragrant cloud that passed over all of Holland."[21] The enormous fires were like the funeral pyre of the fading spice boom, for thirty-five years later the Dutch monopoly was broken by the English. Spices had become more available and less valuable. By the end of the eighteenth century the VOC was on its last legs, exhausted from internal dysfunction and debt, the latter largely a result of the many military conflicts in Java and the other islands.

But the Dutch had a major foothold in Indonesia, for Batavia had been founded, and thanks to Coen's efforts the city "rapidly developed into the foremost European military, naval and commercial base in Asia, far outstripping Goa and Malacca." As an enclosed and fortified city, it did not have much contact with areas that lay inland, but

> from the first it served as the general rendezvous for Dutch ships and cargoes converging from the outlying parts of the Indonesian archipelago, India, the China Sea, and Japan. It was also the principal Dutch military garrison in the East Indies and in the seventeenth and much of the eighteenth century, Batavia constituted the largest concentration of Europeans anywhere in Asia. The town acquired [all the usual civic institutions] of Dutch towns of the time. By 1700, there were about 6,000 Europeans at Batavia, almost as many as were then to be found in Dutch South Africa.[22]

Interestingly, Israel also writes that even though Batavia held the largest concentration of Europeans in Asia in the seventeenth and eighteenth centuries, the city "never developed an economically independent Dutch burgher class." Jean Gelman Taylor explains that the Europeans and local rulers did not consider themselves to be part of the established elite, but were inclined "to retain their identity as immigrants and their dependence on Europe, whilst the Eurasians [the people of mixed birth, the so-called Mestizo class] were divorced from the symbols of status of the colonial elite."[23]

The Mestizo or Eurasian group quickly outnumbered the European elite. Taylor writes that Dutch soldiers, an uneducated and displaced group, usually took native women as their partners and that they did "not pass on a typically Dutch bourgeois culture to their wives, mistresses or children."[24]

As early as the seventeenth century, Coen, who so eagerly hoped to grow the colony with native Dutchmen who would stay indefinitely, complained of the greedy opportunism of the Dutch, who were unwilling to put down roots in Batavia. Coen's criticism was to be heard throughout the colonial period and certainly was the prime reason for my family's presence in the Indies. In a letter to his VOC directors, Coen wrote that while Batavia was thriving inside and outside its city walls, the Dutch burghers were not interested in these local developments: "All they want is to grab riches in the easiest possible manner, so they can fritter them away in the Netherlands, instead of committing themselves for a while to stabilize Batavia."[25] In part, this also had to do with the limitations the VOC put on settlers. The newcomers were not allowed to engage in free trade or become entrepreneurs because the VOC ran the monopoly and was the only employer in town. "Drained and depressed by the muggy pall that hung limply over the settlement," these newcomers would not stay long in a town where disease "was rife, the canals swarmed with mosquitoes, and the midday heat was so intense that even [the VOC] did not require its clerks to be at their desks at noon."[26]

The high standard of living in the Dutch Republic, among the highest in Europe, also presented a problem for the Dutch colonization attempts around the world. Men who were thriving in Amsterdam would not risk hearth and home for an uncertain voyage to the

East or West Indies. Only people who had nothing to lose—the poor, destitute, criminal, and displaced—signed on with the VOC as a last resort. Coen was well aware of this and therefore suggested that orphans without "relatives, fortune or ties of sentiment to draw them back to Holland" might make good candidates for emigration.

As for the few Dutch women who did risk the journey and the diseases of the tropics, they would, in the words of Governor-General Hendrik Brouwer, "never stop complaining until they can return home and appear before their old acquaintances in their new riches." Besides, Brouwer implied, Dutch men were better off with indigenous women because "their children are healthier, and the women have fewer demands."

Apparently, by 1652 the VOC decided that Dutch women were not the solution but the problem and that unions with Asian women should be encouraged. The matter was hereby settled for the next two hundred years, which means that the oldest Indies clans may go back to Dutch men and women but that most Indies families derive from white male immigrants and Asian or Eurasian wives, some of whom were slaves.

In these mixed unions it was obligatory for the indigenous woman to learn Dutch and take on a Christian name, while she, if she were a slave, would be freed. Unlike the white elite of the British Empire, who frowned upon mixed marriages, Dutch men seemed to prefer Asian women as they had fewer material wants than European women. In addition, Asian women would not persuade their husbands to repatriate, their Eurasian children thrived better in the tropics than their European counterparts, and Eurasian children did not need to be sent back to Europe for their education. Taylor adds: "Thus through marriage Asian women joined the European community, bearing Dutch names and assuming their husbands' nationalities. [As a result] the dominant cultural influence in the household was Asian."[27]

Consequently, eighteenth-century visitors to the colony were struck by what they saw as Asian, not European, habits and traits in the ruling families of Batavia. They were shocked that women chewed betel, bathed several times a day, and were, in the visitors' view, much too indolent. Dutch visitor Nicolaus de Graaff writes: "These little ladies, in general Dutch but also Half-Castes and Mestizas, and especially in Batavia . . . let themselves be waited on like princesses. . . . [They are so lazy] that they will not lift a finger or anything. . . . [They are even too lazy] to raise their own children[, but all they do is] chew betel, smoke, drink tea or lie down on a mat."[28]

In the nineteenth century the lifestyle in the Indies had not changed much. Johannes Olivier writes: "The European avoids all strong physical exercise. There is a rule in the Indies that it is better to stand still than to amble, better to sit than to stand, better to lie down than to sit and better to sleep than to be awake. . . . The longer one stays here, the slower one becomes, one starts to speak Malay, one does not want to get up in the morning, one allows oneself to [be massaged] and one sits or lies down half the day, dressed in *sarong* and *kabaai* while smoking a cabal pipe."[29]

It was into this world that my newly arrived great-grandfather was launched. As he walked or was carried or driven through its dusty streets, late-nineteenth-century Batavia was changing from a big and luxuriantly green park into an urbanized and cosmopolitan town: sandy roads were paved, streetlights appeared, and the horse tram was replaced by the electric tram. Large European department stores (*maisons*) with cafés, restaurants, and lamplit shop windows were built. Batavia became a modern, posh city; Otto Knaap writes: "Batavia is a fancy city, a fanciness that is really quite ridiculous, because Indies society is largely made up of opportunists; it is not scandalous so much as commendable that for example, someone whose father sells currants and raisins in Holland can work himself up here to a position of power and authority."[30] Despite this influx of young opportunists like my great-grandfather who were seeking their fortune in the "new" and bustling city of Batavia, Rob Nieuwenhuys writes that the old Indies habits (carriage rides by moonlight and sitting on the open verandas enjoying the evening cool) remained.[31] It is at this moment in time, albeit in Surabaya, at the other end of Java, that my family history begins.

Chapter 2

CREOLE ROOTS

Your blood may not be mixed, but your spirit is.

Aya Zikken, *De Atlasvlinder* (1958)

The stories of the seignorial manner of the Mestizo class are revealing because they so compellingly resembled the indolent lifestyle of my Creole great-grandmother. I follow Jean Gelman Taylor's definition of a Creole as a European who was born in the Indies but had European parents. This was the case with my great-grandmother, the mother of my grandfather, Jacques Francken. Jacoba (Coba) Johanna Huberta Kervel was born in 1863 in Surabaya, the major port city of eastern Java.

According to my mother, Grandma Francken was a statuesque woman who was surrounded by servants all her life. My mother elaborates: "She was not very active and I never saw her walk! She did not seem to like children, was strict, reserved, and very stingy." My mother's cousins confirm my great-grandmother's sedentary lifestyle. One of them says, "I only remember her as a very old lady with a great number of double chins. She always sat in the same chair, behind a table, and I remember wondering how she made it to bed at night."

It is much too easy to condemn the ancestors one knows only through family gossip. In the many random readings in which I indulged in my early research, Lyndall Gordon's words resonate with me when I tried to imagine my great-grandmother's fixed pose: "Well-bred women in that period adopted a frozen manner. It was a sign you were a lady, a creature of low vitality and virtuous reserve. . . . Florence Nightingale reports that when middle-class mid-Victorian women went to bed at night they felt they were going mad and were obliged to lie down by day in an effort to subdue themselves to modish icons of domestic devotion and frail femininity."[1]

The only picture I initially had of Coba was the one that was printed on her little black-and-white "In Memoriam" card (see fig. 2.1). In contrast to the chilly impressions her grandchildren conveyed to me, I was struck by her friendly face. She has a playful smile, and her one eyebrow is lifted as if someone has asked her a question that she wants to ponder for a little while. She has a broad forehead, and her eyes are too far apart. Her lips are full, her cheeks meaty, and her teeth big. "A horse's head," one of my mother's cousins tells me.

Much later I obtained a photograph of my great-grandparents walking down a garden path (see fig. 2.2). The picture was taken in 1928, and this time Coba is not glued to her seat but seen ambling

Figure 2.1: Coba Francken (1863–1949), great-grandmother of the author. *Source: Laurine Francken-Hollander* Figure 2.2: Coba Francken and her husband Jacques Marinus Wilhelmus (JMW) (1850–1929) in 1928. *Source: Harry Francken*

next to her painfully thin husband, who would die a few months after the picture was taken. Coba wears an expensive, stylish winter coat and a typical twenties hat pulled over her eyes; it gives her a mysterious, ominous look. Coba Francken was certainly no society beauty, but maybe feminine beauty was defined differently in colonial Surabaya, a city that at the beginning of the twentieth century was described as a metropolis by the Dutch author C. M. Vissering. In her travelogue, she mentions the Surabaya city gardens and the Grimm Restaurant with its marble floors, potted palms, and Indies waiters dressed in immaculate white cotton. "In this restaurant," she notes, "one finds absolute peace and quiet," and it is cosmopolitan enough to outdo the "urban banality" of restaurants in Vienna, London, Berlin, or Paris.[2] Somehow, it is easy to picture my formal great-grandmother in these sophisticated colonial surroundings of servants and glamour.

Today not much of the former glitz remains. Surabaya is primarily an industrial city and port. By 1900, it had become the biggest town in the East Indies, bigger than Batavia. Aletta H. Jacobs, the first woman physician in the Netherlands, visited the Indies in the early 1900s and wrote about the city in the Dutch newspaper *De Telegraaf.* Her impressions of Surabaya are a little less flattering than Vissering's: "Surabaya is a city of trade . . . One notices this because of the crowded, busy and dusty streets, the high, ugly buildings which are business offices, and the mingling of the Chinese, Javanese, Arabs, and Europeans."[3] One should point out here that the dusty streets were sprinkled by coolies who carried about large water pots all day long. Jacobs continues: "Surabaya is not beautiful. . . . One lives here to do business, to make money. If one is successful at the latter, one hurries out of here, either back to Europe or to a better place in Java where one can retire on hard-won capital."[4] The Dutch novelist Louis Couperus, who visited the town in 1921, called it "a dirty city full of pretensions and greed."[5]

The Dutch journalist D. C. M. Bauduin makes the distinction between the lower city and the upper city. The lower city is the industrial part, crowded with traffic jams, swarms of people of all ethnicities, dark alleys, open sewers, and dusty slums. He adds in a rather prejudiced way: "In stinking, dirty *tokos* in which yellow faces grimace, one hears the clicking of the beads on the abacuses of the Chinese; they trade and barter everything that has any value in this world."[6]

After the Dutch colonials, like Coba's father (see fig. 2.3), worked in the lower city all day long, they would return to the upper and outer city, where there were endless boulevards with electric trams and white villas with red roofs. Unlike the slums of Surabaya, these homes had leaded glass, drapes, and marble on the floors. Coba was a sugar heiress. Her father had done well in sugar, possibly through owning sugar mills, because at the time the Kervels were in Surabaya all plantations were still run by the state. The Kervels' sugar fortune was not based on the "blood money" of the VOC, but was acquired by what came after it, notably the Nederlandse Handelsmaatschappij (NHM).

When the VOC went bankrupt in 1799 due to corruption, greed, nepotism, mismanagement, and debt, the imperial hegemony of the Lowlands was already a thing of the past. Overseas trading posts had been lost, and within the Indonesian archipelago Dutch dominance was limited. As Beekman argues, "The Dutch wanted a mercantile monopoly, not political annexation; their objective was the bottom line, not physical dominion."[7] Even the main island of Java, the focus of Coen's successors, was the scene of many internal conflicts and ethnic strife. Not until the efforts and ambitions of Governor-General Herman Willem Daendels (1808–11) was the Javanese infrastructure improved to the point where it finally became possible to reach all corners of the island via land, rather than sea.

Daendels, who served under King Louis Napoleon (Napoleon's brother and king of Holland during the French occupation), was succeeded by Governor-General Jan Willem Janssens, who had to concede defeat to the English when they showed up in Batavia with twelve thousand troops.

During the brief English interregnum Governor-General Thomas Stamford Raffles (who was later to found Singapore) took over the

Figure 2.3: Coba's father, Koos Kervel (1828–1895). *Source: Tineke Francken-Everard*

reins. He successfully pushed for many reforms, abolished forced labor, gave more legal status to the Indonesians, introduced financial reform, and initiated the land rent system.

While both Daendels and Raffles were more enlightened than their predecessors, under both there was a further breakdown of indigenous power structures. While members of the Javanese aristocracy were allowed to keep their positions, they were robbed of their sovereign rights and had to accept a dual Dutch-Javanese hierarchy. Thus, every Javanese regent was "assisted" by a Dutch resident, and although the Dutch were somewhat respectful of indigenous power structures and *adat,* they also used the aristocracy to collect taxes and land rents, and demand revenue from harvests.[8]

In 1814 the Indies were returned to the Dutch. The son of King William V of Orange, William I of the Netherlands, who had fled to England when France invaded Holland under Napoleon, became the new commander-in-chief and colonial legislator. At this point Holland was hardly the colonial powerhouse it had once been. Exhausted by war and economic depression, it had lost most of its overseas trade to England. Because the VOC had been a state monopoly, private landowning, entrepreneurship, or private trade had never been encouraged or stimulated in the Indies. To prevent a total loss of the Indies trade, Herman Muntinghe, a member of the Council of the Indies, urged William I to take measures. Muntinghe called for the founding of a new shareholder organization that would promote agricultural cultivation to produce tropical products for a low price. On March 29, 1824, the NHM was founded, selling shares and locking in the interest rate at 4½ percent. The king himself invested four million guilders in the NHM.

Lacking the VOC's strengths, such as owning the latest in ships, shipping technology, and accessible harbors, the NHM was unsuccessful at first. The 1825 economic crisis at home aggravated matters, and the NHM went nearly bankrupt. The company was then reorganized, moved from The Hague to Amsterdam, and by means of strict state control, more efficient management of deliveries, the transport of soldiers, and the sale of colonial products, became the sole "banker, commissioner, and business observer of the Indies government and trade."[9] Although this meant a rebirth of a market of colonial products, the NHM did not become fully profitable until an advisor to the king (and later governor-general), Johannes van den Bosch proposed that the trading company resort to the monopolies and labor-cultivation practices of the VOC. As with the former VOC, the *cultuurstelsel,* or cultivation system, was based on a government monopoly. Private landowning and enterprise were made impossible, and soon NHM came to stand for "Niemand Handelt Meer" (No One Trades Any Longer). Nevertheless, between 1830 and 1840 NHM shares jumped spectacularly, from 5.9 percent to 50.4 percent.

Van den Bosch, who knew that the Javanese did not like "to work under the supervision of Europeans" but preferred to "be directed by their own chiefs," stayed within the parameters of the system to bring about a forced harvest quota, a percentage of which was destined for export and sold to the Dutch for the market in the Netherlands. This market included tea, coffee, sugar, tobacco, cotton, cochineal, pepper, and cinnamon.[10] Van den Bosch's view of the Javanese was steeped in racism; he considered them "childlike," lazy, and in need of firm domination. The cultivation system resulted in slave labor conditions, "in which the peasants had to work two hundred days a year, unpaid, for the government [and, as such] the Dutch were establishing [a] tradition of exploitative commercial imperialism, which was to be widely followed in Africa, especially by the Belgians," Paul Johnson writes.[11] "In Indonesia itself," Johnson says, "where [the Dutch] were already absorbing other islands in addition to Java during the 1820s, they were setting the pattern of white-native hatred which was to mold this vast and populous country during the crucial decade of the 1940s and beyond."[12]

This white-native hatred would have catastrophic consequences for my family later on, and it might have had its roots in NHM and the cultivation system practices, activities that Coba's father (Koos Kervel) engaged in either directly or indirectly. As a friend of the Dutch king, Kervel might have owned NHM shares, and he definitely was involved in sugar selling or exporting.

The putting together of these facts made me uneasy. Multatuli's *Max Havelaar* (1860), "the book that killed colonialism," exposed the evils of the cultivation system: was Koos Kervel another Droogstoppel, the bourgeois villain in the book whose only joy in life was the pursuit of hard guilders? Did Kervel sow the seeds of the killing of his own great-granddaughters so many years later in 1945? It is a sensitive question that my family would certainly deny, just because they are defensive about it. Granted, Kervel may not have been a Droogstoppel at all, and his involvement with NHM may have been minimal, but feelings of awkwardness remain.

I decided to consult the family tree again. While Van den Bosch's cultivation system was in place from 1830 to 1870, Kervel would have profited from it only at the tail end of this period, for he was only two years old when it was established and forty-two years old when it ended. What his father or father-in-law did in the Indies is completely unknown, although they might have contributed to the kind of situation that the colonial critic L. Vitalis sketched: "On the roads as well as at the plantations one does not meet people but only walking skeletons, who drag themselves with great difficulty from one place to another, often dying in the process. The Regent of Suka-pura told me that some of the laborers who work in the plantations are in such a state of exhaustion that they die almost immediately after they have eaten from the food which is given to them as an advance payment for the produce to be delivered later."[13]

The fact that there was practically no Indonesian middle class certainly was an alarming premonition for the revolution that lay ahead.[14] Although my ancestors were entrepreneurs rather than the architects, implementers, and enforcers of the despicable cultivation system, they were imperialists and colonists whose money was contaminated: "When I had just arrived in Europe, someone cautiously suggested to me that my parents must have stolen their money in the colonies, because otherwise they couldn't be so wealthy," Ducroo, the alter ego of Dutch writer Edgar du Perron, says in *Country of Origin* (1935). At the end of the novel Ducroo also says, "I'm now forced to admit that for more than thirty years I have lived quite happily on money that was tainted."[15]

As I was dwelling on the skeletons in my ancestors' closet and trying to return to the narrative thread that I started with Coba, one of my aunts happened to run into Harry G. M. Prick, the biographer of well-known Dutch author Lodewijk van Deyssel (1864–1952), who was a contemporary of my great-grandmother as well as a friend of the family. When Van Deyssel's biographer found out that my aunt's grandmother was Coba Kervel, he told her that Van Deyssel thought she was "a great kisser," an image that clashes with my impression of the passive old lady in the front parlor. I was not aware of the link with Van Deyssel, so I immediately turned to the oeuvre of Van Deyssel and Prick's biography of him.

As it turns out, after Coba was born in Surabaya, the Kervels went on leave in Amsterdam, where they came to know the Van Deyssels. In his memoirs, Van Deyssel mentions that the Kervels lived at Vondelstraat 75, right by the entryway of the Vondelpark. I told my friend Maureen, who lives in Amsterdam, to bike by the house in the Vondelstraat and see what it is like. She e-mailed me the next day and told me it is beautiful, big ("spacious," Van Deyssel writes), and has a large sunroom with a gorgeous view of the Vondelpark. "By far one of the grandest places in the Vondelstraat," Maureen wrote.

Van Deyssel elaborates in his memoirs that Koos Kervel was married to Miss Laurina van Krieken (see fig. 2.4) and that they went

Figure 2.4: Coba's mother, Laurina van Roessing van Iterson (van Krieken)-Kervel (1824–1891). *Source: Tineke Francken-Everard*

back to the Indies in 1879–80 to prop up the family's "sizeable sugar fortune." This seems plausible: H. W. Dick writes that in spite of the 1880s collapse of sugar prices "caused by the rapid growth of beet sugar production in Europe . . . the industry emerged stronger than ever before."[16] Nonetheless, because the Agrarian Law of 1870 made it easier to own and develop land, Kervel may already have had his eye on the cultivation of coffee in the nearby highlands, or Oosthoek (eastern corner), of Java.

Coba was seventeen years old when the family returned to the Indies. Before leaving, she had been playing croquet with Van Deyssel *and* she had been kissed by the budding author. Or, as Prick writes, because she was taller than Van Deyssel, Lodewijk had kissed her "under her ear, an awkward spot but that did not matter as he had finally kissed her."[17] Whether she reciprocated the kiss, I was unable to verify, so her being a "great kisser" may well have been an embellishment on the biographer's part.

I did, however, obtain a delicious glimpse of Coba's older brother Anton in Van Deyssel's autobiographical coming-of-age novel *De kleine republiek* (1888). Van Deyssel's alter ego, Willem, is friends with Arthuur Meerel (based, according to Prick, on Anton Kervel), who said forbidden words like "damn" and showed him "dirty" pictures of women "with naked necks and exposed collarbones." The Meerel (Kervel) family was obviously more well-to-do than Willem's family; Willem wears Arthuur's hand-me-downs, and when the two boys travel by train to their boarding school, Rolduc, Willem becomes irritated by Arthuur's airs and his flaunting of his fancy leather gloves.

There are even rare peeks of my great-great-grandparents: while Mrs. Meerel is an indulgent, heavyset lady who feeds the boys cream-puffs, Mr. Meerel is annoyed when Arthuur starts crying on the train. Arthuur wants to tell Willem he is being sent to boarding school because he has been naughty. Mrs. Meerel tells Arthuur not to tell: "I would keep your secrets to yourself. Willem must have been naughty, too, haven't you, Willem, but once that has passed, it is over and one should not speak about it anymore." Arthuur says,

"But mommy, you have raised us all the wrong way," which triggers objections by Mr. Meerel and Arthur's subsequent crying fit.[18]

I thought it was poignant that this rare fragment of my great-great-grandparents' lives, preserved by the pen of Lodewijk van Deyssel, revolved around the silencing of certain events that happened in the family, just as it is ironic, or maybe fitting, that this story begins in Surabaya, as it will also end there. While my great-grandmother's roots were in Surabaya, three of her very own grandchildren found themselves uprooted, abandoned, and unprotected in one of Surabaya's exclusive colonial neighborhoods during the outbreak of the Indonesian Revolution.

It is not known if my great-grandfather, who was new to the colony, first met my great-grandmother, Coba, in Surabaya. My great-grandfather, Jacques Marinus Wilhelmus Francken (JMW) came from an upper-middle-class family in Leiden, the Netherlands. Why he left for the East Indies, possibly with some of his brothers, is not entirely clear. Bauduin lists the "obvious" reasons why young men took off for the Indies: they had either failed in the Netherlands or were attracted to a life of pioneering in the Indies. They might have felt hampered by opportunities in Holland, have failed academically, or simply have been craving adventure. When I looked up the Francken family tree, I saw that two of JMW's older brothers went to the Indies before him and even died there. One was a Chinese interpreter who died at the young age of twenty-six in Surabaya, while the other died in Malang in 1923. Maybe these brothers were considered the pioneers in the family. Their younger sisters were far from that: two of them became nuns in a convent close to home.

Incidentally, adventurers and opportunists were not at all welcomed by the colonial government. Dutch writer A. Alberts writes: "They feared the emergence of a societal group which, in the English-language colonies, was called 'poor whites.' To put it crudely, they wanted to prevent the growth of a white proletariat."[19]

Although "white trash" was shunned, the East Indies were nonetheless a magnet for what Du Perron called opportunistic career climbers, young men with a decent upbringing who were trained at the University of Leiden to speak some Malay and know the basics of Dutch and Islamic laws. JMW had studied in Leiden too, possibly with the objective of becoming an official in Java.

Java, the jewel of the Emerald Isles, turned out to be the great moneymaker for the Dutch Treasury. Ricklefs writes that "from 1831 to 1877 the Dutch home treasury received 832 million guilders. Before 1850, these remittances accounted for about nineteen percent of Dutch state revenues, in 1851–60 for about thirty-two percent and in 1860–66 for about thirty-four percent."[20]

The revenues from the Indies during the cultivation system revived the economy in the Netherlands. Ricklefs writes that debts were paid, taxes lowered, and the Dutch infrastructure was improved and built (the Dutch Railway System in particular), "all on the profits forced out of the villages of Java [while] returning significant benefits to only a small stratum of indigenous [Javanese] society."[21]

While Java was milked, little of the money went back into roads, hospitals, and schools on the island itself. The extravagance of it all may have been symbolized by the decadent lifestyle of the colonial ruler-in-chief, the governor-general. He lived in a luxurious palace in Buitenzorg (present-day Bogor) and made twice the salary of the president of the United States at that time plus more than half of his salary's amount for parties, receptions, and other incidental expenses.

Admittedly, my great-grandfather was no representative of the Dutch government but a private entrepreneur. In the course of the nineteenth century it became clear that people like him could make a nice little profit as the result of the Agrarian Law of 1870, which opened up the Indies to private landowners. The opening of the Suez Canal in 1869 and the improvements of the passenger ships occasioned a new wave of migrants. "By 1885," Ricklefs writes, "the proceedings from private plantations in the Indies were already ten times higher than those of the state plantations."[22]

I should add here that the cultivation system, which generated so much money for the Netherlands' treasury, came under attack during the rise of the Liberals, who came to power in 1848. The Liberal Party wanted to do away with protectionism (Dutch products carried lower import duties) and stimulate private landowning and enterprise, which finally materialized in the Agrarian Law. Under this law private citizens could lease land (the government would still own the land) for seventy-five years and start the cultivation of crops. Land that belonged to the indigenous villages or individuals could only be rented for shorter periods.

There are no details as to when my great-grandfather (see fig. 2.5) left for the Indies, but the family believes that it was before the opening of the Suez Canal. This means that he would have taken the train from Amsterdam to Genoa, from where he would have crossed the Mediterranean to Egypt. When he boarded in Genoa, the atmosphere of the Indies would already have been tangible, as he would have seen Sudanese staff with turbans on their heads and babus dressed in sarongs.[23] In Egypt the passengers would cross the desert to the Red Sea, where a boat waited to take them to Batavia across the Indian Ocean.

The date Van Deyssel mentions in relation to the Kervels' departure for the Indies, 1879–80, suggests that JMW might have arrived

Figure 2.5a and 2.5b: JMW as a young man. *Source: Harry Francken*

at around the same time or maybe even later, meaning that he would have traveled via the Suez Canal.

Whatever the itinerary, after an exhausting equatorial journey that took weeks, the first sighting of Java must have been a welcome change. The American author Eliza R. Scidmore described the arrival in Java as follows:

> In the earliest morning a clean white lighthouse on an islet was seen ahead, and as the sun rose, bluish mountains came up from the sea, grew in height, outlined themselves, and then stood out, detached volcanic peaks of most lovely lines, against the purest, pale-blue sky; soft clouds floated up and clung to the summits; the blue and green at the water's edge resolved itself into the groves and the lines of palms; and over sea and sky and the wonderland before us was all the dewy freshness of dawn in Eden.[24]

That first night in Java might have been magical for my great-grandfather. Leaving the sounds of the sea and the ship behind him, he must have fallen asleep while listening to the buzzing of mosquitoes, the scream of a lost parrot, the rustling of the palm leaves and tall ferns, and the sudden thud of the occasional coconut falling to the ground. JMW was young and doubtless very eager to start his life in the Indies.

When my great-grandfather arrived in the humid city of Batavia, Europeans were no longer living in the harbor or the oldest part of town. From the moment the first Dutchmen came ashore in the seventeenth century, Batavia, or rather Jayakĕrta, was a swampy, unhealthy spot where many Europeans died of swamp fever, which came to be known as Java fever. It took the Dutch almost two centuries to realize that they had to build their homes higher up and that their houses had to have an open structure for adequate ventilation, to prevent mold and avoid disease.

The American scientist David Fairchild described the Batavia of my great-grandparents as a sleepy little town that had at its center the Koningsplein, which was surrounded by ficus trees.[25] Aletta Jacobs stayed in a hotel that looked out over the Koningsplein: "Don't think for one moment," she writes, "that this square resembles its namesake in Amsterdam. Here the square is a vast, green meadow with cows and other animals. Across the busy and broad gravel road that separates us from the square, Batavia's population files past our porch."[26] The latter are, according to Fairchild, "turbaned Javanese [wandering] barefoot, swinging their beautiful bamboo hats, or carrying on their shoulders long bamboo poles with baskets at each end. Tiny ponies trotted along, pulling some white-clad official sitting back to back with the driver in one of the two-wheeled carts called dos-à-dos."

But Batavia was not the final destination for JMW. To travel inland, one had to apply for a registration card within twenty-four hours of arrival. Before he took off, my great-grandfather must have enjoyed the colonial and grand hotels, like the Hotel Des Indes, of which only the version in The Hague exists today. These hotels had, just like the homes, spacious porches or verandas where guests liked to relax in Indies leisure wear or Japanese kimonos. "It was a world of opposites," writes Karel Woltering, a friend of my family: "the closed house in Holland and the open verandas in the Indies." Fully clothed in the Netherlands and the fewest clothes possible in Java. Bland food in Amsterdam and spicy food in Batavia. White people here, "black" people there.[27]

The hotel rooms my great-grandfather stayed in had beds that were made without sheets or blankets because of the high temperatures, even at night. These beds would usually have the appropriate mosquito netting as well as body pillows to stem excessive perspiration at night. The English named these pillows "Dutch wives," a reference to the fact that in earlier colonial days the Dutch had to make do without their women and hug their big body pillows instead. At all times the rooms were well ventilated to prevent mold from forming on walls and floors. After his stay at these hotels, JMW may have crossed Java, or perhaps he never touched down in Batavia, but stayed on the ship, which might have made a stop at Surabaya.

The story goes that JMW met his future wife in one of the sugar factories owned by her father in or around Surabaya. The American naturalist Albert Bickmore visited one of the sugar factories outside of Surabaya in 1868 and provided this account:

> As we neared it, several long, low, white buildings came into view, and two or three high chimneys, pouring out dense volumes of black smoke. . . . The "fabrik" (factory) was in the rear. The canes are cut in the field and bound into bundles, each containing twenty-five. They are then hauled to the factory in clumsy two-wheeled carts called *pedatis* with a yoke of *sapis* (cattle). . . . The mode adopted here of obtaining the sugar from the cane is the same as in our country. It is partially clarified by pouring over it, while yet in the earthen pots in which it cools and crystallizes, a quantity of clay, mixed with water, to the consistency of cream. The water, filtering through, washes the crystals and makes the sugar, which up to this time is of a dark brown, almost as white as if it had been refined. . . . After all the sugar has been obtained . . . the cheap and impure molasses that drain off are fermented with a small quantity of rice. Palm-wine is then added and from this mixture is distilled the liquor known as "arrack."[28]

The word "arak" carries a familiar echo. I have always heard that word in my family but never knew what they were talking about. Bickmore tells me it resembles rum and that it was considered "the most destructive stimulant that can be placed in the human stomach, in these hot regions." Arak was already around before the first Dutchmen settled in Java—the drinking of arak was much safer than the drinking of water, which was frequently contaminated. The Dutch "started the day," Bernard Vlekke writes, "by drinking a fair-sized glass of gin on an empty stomach." "Our nation must drink or die," wrote Coen in 1619. The same "medicine" was taken frequently during the day. It is no wonder that the drinking of arak has been called "the principal industry of Batavia," and when the British arrived at the beginning of the eighteenth century, captain Woodes Rogers reported that his men "were hugging each other and blessing themselves" for having come to "such a glorious place for punch."[29]

Smoking, and in particular pipe smoking, was also popular in the Dutch East Indies. The pipe-smoking colonials sometimes mixed their tobacco with opium, a habit that the Chinese adopted and turned into a thriving opium trade. The use of stimulants was a welcome diversion to combat a general sense of discontent—to escape the heat, boredom, and lack of entertainment and culture, people sought oblivion in alcohol, tobacco, and opium. My great-grandfather liked his *borrel* (cocktail) and maybe even drank too much; his grandchildren, my aunts and uncles, remember that he hid his glass under chairs and behind curtains when Coba happened to walk in.

What was JMW's first encounter with his future wife in that sugar factory like? Was it noisy, was the air filled with the sweet scent of sugar? How and when did they fall in love? And did they in fact fall in love? Was their marriage as sugary-sweet as their first meeting?[30] Although the romantic in me likes to believe in love at first sight, it is more likely that Coba, the affluent sugar heiress, was a great match for JMW from a financial point of view. According to Jean Gelman Taylor, this was a typical pattern in Indies society that went back to the days of the VOC: "The crucial family links were not those between father and son but between a man and his in-laws. At the heart of the Indies clan were women, locally born and raised, who brought men into relationships of patron and protégé as father-in-law, son-in-law, and brothers-in-law."[31] Thus, Taylor believes that Indies society was not patriarchal but matriarchal and matrilineal. Because fathers sent their sons to Europe for their education, the property and landholding were passed on to the daughters, who often stayed behind and married Dutch newcomers to the Indies.

Because of their position of power over the Indies estate, matriarchal clans called the shots and sought out husband material among the newly arrived Dutch males from the Netherlands: "The clan enfolded the newcomer in a network of immigrants with locally born wives, Mestizo and Asian kin. At the same time, the clan eased adoption of Indies manners for the newcomers."[32]

Johannes Olivier, who wrote on the Indies lifestyle, claimed that it was a common practice for Dutch newcomers to marry into money: "If one wants to make a dazzling fortune rapidly one should meet with one of the many daughters which the gentlemen *oudgasten* [longtime Dutch residents] have had with their native slaves and women. [Even though they are illegitimate children,] they receive a great inheritance and money makes everything right." Marriage to these women is easy, Olivier writes, "for husband and wife each live in a separate part of the house and only see each other at big dinners. . . . Marriage is a great means to get ahead."[33]

Considering JMW's quick business successes and rise in the ranks, it seems more than probable that he married Coba soon after getting to Surabaya and that his settling into Indies society and the local economy was greatly facilitated by the wealth and network of his father-in-law. JMW was certainly not the only one who was absorbed by an Indies clan the moment he got off the boat. With the passing of the Agrarian Law, the abolishing of the cultivation system, and the loosening of immigration restrictions, a great many Europeans started arriving in Java: in 1872 there were 36,467 newly arrived Europeans, and in 1900 the number had more than doubled, to 75,833.[34]

But not all newcomers were, like my great-grandfather, absorbed and accepted into Indies society. Because of the great influx of new migrants, a society of expatriates coexisted next to the older Eurasian culture. It was around this time that the distinction was made between so-called *blijvers* (those who stayed more or less indefinitely) and the *trekkers* (those who went back to Europe after a few years). The trekkers shunned the Indies lifestyle and abhorred "Indianization" as a form of degeneration. Dutch writers Bas Veth and Johannes Hennus both commented that mixed marriages led to "verindischen" (Indianization), which, in turn, resulted in a loss of Dutch values and supposedly caused idleness, arrogance, an obsession with money, rank, and precedence, as well as illiteracy.[35] Louis Couperus noticed in 1921 that the indigenous *rijsttafel* was spurned in favor of wintry Dutch dishes such as heavy pea soup. The rijsttafel, according to the trekkers, would only lead to degeneration: "To prevent Indianization, obesity, and laziness, the European abolishes the *rijsttafel* and demands a lunch that he could not eat in the fatherland unless it was really cold and only then if he had skated for hours."[36]

As for the blijvers, they extolled Batavia over Amsterdam, Paris, and London as being more enlightened, more refined, and more hospitable. The relationship with the mother country and government in The Hague was tense: Indies people felt patronized by the government in The Hague, which, albeit far removed from Batavia, had far more authority than the Indies Council and the governor-general. The Hague was seen as a village, Busken Huet wrote, and the Indies were "too large, too removed, and too foreign to be governed by such a parochial place as The Hague."[37]

It is impossible to make assumptions as to how my great-grandparents behaved between the polarities of blijvers and trekkers: was JMW receptive to and did he identify with Indies culture, or did he cling to his European roots and culture? I cannot be certain about this, but I presume that, in spite of my great-grandmother's Indies roots, the family identified itself as European and as trekkers. The fact that the Indies have been such a forbidden subject in my family may well be an indication, if not a conscious attempt to deny and hide any form of Indianization that might have taken place at the time the family was there.

While JMW was a relative newcomer, I wondered how long the Kervels had been in the Indies. Consulting Coba's genealogy by writing the Foundation of the Stichting Indisch Familie Archief (Indies Family Archives; SIFA) in The Hague, I found that Coba's father Koos was born in The Hague as the son of Leonard Frans Kervel and Adriana Pauls. Coba's mother (the lady who fed Willem and Arthuur creampuffs on the train en route to their boarding school) was Laurina Frederika Theresia Roessing van Iterson. She was born in Heusden and married her first husband, Albertus Gerrit van Krieken, in Surabaya. They had one daughter, Jeanetta Agnieta Huberta van Krieken, who was also born in Surabaya. One year after Van Krieken died, Laurina married Koos in Probolinggo, a coastal town east of Surabaya where she had been living with her first husband. Like Koos's parents, Laurina's parents clearly show no Indonesian connection: they were Elias Cornelis Roessing van Iterson, who was based out of Heusden, and Susanna Gerardina van der Pol, who was born at Berkenrode, near Heemstede.

After Laurina married Koos at the age of thirty-one, they had eight children together. That seems like a lot of children in a short amount of time, although it was not out of the ordinary to have that many, even for a woman already well into her thirties and forties (Laurina had Coba when she was thirty-nine).

One genealogical mystery is that one of my mother's cousins clearly remembers an aunt, a younger sister of Coba, who lived in the Indies most of her life and went by the name of Eugenie. The genealogical records show that Coba had one half-sister (Jeanetta) and four full sisters (Maria, Laurina, Adrienne, and Lucia), but no Eugenie. Aunt Eugenie usually had a blanket over her legs because she had no legs, and once one of my mother's cousins, trying to peep underneath the blanket, asked her, "Dimana kaki?" (Where are your feet?), to the embarrassment of the adults. Who was this Eugenie—could she have been Koos's illegitimate child? Or was she a more distant family member whom the Kervels had taken under their wing and whom everyone referred to as "aunt" even though, strictly speaking, she was not an aunt?

Just as in families of the American South family identity, the sense that you were part of a clan and had certain responsibilities and duties toward your family, was extremely important in the Indies.[38] As the literary critic E. M. Beekman has pointed out, there are many more similarities between Indies families and antebellum Southern families. Aside from the fact that both societies were mostly agrarian and biracial in nature, particular aspects such as hospitality, gossip, chivalry, family honor, black magic, interracial sex, and a sophisticated oral tradition (derived from long nights of storytelling on the porch) were prevalent in both societies.

Apart from stories on the porch, there were also carriage rides and balls in my great-grandparents' time. Dancing was popular, but after the dance was over the men joined the other men to smoke Javanese cigars while the women practiced their French. At home they were probably waited on by four to six servants. In the kitchen there was a cook and for the children there were nursemaids. I also know that Coba had a chauffeur until she died.

While indolence and the pampered lifestyle of the ruling class are a recurring theme in the accounts of visitors, Dutch author and newspaper editor Conrad Busken Huet complained more about the boredom and the gossip that prevailed in a society that was devoid of any form of highbrow culture: "One hardly meets intellectual or literate people. The conversation revolves around cancans and those who have been in the Indies the longest time dominate it. Everyone knows everything about everybody. Hence the *ennui* of a people whose only aim is to kill time."[39]

Willem Walraven, a bookkeeper and journalist, also complained about the lack of culture, a feature of European life he missed most. To him the Indies was a place for shallow and materialistic people: "For them the Indies delivers where Europe does not. The convenience and the space. The absence of cold and dampness. The cheap servants. . . . Oh, this is a place for materialists, a real bourgeois country . . . but there are good things too, like *bahmie* and big bottles of beer!"[40] Kees Snoek, the biographer of the Dutch novelist Du Perron, called the Indies' cultural life a "pseudoculture" of *leestrommels* (reading trunks with magazines that circulated among the Dutch), orchestras, dances, itinerant theater, and music ensembles.[41]

Maybe the most striking and deplorable thing about the time in which my great-grandparents lived was the exaggerated sense of superiority of the Dutch over the Indonesians. In a manner of speaking, the Dutch were "guests"—an immigrant minority—yet they behaved as if they were equals of the Javanese aristocracy. In pictures from the time, Dutch families pose formally, dressed in white or in the Indonesian clothes, while their servants sit cross-legged on the floor, at their feet. Dutch novelist Augusta de Wit observed that, as late as 1900, "it was customary for lower-class Indonesians to squat in the streets, hands clasped, before passing Europeans, giving them the deference due a Javanese of rank, whilst even Western-educated Indonesian members of the colonial civil service were expected to sit on the floor before the Dutch officials to whom they reported."[42]

Many Dutch people took the Indonesians' obsequiousness for granted, and there were few colonials who considered it obscene or ridiculous. The Dutch writer Walraven was an exception. The relationship between the "small-minded motherland" and the "majestic colony" reminded him of "a parsimonious cleaning lady" who came to rule over "the life of an Olympian god." As Walraven's biographer, Frank Okker, has argued, Walraven was one of the few Dutch writers who genuinely believed that the Europeans did not belong in the Indies and that they were too busy robbing the Indonesians, who lived in great poverty already. "Our presence here," Walraven argued, "is based on injustice."[43]

But is it fair to condemn an entire society with the advantages of hindsight rooted in a more enlightened postcolonial world? My great-grandmother's birth and childhood in an extremely feudal, hierarchical, and colonial society was as accidental and beyond her control as my great-grandfather's early life in Leiden had been. However, with all the information that we have of colonial Indonesia and the Mestizo culture, it is not so surprising that Coba's grandchildren remember her as an extremely immobile grande dame who seemed glued to her chair.

Servants were never common in the self-made and egalitarian burgher society of the Dutch. Because of that, my great-grandmother, who had been born and raised in an Indies family, must have been a somewhat different, alien creature in her large house in Holland later on in her life. Whether she resisted it or not, my great-grandmother was probably more Indianized than she or her family would ever own up to being.

Chapter 3

TOSARI TRAGEDY

> To be a child, a happy, playful child again, to play barefoot
> in the river in front of the house of the Assistant-Resident
> ... to indulge in the fruits, the birds and the animals ... to
> indulge as only a child can in Java, a child that can play in
> the large grounds, in the gardens by big rivers.... a child
> that can climb in the trees with the big red blossoms.
>
> Louis Couperus, *Of Old People and the Things That Pass* (1906)

In 1885, at a plantation in or near Malang, Coba Kervel Francken gave birth to her first child, a daughter, Laurina (Laurine) Jacoba Maria Frederica Theresia Francken. She was twenty-two, and her newly married husband was thirty-five. Eighteen months later her first son, Henri (Harry) Maria Mathieu Francken, was born.

After Surabaya, Malang is currently the biggest city in eastern Java. Around the time the Franckens were there, Malang, which is at a higher altitude than Surabaya and therefore cooler, was being developed by the Dutch for the cultivation of rubber, coffee, and cocoa. The American art historian John van Dyke, who visited Malang in 1929, wrote, "It is a city in a wide valley surrounded by great mountains, a city of fine streets, with overhanging foliage, parks with huge waringin trees, good houses, lawns, flowers, a picturesque river with high bridges, a fine climate, and lastly ... good hotels, good drinking water, and a fine swimming pool."[1]

It is safe to assume that when my great-grandparents landed there, Malang was a "new town" with European-style bungalows on tree-lined avenues. Why Malang? The family must have owned land there, bought by Coba's brother-in-law Herman Everard, who was married to Coba's half-sister Jeanette. Herman came to the Indies after working for an Amsterdam firm as an apprentice. He had worked very hard, and when, at the end of the year, he was rewarded with a mere watch, he decided Holland was not for him anymore and took the boat to the Indies. By the time Coba and her husband settled in Malang, Herman was the director-in-chief of a number of plantations. Two of these were coffee plantations, Sumber Aju (near Malang) and Kali Jompo (near Jember). In exchange for inspecting the land, my great-grandfather had received ten shares of the original stock. He was there too when the land was prepared for cultivation, which was no easy feat. The dense vegetation of the tropical rainforest had to be cut down, after which the soil was checked and a master plan was drawn up to determine where the different buildings, factory, roads, and gardens were to be located. Jaap van der Zwaag writes in *Verloren tropische zaken* that the terrain would then be divided up in squares by laying out one line from north to south, the other from east to west. Further squares would be planned out, meaning the further cutting down of big trees and bush, which housed thorns, snakes, leeches, scorpions, and other poisonous animals. Indonesian laborers, sometimes dressed in no more than loincloths, would perform this backbreaking labor with small knives and axes.

Once the land had been cleared, it would be plowed with a *pacul* (a kind of sharpened hoe), and drainage and terraces (if necessary) would be put in. The coffee gardens would have protective roofs, made of palm, fern, or grass leaves. Van der Zwaag explains that these shade covers were meant not to keep the coffee plants cool but to keep the soil cool so that soil bacteria could not eat the humus. The leaves falling from these shade trees would in turn replenish the humus layer.[2]

Little is known of Sumber Aju. Evidently it did not thrive and was sold soon after it was bought.[3] This may have coincided with the birth of Coba's third child and second son, Herman (Mannes) Jean Marie Francken, in 1888. At that point the family found itself at the Limburg rubber plantation in Limburg, south of Malang and southwest of Turen. Did my great-grandfather have to learn more about the growing of rubber at Limburg?

Chronologically, this seems about right: in 1884 sugar prices slumped and the booming crops were coffee and rubber. When the price of coffee tanked as well in the late 1880s due to competition with Brazil, JMW must have placed his bets on rubber: "The demand for rubber from tire manufacturers was growing steadily, and it was obvious that the supply of rubber collected from trees in the wilds of the tropics could not meet the demand. As a consequence, the price of rubber went up: in the boom years of 1910 to 1912 it reached the price of more than $3.00 per pound. No wonder that owners of estates with unprofitable crops turned to rubber!"[4] Many coffee planters also switched to rubber because of the many coffee blights. Thus, over a period of twenty years rubber cultivation in Java rose from seventy-five thousand hectares in 1910 to five hundred and seventy-thousand hectares in 1930.[5]

Although rubber was cultivated rather late in the nineteenth century, it became the archipelago's most productive crop, and by 1930 "Indonesia was producing nearly half the world's rubber supply."[6] Because rubber was a relatively new crop, many planters had to learn from places like Buitenzorg, which had extensive botanical gardens and a research station. The Limburg plantation land was discovered by my great-grandfather, who, after having learned about rubber cultivation, became the administrator of Limburg and turned it into a success for the family. The 1945 book *Science and Scientists in the Netherlands Indies* contains a black-and-white photograph of the Limburg estate, showing a compound of low buildings surrounded by neatly organized rubber groves. It is somewhat likely, although by no means certain, that the family then bought Limburg and, as a reward for discovering the excellent land, my great-grandfather might have become the main shareholder of the limited liability company of Kali Jompo, near Jember, in eastern Java.

At first I had no concrete information on Kali Jompo, as the company archive was lost during the war and the restive postcolonial period that followed it, but the International Institute of Social History in Amsterdam lists a number of annual reports, the earliest one dating back to 1926. The later reports actually give the acreage and the terms of the land lease. Kali Jompo had two long-lease contracts, one dating back to September 30, 1884, consisting of 372 hectares (938 acres). This lease was for seventy-five years and was to end on September 29, 1959. The other contract went back to August 13, 1890, and consisted of 52 hectares (130 acres). This lease was for sixty-eight years and would end on September 28, 1958.

Curiously, in 1891, when my grandfather, Jacques Willem Eugene Ferdinand Francken, was born, the family was not living in Limburg or Jember but in Jombang, a major hub for sugar cultivation. Had my great-grandfather abandoned rubber. or had he been asked by his father-in-law to run one of the sugar plantations or factories?

My grandfather Jacques was Coba's fourth child, and I assume that at this point in time she may have looked a little bit like Aunt Ruyvenaar in the novel *De Kleine Zielen* (1901) by Louis Couperus, a Dutch writer who had grown up in an Indies milieu similar to my grandfather's: "Auntie was a rich *nonna* in sugar. . . . She was heavy and fat like a Hindu idol, wearing big diamonds; and yet she had something sweet and friendly as if she were about to promise a delicious *rijsttafel*. . . . She had something that had to do with living well materially, something puffy with soft, dark eyes."[7]

When my great-grandparents were in Java raising their children, they still lived the life that Scidmore described in her book on Java, of beautiful and spacious homes with verandas and tropical gardens. At night the family would cool off on the verandas by the light of lanterns. When Scidmore rode past such homes in her carriage, she remarked that these candlelit homes in the dark of night were the genre paintings of life in the Indies that ought to have inspired a tropical school of Dutch painters.

How did the Dutch entertain themselves when the museums and concert halls of Europe were so far away? Every family had the earlier mentioned *leestrommels,* in which one could find European magazines that the Dutch community shared. The Dutch may have been more active culturally than the British in India, who were passionate about their tennis, golf, cricket, and horse races. People met each other at social clubs and went to receptions, and the bigger towns put on musicals and operas. There were also weekly concerts at the *Harmonie* and *Concordia* clubs, where the men would dance in tails or uniforms while the women wore the same heavy velvet they would have worn during cold evenings in Amsterdam (some believed that the heavy clothing formed a protection against tropical germs and diseases).

As for Jombang, the name of the town I first discovered on my grandfather's tombstone in Bloemendaal, I got to see the place through the eyes of Willem Walraven, who visited the sugar town on the eve of the Second World War. Because Jombang's soil is enriched with the sediment of the Brantas and its side rivers, Walraven writes, the grass is "fertile" and the soil "greasy." For this reason Jombang became a center for sugar cultivation and factories.[8]

There is something strangely melancholic about Walraven, who ambles through the deserted town where no European is to be seen and where even the Dutch club, called *soos,* short for *sociëteit,* is empty, like an abandoned ship. The heyday of sugar was over in 1939, and the ghost town of Jombang was there to prove it. The soos, which my great-grandparents would have visited, is described like a relic, not demolished but "well-maintained," Walraven writes, "as if one hoped that the days would come back when complete operas with entire orchestras would perform for the white elite." By 1939, ten years before Indonesia's independence, Jombang's era of sugar, profits, and empire had come to an end.

The golden years, which my great-grandparents must have known intimately, became known as *tempo dulu* or *nostalgie tropique,* and the yearning for them was as strong as that for that lost era of moonlight and magnolias of the antebellum American South. For my grandfather this sentiment was probably symbolized by his boyhood years in the midst of a tropical and natural abundance that no Dutch child could ever replicate in Northern Europe. The novelist Jeroen Brouwers, who also grew up in the Indies, invokes that nostalgia in many of the childhood scenes in his autobiographical novels. He associates *tempo dulu* with the Edenic quality of Java's nature, which surrounded him as a child. Later on, only accessible by memory, it became a kind of Atlantis that would be submerged (and never rise again) when the war started and Indonesian independence became a fact.

Coba's fifth child and fourth son was André Marie, of whom I merely have his year of birth: 1895. Two years later the family was back where they had started, in Malang, where the youngest son, Ferdinand (Peddy), was born in 1897. The reason André's place or precise date of birth has not been handed down in my family may well have to do with an unfortunate event that happened in 1899. The Franckens had planned a vacation that year to Tosari, a location in the mountains with an exclusive hotel. The place was well known for its clean air and good living. Most Europeans did not tolerate the heat very well, so "going on vacation in the Indies meant going to the much cooler mountains."[9] The Franckens' destination in the mountains was located on the slopes of Mount Bromo, one of many still-active volcanoes in Java.

Travel in those days happened in little carriages called *sados.* "Coolies," mostly Chinese or Javanese servants, would follow on foot with the luggage. In an old travel guide I found that you could travel from Tosari from Malang within an hour and a half by car. After the ride up you could relax, cool off, and eat avocadoes, which were not native to Java but imported from Florida. Aletta Jacobs would make the same trip to Bromo in the Tengger Mountains in the 1910s: "It was a beautiful country road past big vegetable, fruit and flower farms, past coffee plantations and cornfields and with a constant view of the mountains."[10]

In the mountains, the journey would go past "dazzling ravines" and mountain paths hewn out of the hard rock.[11] The mountainscape was both lovely and terrifying, for in the background the volcano pounded and roared. I doubt whether Coba, who was known to sit all her life, would have undertaken the trip to the crater itself. Vissering mentions that on the hike up the path was sometimes so steep that one's feet pointed upright at a 90-degree angle and one had to stoop and lean forward to preserve balance. Because the Franckens were a large family with small children, their ultimate destination may more likely have been the beautiful hotel in Tosari. Tosari is more than five thousand feet up and, according to Eliza Scidmore, offers "one of the most famous views in Java, with the plains, the sea, and groups of islands in one direction, and the great Bromo, smoking splendidly, in another."[12]

The hotel itself offered interesting views too, and Vissering went so far as to call it a Garden of Eden. It was surrounded by gardens with all sorts of plants and flowers: cacti, cypresses, yuccas, hydrangeas, heliotropes, and white roses. There were vegetable gardens, tennis courts, and stables.

Aletta Jacobs was also pleasantly surprised by Tosari: "Tosari is known as the Darjeeling of Java. . . . It is covered in roses and the place is ideal for the relaxation of unsettled nerves. . . . The mornings are especially lovely. In the afternoons there is usually a dense fog which feels cold and wet. [It] is the most popular spot in Java for a cosmopolitan crowd. One plays tennis, walks around to be seen, there is some flirting going on, people make trips together and indulge in everything that occurs in *un monde où l'on s'amuse*."[13]

This cosmopolitan crowd must have formed a contrast with the native people of the Tengger plateau, Hindus who walked around with colorful headscarves and ash marks on their foreheads. According to Jacobs they were a "curious" people, and "less civilized" than the Javanese because of their "improper" clothing, which sometimes meant no clothing at all.[14]

The hotel in Tosari also served as a sanatorium. The high and pure mountain air was supposed to have a medicinal effect on the growing number of TB patients. On the Internet I found an old picture of the sanatorium/hotel, which looks like a dark wooden chalet in the Swiss Alps. The English author Somerset Maugham stayed there in 1921, and a postcard he mailed to his friends shows white people lounging on deck chairs as if it were a mountain ridge in Austria instead of Java. Vissering describes the mountain air as champagne that "bubbled" through one's veins. She further mentions that all around the Indonesians had left gifts of rice wrapped in palm leaves, flowers, and even money to please the mountain deities.

Had the little four-year-old André picked up some of the money or the rice? Had he broken a spell that would turn fate against him? Or was it the datura bush, the kecubung plants with the big white flowers, also known as witches' flowers, which are planted all along the way to Tosari? The Javanese believe these bushes can be fatal; there are stories that the pollen from the flowers, if blown out over someone who sleeps, can trigger coma, paralysis, or sickness.[15]

According to the family, André had slept in a room where a diphtheria patient had lain. In the nineteenth century, diphtheria was one of the most dreaded deadly diseases; its ability to spread easily often led to pandemic outbreaks. Diphtheria is an upper-respiratory-tract illness that leads to high fever, nausea, vomiting, and difficulty swallowing and breathing. In the developed world it has been virtually eradicated through the DPT vaccine, but until the late 1800s there was no cure.

Within a week André had a high fever and a swollen neck. I can imagine the consternation in the hotel room and the noisy volcano in the background. While there must have been doctors in Tosari because of the sanatorium, either there was no antitoxin or it arrived too late, and the little boy died, suffocating in Coba's arms. Apparently my great-grandmother became hysterical and may have been sedated. My great-grandfather and grandfather went on horseback down the mountain to fetch a little coffin.

My mother thinks that the quick burial had to do with Islamic law, but it seems more likely that people were buried swiftly because the decomposition process in the tropics is much more rapid. No one knows where the little one was buried. "Oma [Grandma] Francken refused to talk about it later on," my mother writes in an e-mail. She also tells me the story that my grandfather, years later, had to bury his oldest stillborn daughter on a somber autumn day in Holland. Would he, amidst the falling leaves and rain, have thought of the journey on horseback with his father in 1899, when he helped carry up the little coffin to the hotel? My mother thinks he processed neither event adequately: "He never even mentioned these deaths."

Once the coffin arrived, the family must have prepared for a burial with a Catholic priest present. How did they say good-bye in the foggy atmosphere of Tosari? Were they aware of the Hindu superstition that says that when Mount Bromo roars, it is ready to devour a young child? What was the burial like, and how does one say good-bye to a child who at four, has reached his most adorable age? What went through his siblings' minds? Laurine was fourteen at the time, almost a young woman, Henri was twelve, Mannes ten, Jacques eight, and little Ferdinand only two. They went up the mountain with six children and came down the mountain with five.

I wondered why there is not a single picture of André and why we do not know his place of birth or where exactly he was buried. What did he look like, this Dutch child who knew so little of the country of his parents, a place of polders, canals, and windmills—all he knew and the last thing he would know was the color of the roses, the cacti, the heliotropes, and the discontent of Mount Bromo.

What was it like for my great-grandmother to return to the house in Malang without the missing child? Did the house carry many memories of André? Did she, when she saw her other boys running barefoot through the creek, playing with the water, and making little sailboats out of coconut shells and palm leaves, only see the child who was no longer there? Did her servants tell her that at sunset André's spirit was still there, hovering somewhere among the waringin trees in the back? Had memories become dearer and more real to Coba than the routine of the unforgiving heat and the numbing boredom of everyday life in the tropics? Did Coba and her husband want to leave because of André's sudden death, or was the decision to repatriate made because the boys were at an age when they needed good schools?

Whatever the cause of their departure, in 1900 the furniture was sold at a *vendutie* (auction). Bauduin explains that these auctions were held because transport of the furniture would be too costly, while the Indies style of furniture would not match a European interior.[16] While the furniture was carried out of the house, the Francken sons, Henri, Mannes, Jacques, and Peddy, were told to say good-bye to their *babus,* who had been sleeping on thin mats on the floor beside their beds. They probably also had to put on socks and shoes for the first time—socks that itched and shoes that pinched, for these children had been running around barefoot all their lives. All they knew were the bright colors of the jungle, the smell of the coconut oil that their babus used on their hair, the pungent aromas of the rijsttafels, the drum of the monsoons on the tin roofs of the verandas, and the cries of the monkeys that jumped from tree to tree. Holland would be the opposite: cold, gray, flat, clean, disciplined, sterile, and dull. When my grandfather went to Jesuit school in Katwijk and started learning his first Latin conjugations and Greek alphabet, he must have missed the colorful paradise he had left behind. An Indies childhood was something that people carried with them for life. In many cases, this chunk of tropics nostalgia would grow larger in their minds the more removed they were from it.

I. P. C. Graafland, who wrote under the pseudonym Creusesol, argued that tropics nostalgia was most pronounced when the cold fogs and rains of Holland pervaded everything else: "Voilà, right next to your hearth in Holland you behold in your imagination, framed by the mists of time, a panorama of that country, of that rich, lovely, splendid island, our Java! There is a story that says that the volcanoes of that island have powerful magnets inside of them. These magnets are at their strongest when people are surrounded by Dutch fogs and when the skies hang leaden above a dismal winterscape."[17] I assume that my grandfather thought back to the Indies often, even though he did not talk about it with his family. It would be more than twenty years before Jacques Francken would return to his country of origin.

Chapter 4

A NEW CENTURY, A NEW AGE

> She was a child of two worlds, of two eras. Though her
> blood was pure, she was a stranger at home and a stranger
> in that other world. And that was the curse of the Indies.
> It was not that you sacrificed fifteen or twenty years for
> the sake of an easy old age. No it was that you were rooted
> up and transplanted, and while you yourself hungered for
> your native soil, your children were different.
>
> Madelon Lulofs, *Rubber: A Romance of
> the Dutch East Indies* (1931)

The trip to Europe must have triggered profound culture shock in my grandfather, who was around nine years old at the time. After a tropical childhood in which the bright colors of nature, penetrating smells, and intense heat were the dominant forces, the gray, colorless, and cold climate of the Dutch winter and the flat landscape would have given him the impression that he had lost paradise forever. Many writers who grew up in the Indies remember the alienating sensation of arriving in Holland for the first time. They had lost another world that would never come back but that would generate a constant memory making and a profound nostalgia. Jeroen Brouwers found his first sight of Holland disappointing as he did not see the stereotypical windmills, tulips, or farmers in wooden shoes. To escape this new reality, he, together with Du Perron and others who were born in the Indies and who felt uprooted upon arriving in Europe, almost immediately escaped into the memories of the world they had left behind.[1]

The transition from relative freedom to the drab discipline of Catholic school may have been very disorienting for my grandfather and his siblings. The Dutch novelist Hella Haasse, who also grew up in the Indies, writes about the awareness of "being different" and not blending in with the Dutch who had grown up in Holland. In her novel *Heren van de thee,* one of the characters, Jenny notices, "Mommy is born in the Indies, in Semarang, and me too, we are all born in the Indies, except for poor little Betsy. When we were in Holland, I noticed that we were different. We are white and blond and yet we are not Europeans. I immediately notice it with people like us."[2]

For many Dutch people and Eurasians who repatriated to Europe, Holland was almost too vast a contrast. When the well-known Indonesian writer Pramoedya Ananta Toer spent some time in the Netherlands, he compared the organized and rule-ridden country to a coffin: "Alles is *geatoerd*" (everything is arranged). The historian Willy Meelhuijsen said essentially the same thing when he told me in a letter: "In Holland you find more hedges, ditches, and gates than wilderness."[3]

As my grandfather had to get used to socks, shoes, a wet climate, a colorless polder landscape, and the rigorous academic discipline of the Jesuit secondary school where he learned to love the classics, the Indies entered a new era. While the Agrarian Law of 1870 and the abolishing of the cultivation system had improved general conditions somewhat, the tax system was such that improved infrastructure and entrepreneurial activity in the Outer Islands, all of which benefited European plantations, mines, and industries, was paid for by the Javanese rather than the Europeans.[4] This disparity did not go entirely unnoticed in Holland. Supported by liberal politicians such as W. R. van Hoevell and the publication of *Max Havelaar,* in 1899 C. T. van Deventer published a critical essay, "Een eereschuld" (A Debt of Honor), in the literary magazine *De Gids.* He argued that it was high time to pay back to the Indonesians what the Netherlands had extracted over the years. In 1901 Queen Wilhelmina ordered an investigation into the welfare of the Indies, which led to the Ethical Policy. With this policy, which aimed to improve local conditions by investing in schools and such, the colonial government's debt of forty million guilders was also remissioned by the Netherlands government so that Batavia could start with a clean slate, without further indebtedness to the mother country.

Actions speak louder than words, however, and unfortunately the Ethical Policy consisted more of words than of actions. According to Ricklefs, actual economic development and indigenous welfare were limited to infrastructure projects. Other potential good intentions and policy changes were undermined by the exponential population growth. In 1900 the indigenous population of Java and Madura had reached the 28.4 million mark, from about 5 million at the end of the eighteenth century. By 1920 that number had increased another 6 million, so that "nearly 70 percent of the Indonesian population . . . was living in Java and Madura" (which made up only 7 percent of the total land area of Indonesia). The population growth was most disastrous in the big cities, where most of the people lived in shantytowns and huts without proper sanitation. During the monsoons these homes would flood, causing malaria, cholera, and typhoid fever outbreaks.

The challenge for the colonial administration was that in order to feed, educate, and provide adequate health care for such a rapidly growing population, one needed, besides a thriving economy, an efficient set of policies to keep up with the demand for essential services. The Ethical Policy, however well intentioned, fell short on most counts. In 1930, for example, there were still only 667 doctors in Java.[5]

Education, one of the main emphases of the Ethical Policy, was dominated by Snouck Hurgronje's "Association Theory," which had the objective of giving the Indonesian elite a Western education so that Western values would trickle down to the general population and win out over, or at least compete with, the influence of the growing Islamic nationalist movement. Mass education was supported too, but the education of women was not pursued.

While more Indonesians had access to education in Dutch at Hollandsch-Inlandsche schools (HIS), few reached Hogere Burgerschool (HBS), secondary school, which prepared students for university; even fewer were sent to universities in the Netherlands. In

1905, Ricklefs writes, no more than thirty-six Indonesians entered HBS. The first local university-level schools became available after the 1920s: a Technische Hogeschool (engineering school) in Bandung and a Rechtshogeschool (law school) and a Geneeskundige Hogeschool (medical school) in Batavia.[6]

Most likely the Franckens left in 1900 because Europe was a better place for the continued education of their sons and only daughter. Of course Europe itself was, at the time, on the cusp of modernity. Exciting new developments in technology and science made headlines in the newspapers of the time: the Curies discovered radium and Röntgen implemented X rays. Marconi introduced wireless telegraphy—the radio. Malcolm Bradbury writes: "All the great cities of the West were changing, rebuilding, electrifying, modernizing, adopting new civic styles of architecture and taste, showing the spirit of the *belle époque,* art nouveau, and *Jugendstil.*"[7]

On a more mundane level, outhouses became a thing of the past as indoor plumbing, along with central heating, revolutionized the domestic sphere. Horse-drawn carriages began to be replaced by automobiles. Electricity, the telephone, and the first airplanes became some of the great modern innovations. My grandfather must have marveled at all these new Western things—having grown up in Java, he was, as in a time machine, catapulted from a predominantly rural country into a modern world of futuristic, alien, and strange new phenomena. Did this increase his sense of exile and not belonging, or did my grandfather embrace the brave new world of Western Europe?

The great breakthroughs in technology and industry had consequences for Kali Jompo too, where a cousin of the family, Jos Everard, had become the administrator. "Between 1880 and 1910, the three great developments wholly dependent on rubber—electricity, bicycles and cars—increased the demand for rubber to a near-doubling every five, then every three years."[8] After the economic downturn of 1890–96, the new century was promising, and the production of rubber contributed to an increased export and import boom, as reflected in the number of steamships that moored in Batavia's harbor: from 487 in 1885 to 1637 in 1913.[9]

As my grandfather and his brothers went to school and excelled at soccer for the Haarlem soccer club HFC, Kali Jompo continued to thrive under Jos Everard. Although there is no Kali Jompo archive, the Royal Library in The Hague has an online newspaper archive, and in the countless columns of financial news I found regular reports on the number of Kali Jompo Robusta coffee bags and rubber deliveries that arrived in the Netherlands. Because Kali Jompo became a public company in 1910, with shares that could be sold and bought on the Amsterdam stock exchange, all deliveries had to be registered, whether it was 5 bags of coffee from one ship or 251 bags from different ships. Dividend payments were discussed and determined at the annual shareholder meeting in Haarlem, over which my great-grandfather, JMW, presided. In Jos's years these dividend payments hovered between 10 and 20 percent.[10]

Back in Indonesia, few of the workers who picked coffee beans and tapped rubber at Kali Jompo truly benefited from the surging wealth of the new century. Even though the situation in East Java was better than average, with higher wages, P. Brooshooft accused directors like my great-grandfather of "solely" being interested in "large profits or dividends" while putting "the thumbscrews on the managers to economize as much as possible on wages and other expenditures. There is for example the scandalous situation," he says, "where coolie wages, which were lowered because of the sugar crisis [price decline] in 1883 by an average of five cents per day, have not been increased again, although the sugar industry now shows great profits. The owners, however, keep their money boxes as tightly closed as the deaf ear they turn to the voice of justice."[11] I cannot help but believe that Jacques Francken, who would succeed my great-grandfather in 1917 as Kali Jompo's director (shortly after he obtained his law degree from the University of Amsterdam), was no better than his father or his grandfather Koos Kervel.[12] For all I know they were all Droogstoppels for whom there was but one religion and one god (as Multatuli cried out): the religion and god of the hard guilder and the bottom line.

While the Ethical Policy was in many ways ineffective, it did create room for Indonesian emancipation and did shed light on the great disparities between the European elite and the indigenous underdog. The Budi Utomo organization, accepted and condoned by the colonial government because of its moderate progressivism, tried to press for educational and economic reforms but was soon competing with more aggressive organizations such as Sarekat Islam (Islamic Union), which grew quickly and sparked off violence in several villages in 1913 and 1914.[13]

Increasingly, Indonesians became aware of the essential inequality between the colonizers and colonized. Vissering picked up on it when she overheard a young Indonesian blurt out: "I hate the *totoks* [Europeans]. They are invaders who come here to become rich. I hate them! What are they doing here? All they do is look down on us." Vissering then says: "The boy verbalizes what one feels when one deals with his fellow Indonesians: hatred, repulsion, and jealousy."[14] The Dutch did not completely ignore the growing resentment and restlessness of the Javanese. Pressured by a number of Indonesian factions that have been mentioned already, the colonial government allowed the formation of a Volksraad (People's Council) in 1916. This was the first step in the direction of self-governance, even though the People's Council had no autonomy in the beginning.

The First World War broke out when Jacques Francken was still studying law in Amsterdam. The twentieth century, which had begun with so much promise, would get stuck in the mud of the killing fields of Flanders and Verdun. The Netherlands remained neutral in the conflict. This was both a blessing and a curse, because when the Germans started the Second World War, the Netherlands, which had not modernized its army, was conquered in a matter of days. But during the First World War the country remained untouched, even though the Dutch saw German Zeppelins, armed with bombs, fly over. Jacques and some of his friends would occasionally go to the border with Belgium, from where they could hear, in the distance, the explosions of the absurd trench warfare.

Because Holland was hardly affected by the war, Laurine and her brother Ferdinand (Peddy, a nickname he had from early childhood because Indonesians pronounce "f" as "p") returned to Java in 1914.

Peddy was only seventeen and still enrolled at Latin school. Laurine was twenty-nine years old and considered old because she was still unmarried. That same year she would marry Jos Everard, a first cousin and Kali Jompo's administrator. The fact that Jos was family and that Laurine was older than the average debutante raises speculation about whether the match was arranged. If so, one feels sympathy for Laurine Francken, who, on the steamer headed for the Indies, must have waited in anxious anticipation. The last time she had seen Jos, she was fifteen and he was twenty-nine. This age difference may seem substantial, but it was more accepted in those days, just as it was more normal for cousins to marry cousins, often with the intent to keep (Indies) wealth inside the family.

In a family album I found an old picture of Laurine, taken before she met Jos in eastern Java. She looks like an apprehensive English boarding-school girl. Her outfit, a white hat with a black rim and a white cotton dress with a black bowtie, makes her look younger. Behind her stands her chaperone, Peddy, dressed in white and seemingly protective of his older sister. The picture was taken in the garden of Peddy's and Laurine's aunt and uncle, the Stuckys, who lived in Malang (and who also posed in this picture).[15] Compared to the relaxed and somewhat complacent posture of the Stuckys, Laurine looks tense. Was she mentally preparing for her meeting with Jos? Was she thinking about what her life would be like as a planter's wife in the *udik* (country)? Was she at all happy about being back in the land that she remembered so fondly from her childhood? As Laurine and Peddy were traveling down the roads of Java, did Laurine agonize over the Indies wedding she had to plan?

Indies weddings usually took days. The Dutch novelist P. A. Daum talks about such a wedding in *Ups and Downs of Life in the Indies* (1892). The wedding is being held at a plantation, and the groom has hired all the *sados* in town to transport his guests. The house is decorated by the *mandurs* with much greenery and flowers. In the garden a wooden floor is set up on which people dance the quadrille. Inside, a special ensemble plays the arias from all the great Italian operas. Until late at night, guests play cards on the cooler verandas. Lemonade and alcohol are served, both diluted with water. Late at night the men exchange their dark formal wear for the cooler white cotton of the tropics. People eat sandwiches and take sips of champagne. When the second day rolls around, some of the guests rise and run to the *kali* (river) for a morning bath, after which the partying is resumed with more champagne, speeches, dancing, and the smoking of cigars.

Oddly, Laurine did not have her wedding in Malang or Jember but in Haarlem, the Netherlands. What had happened? Why did she travel all the way back to the Indies if she was not going to stay there? When I asked the family about the marriage between Jos and Laurine, I learned that before Laurine came into the picture, Jos had a *bini mudah,* a "wife on the side," who had the curious nickname Snaar (meaning "string," like the string of a violin). Was the existence of Snaar the reason Laurine married in Haarlem? The fact that the family seems to know that Jos went to confession to be absolved and forgiven after he returned from the Indies appears to indicate that Jos's mistress was more or less public knowledge and that Laurine might have insisted on a life away from Snaar in Europe.

It was no secret that Dutch planters in remote areas shared their beds with Indonesian *nyais* (the word could mean both "mistress" and "housekeeper"), who were almost as omnipresent as the *babus* the Dutch relied upon. It was just as well known that the nyai was more experienced, and in some cases more exciting in bed, than the average Dutch woman. According to Rob Nieuwenhuys, 1880s manuals for planters still recommended that the bachelor planter take a nyai to learn the language, habits, and customs of the local population in the fastest way possible.

It was also common knowledge that nyais often made better wives than white Europeans women, who, newly arrived in the tropics, would fall ill or fall victim to the much diagnosed neurasthenia, or nervous breakdown. In fact, neurasthenia accounted for "more than half the Dutch repatriations from the Indies to Holland. . . . Colonial neurasthenia was said to be caused by distance from civilization and

European community [and] some doctors considered the only treatment *le retour en Europe.*"[16]

The social historian and anthropologist Ann Laura Stoler goes so far as to argue that the nyai (as well as the *congai* in Indochina and the *petite épouse* throughout the French Empire) was a pivotal tool ensuring the success of colonial rule:

> Unlike prostitution, which could and often did increase the number of syphilitic and therefore non-productive European men, concubinage was considered to stabilize political order and colonial health. It kept men in their barracks and bungalows, rather than brothels or hospitals or worse, in "unnatural" liaisons with another. . . . Across Asia and Africa colonial decision makers counted on the social services that local women supplied as "useful guides to the language and other mysteries of the local societies." Their medical and cultural know-how was credited with keeping many European men alive in their initial, precarious confrontation with tropical life. Handbooks for incoming plantation staff bound for Tonkin, Sumatra, and Malaya urged men to find a bed-servant as a prerequisite to quick acclimatization.[17]

While this seems to imply that because the nyai had a proper and beneficial function, she was looked upon favorably, she was in fact, in the nineteenth century, the "subject of fantasies as a seducer of hapless European men by means of potions and magic, and popularly suspect as poisoner of the rival or bride who replaced her. Newspapers carried [and sensationalized] stories of alleged murders by *nyais.*"[18]

At the turn of the century more than half of the European men in the Indies lived in some form of sexual arrangement with native women, so it should not come as a surprise that Jos had his own nyai to stay healthy and combat boredom and loneliness. Nor should it be a surprise, with all the nyai paranoia fed by colonial yellow journalism, that Laurine wanted to return to Europe in order to elude Snaar's potential revenge.

Many planters without sexual partners hit the bottle. The planter Rudolf in Hella Haasse's novel *Heren van de thee* observes that planters without partners or nyais often became alcoholics or tried to amass their fortunes as fast as possible so they could return to Europe more quickly. But as the Indies economy flourished at the end of the nineteenth and the beginning of the twentieth century, more Dutch women began to arrive to replace the nyai. According to Rob Nieuwenhuys, the number of Dutch women in the colony rose from 18.7 percent to 40.6 percent between 1905 and 1915. This number would go up even more with improvements in hygiene, health care, and the modernization of the domestic sphere.

The arrival of these Dutch women also involved the decline of the Mestizo culture and, with it, a more definite segregation between Dutch colonials and Indonesians. The Mestizo culture had traditionally served as both a buffer and a bridge between the Dutch and the Indonesians. Mixing with and marrying Indonesians now became more taboo because it led to so-called Indianization and degeneracy. Interestingly, Mannes Francken, who would succeed Jos at Kali Jompo, was to marry a Eurasian when these matches had become more scandalous.

Mannes, my grandfather's older brother, who in Holland had become a celebrated soccer star, took the boat to the Indies in 1916, abandoning his illustrious athletic career. Why did Mannes go, and not Henri, Jacques, or Peddy? Peddy might have been considered too young, Henri already had a business of his own, and my grandfather was still studying law in Amsterdam. Mannes, therefore, who was more interested in business than in books (or a university degree), seemed to be the appropriate successor to Jos.

In 1918 the First World War ended. In the months following the war, my grandfather Jacques was recovering from the Spanish flu: he was one of the lucky survivors of the famous influenza pandemic. The number of people who died worldwide was more than twice the number of soldiers killed during the war. When he became ill, my grandfather was already engaged to Anny Huijsser, whom he would marry in 1919. Their wedding would be of Indies proportions, lasting four days (see fig. 4.1).

On Friday there was a large party at Hotel Funckler in Haarlem. On Saturday there was a formal dance, and on Sunday there was a

Figure 4.1: Wedding picture of Anny Huijsser and Jacques Francken (grandparents of the author). To the left of the bride sits Coba Francken. JMW is standing right behind the bridal couple. The man all the way to the right is Henri Francken, and the man on the left in the rear (out of focus and between two wide-brimmed hats) is Peddy Francken. Enny Francken-Harm, who was the source for this picture, believes that the other two siblings of Jacques (Mannes and Laurine) were in the Indies at the time of the wedding.

reception, followed by speeches and a *schimmenspel* (shadow play). When I found this information in a journal kept by Anny's older brother, I momentarily wondered whether it was a *wayang* play, the Indies shadow play, in which dolls are used. In the Indies, wayang plays were customary at weddings, and the thought that this might have been such a play surprised me a little bit, as it seemed to under-line the Franckens' ties with the Indies, ties they otherwise did not seem to cherish or foster.

Although this story opened with the link between me and my grandfather, my focus shifted when Mannes headed for Kali Jompo after Laurine and Jos returned to the Netherlands. Had the war years, although hardly a cataclysmic event in the Netherlands, af-fected the Indies at all? What could Mannes expect in the 1920s, a decade that acquired the adjective "roaring" and is now mostly re-membered for a certain kind of decadence and excess, preceding the meager years of the Great Depression of the 1930s? What was Mannes's life at Kali Jompo like, and how was it different from when his parents were in the Indies? Had Kali Jompo changed, or rather, since we have had very few glimpses of the family plantation so far, what did Mannes see when he arrived on the mountain with a cabin trunk full of expectations, aspirations, and dreams?

Chapter 5

RUBBER

Many pictures of Indies families in the front or back of
their houses recall a lost world, closed in on itself, forever
gone. But the prewar life in the Indies was much more
dynamic than the images of *tempo dulu* suggest. It was on
all sorts of levels receptive to new styles and adapted itself
quickly to changing circumstances. The rise of American
popular culture with its swing music, loose clothing, and
lively new dances influenced the Indies greatly. The Old
World, Europe, was no longer the sole influence. The New
World, the Pacific, was much closer and very attractive.

Pamela Pattynama, "Movement in the Back Yard:
Daily Life in the 1920s"

Mannes Francken abandoned a stellar soccer career to follow the
Francken family tradition and take the boat to the Indies in 1916.
Couperus confirmed that once one family member had gone off to
the Indies, more would follow.[1] Mannes's fame as a soccer player
should not be underestimated: after almost a hundred years he still
ranks high among Dutch top scorers, and the family story that fan
mail with the address "Mannes Francken, Holland" would always
arrive at the right address may well be true.

As his ship was preparing to leave for the Indies, a jazz band was
playing on the shore. A Eurasian fellow passenger by the name of
Kitty Lorgion, who was headed for the Indies to become a school-
teacher, asked what the hullabaloo was about. She was informed that
it was for Mannes Francken, the famous and handsome soccer idol.
"I don't know Mannes Francken and I don't care for soccer," she

replied, and turned away, but before the ship had reached the Cape of Good Hope (the Suez Canal was closed because of the war), Mannes had won Kitty's heart and the couple would get engaged in a rickshaw in the South African city of Durban. Two years after that, they were married in the Indies.

Although the Netherlands had stayed out of the First World War, the war had cut the Netherlands off from the Indies. This meant that other nations, especially Japan and the United States, became important export markets. Given the emerging automobile industry, particularly in the United States, Mannes and Kitty would arrive at Kali Jompo at an opportune moment in time. The first rubber boom had taken place from 1910 to 1912, and in 1920 and 1921 the price of rubber declined. The price soon improved again, and "rubber planting expanded as never before. This period lasted until 1930, after which date comparatively little planting was done."[2]

The expanding market was reflected in the dividend payments from Kali Jompo: no more than 20 percent from 1910 to 1920; 20 percent in 1923; 50 percent in 1924; 100 percent in 1925 and 1926; 95 percent in 1928; and 65 percent in 1929. The 1927 Kali Jompo annual report, reviewing the particularly good year of 1926, shows that the company made an astronomical profit of 212,438.87 guilders (about two million U.S. dollars by today's standards). The 100 percent dividend was a payment of one thousand guilders per share (no less than ten and a half thousand U.S. dollars in 2008).

The local plantation workers did not benefit from this financial bonanza. The annual report of 1927 does not spell out any salaries of the workers, but a 1924–25 survey by J. H. Boeke, who looked at the different budgets of Javanese farmers, shows that the average annual income was about three hundred guilders (no more than three and a half thousand dollars today). Many farmers could not live off this money and were in debt or had to sell the land they needed to cultivate rice.[3] Harry Francken (Peddy's son) told me in an e-mail that the plantation workers were seasonal workers and that they made more than that skimpy three hundred guilders. I then consulted the 1927 report to try to see what the costs were of the coffee and rubber

Figure 5.1: Rubber
tree at Kali Jompo.
*Source: Harry
Francken*

harvests (as well as the costs of the planting of rubber and preparations of coffee and rubber), for which Kali Jompo would have needed
the workers. This amounts to about fifty-six thousand guilders, which,
divided among about four hundred employees, comes to fourteen
hundred guilders per person, or about fifteen thousand dollars in
today's world. Not a big salary, but remarkably better than the figure Boeke cited. "Besides," Harry said in an e-mail, "I was told that
the workers should not be paid too much otherwise they would not
come back the next day. Typically, they only turned up when need-
ing the money."

While the dividend payments in 1930 were still at 40 percent, in
1931 and 1932 the good times were over—no dividend payments
were made at all.[4] What needs to be noted here is that there has been
a common presumption that investors in the Indies pulled in big

incomes with 15–20 percent dividend payments. Jaap van der Zwaag demythologizes this by claiming that actual payments averaged 6 percent in the period 1900–29, whereas the average from 1930–38 was no more than 4 percent.[5] Clearly, Kali Jompo stock did much better than the average Indies stock, so the Franckens made good money by depending on the cheap labor of Javanese farmworkers.[6]

The 1920s marked the last rubber boom, a period that the Dutch novelist Madelon Lulofs portrayed in her autobiographical and internationally acclaimed novel *Rubber* (1931), which is set in Deli (near Medan, in Sumatra). The success of rubber meant thousands of guilders of extra expendable income, which was, according to Lulofs, spent on "fantastic luxuries" such as jewelry and expensive cars.[7]

But before Mannes and Kitty get settled in at Kali Jompo and enjoy the sudden prosperity, one has to ask whether their marriage was easily accepted by the family. It is striking, for instance, that Kitty, whose family had a strong Protestant tradition, her great-grandfather and grandfather being doctors of theology, converted to Catholicism before she married Mannes. As for Kitty's Eurasian roots, I imagine that any possible objections regarding race would have come from Coba. Both Walraven and Stoler claim that racism came especially from the white women, who were not only "the bearers of racist beliefs, but hard-line operatives who put them in practice. It was they who destroyed the blurred divisions between colonizers and colonized, who encouraged class distinctions among whites while fostering new racial antagonisms, formerly muted by sexual access."[8] Walraven, who married a native woman named Itih, was often furious when he saw how white women treated his wife: "Such things make me mad as hell. I hate the quasidistinguished crowd that calls itself the European community of the Indies and in which you will find the biggest bunglers and the most banal women. [They are] people who know nothing and who might have been lumber traders [in Holland]."[9]

Marrying a native or Eurasian woman was seen as exposing oneself to becoming more like the Indonesians. It was a sure way of "degenerating." If Eurasians, better known as "Indos" by the Dutch, were recognized by the father, they were elevated to a special status (above the Indonesians but below the Dutch), but the majority disappeared into the *kampung* when the Dutch planter had rejected his *nyai,* or left his native wife or mistress behind when returning to the Netherlands or marrying a Dutch woman. Most Indos were known as *voorkinderen,* the abandoned offspring of a mixed match, or, more literally, the illegitimate children who came before the Dutch man married a Dutch woman, with whom he would then have legitimate white children (*nakinderen*). The term, Stoler comments, "was racially marked to signal illegitimate children of a mixed union. Economically disadvantaged and socially invisible, they were sent 'back' to native *kampung* or shuttled into the shoddy compounds of impoverished whites." More often than not, Indos, Stoler writes further, were seen as "the progeny of 'malcontents,' of 'parasitic' whites, idle and therefore dangerous. . . . Concubinage raised the political fear that its progeny would demand economic access, political rights and seek alliance with (and leadership of) organized opposition to Dutch rule."

In reality, however, the Indos would become an extremely marginalized group, so much so that "state orphanages were established to prevent neglect and degeneracy of the many free-roaming poor bastards and orphans of Europeans.'"[10] Like mulattoes in the American South, the Indos often ended up in the no-man's-land between the races, accepted by neither the Dutch nor the Indonesians. While they tried to climb the ranks of the Dutch civil service, as soon as more eager young Dutchmen started arriving in the nineteenth century, the Indos were let go in favor of the Dutch, thus creating resentment, but also in many cases causing Indos to engage in criminal activities involving gambling houses and the opium trade.[11]

In the American South, mulattoes are often referred to as "tragic," and Indos seem to have earned the same reputation, for they were forever hovering between resisting the European and wanting to be seen and recognized by Europeans. Never, however, would they find full satisfaction in either status. In Dutch novels of the time, this wavering position was underscored by Indo characters being unreliable, untrustworthy, and always ridiculous in the way they made so many mistakes speaking Dutch.[12]

When I heard stories about Aunt Kitty—how strict she was, and how much she insisted on manners (manifested by her scolding Mannes for mashing his boiled potatoes with his fork)—I wondered whether this was her way of fighting the Indo stereotype. This would also be in line with Willem Walraven's description of Indos as an extremely self-conscious group: "They are *plus royaliste que le roi,* more European than the Europeans themselves. . . . They look down on the natives, the Javanese, something which we, ordinary Dutch boys from the middle class, who were looked down on by people who had the high stoops with the monumental posts with heavy chains, marvel at and get irritated by."[13]

In all fairness to Kitty, a great number of Indos and Indo families came from the upper classes and better families because of the very fact that they *were* recognized by their European fathers. This was also the case with Kitty—she was well educated, and for a Eurasian woman of her generation that was an exception rather than the rule. Plus she had been to Europe for schooling, a privilege usually reserved only for Dutch or Eurasian males.

But the late 1910s and 1920s were a time of transition. Although "nearly half of the Indies' European male population in the 1880s were [still] unmarried and living with Asian women," nyais became less common at the start of the new century because more Dutch women arrived in the colony.[14] "Dutch women," Elsbeth Locher-Scholten writes, "were the new civilization offensive, driving the *nyai* to the back porch and finally off the property. The Dutch women were there to teach manners and morality, and as such this served the awareness of the new Ethical politics well. . . . After the 1920s the number of Europeans who lived with a concubine went down greatly."[15] Curiously, Lulofs writes that nyais were more accepted and not necessarily perceived as "sexually depraved." The housekeeper system was tolerated. "Women at the club . . . had come to appreciate the necessity of the arrangement and no longer looked upon the bachelors as immoral characters."[16]

Kitty was an educated Eurasian woman from a respected family, so I do not think the marriage was necessarily stigmatized or unusual. Maybe Mannes was more drawn to Asian women because of having been raised by loving *babus* rather than by his own more detached mother. He also knew that the life of a planter's wife was not a bed of roses and that a Eurasian woman, like a nyai, would not be bothered as much as a Dutch wife by the boredom, loneliness, and nervous disorders associated with plantation life. The boredom of the planter's wife is a constant motif in *Rubber*. "Don't you understand how terrible it is?" Renée exclaims to her planter husband. "Always to be in this house with nothing round me except this dreadful rubber! . . . In Holland it's all so different. There you have people to help you—your parents, some real women friends. . . . Here you must work it all out by yourself. Everyone stands on his own. . . . Everybody thinks only of his own advantage. Promotion as soon as possible. And then off as soon as possible. It kills every chance of friendship."[17]

But Kitty was no twenties flapper like Renée and did not need to get her kicks at the Dutch club or the *soos*. Relatives and a friend of the family confirm that Mannes, and later Peddy and his family, avoided the *soos*, the petty politicking, and the easy promotions among the Dutch elite. Kitty, and later Peddy's wife, Fré, were not into gossip or club dances; they were part of a group of women who were busy taking charge of housekeeping and the education of their children. Marjolein Francken wrote me: "My mother [Kitty] made one room into a classroom and taught my two brothers and two sisters. It was a proper classroom with desks and a black board (sent from Holland). She was a very good teacher and very strict. No nonsense!"[18] Rather than being a social butterfly, Kitty was the backbone of the family and took on most of the responsibilities at home: "My parents," Marjolein wrote, "loved each other very much but she was the boss. When there was trouble, my father used to say *Oremus* (let us pray) and disappear into the gardens."

After thinking about Kali Jompo and hearing a few stories, I wanted to know what it looked like. Marjolein sent me some wonderful

Figure 5.2: Main house at Kali Jompo in 1928. *Source: Laurine Francken-Hollander*

family snapshots in addition to five minutes of silent film of the plantation, shot in the late twenties.

Because of my past research interest in the American South, I had the wrong impression of what an Indies plantation looked like. As soon as I heard the word "plantation," I automatically thought of stately mansions with neoclassical columns, Spanish moss, magnolias, Southern belles, mint juleps, and a kind of Biedermeier sentimentality that is not at all apropos for the simpler—much simpler—and more primitive plantations in the Dutch East Indies. Half the time they did not even call them plantations but "gardens," and the administrator's house was not referred to as a villa, but was usually called a bungalow. Kali Jompo is no more than that, a bungalow with white-plastered walls, a flimsy corrugated roof, and cheap wicker chairs on the veranda (see fig. 5.2).

Nonetheless, there is one glamorous picture of Mannes and his whole family in front of their Studebaker. Mannes and his English employee John Mills are dressed in white suits, while Mannes's sons are dressed in sailor suits. Kitty is not wearing the traditional sarong that the chauffeur and gardener, Abdul, who is standing off to one side, is wearing. She is dressed in an American-style twenties dress and

Figure 5.3: Mannes and Kitty in front of their Studebaker. The chauffeur on the right is Kassidin. *Source: Marjolein Francken-Jaquet*

on her head she has an alluring wide-brimmed hat. She looks Western rather than Asian, Dutch rather than Indonesian (see fig. 5.3).

As soon as I pushed Marjolein's videotape into the VCR, I was absorbed by the black-and-white images that shot by at high speed. The fast tempo endowed the parading characters in the film with the kind of staccato movements and gestures that remind one of Charlie Chaplin and Buster Keaton movies. And then it was over already, the film turning black, after which the TV showed its customary blue. I rewound and watched it again.

I saw a handsome man, not too tall but slender and friendly, as he came down the stairway of the open veranda in front of the house. He was pulling his giggling kids along toward the camera. They all held hands, as if in school, but also seemed excited, self-conscious, and nervous. There were two boys and two girls, all a year apart, it seemed, and they were being encouraged to "perform" by the white servants who stood at the periphery of the frame. Aunt Kitty was doing the filming. Marjolein explained in her letter that Kitty was pregnant with Marjolein and therefore did not want to be filmed. Was this more of Kitty's Indo (and exaggerated) sense of propriety?

For a moment Mannes took off his Aussie planter's hat, as if impersonating Charlie Chaplin, and then I saw more of his gorgeous good looks. His friendliness, his charisma, and his relaxed glamour were something that I could not retrace in any of the pictures of my own grandfather. Every picture I have of Jacques Francken shows his stockiness, his rigid seriousness, and the seemingly burdensome depths of his responsibilities as Kali Jompo's director (see fig. 5.4).[19]

I rewound the film for a third viewing. I had already become quite attached to Mannes, who seemed to be interacting with his children in a warm and effusive manner. He was laughing at the little girls, who had big white bowties planted on top of their thick dark hair, cut in a charming bob. The girls and boys looked slightly Asian. It seemed an interesting mix: the exotic and elegant features of their Indonesian background were counterbalanced by the more down-to-earth solidity of their Dutch roots.

Did my grandfather act in the same way around his children? When I interviewed my mother and her siblings, I came away with the impression of a father who was very authoritarian, strict, very Catholic, at times temperamental, introverted, and possibly depressed. Jacques Francken did not seem to have Mannes's happy-go-lucky attitude. While *Gropa* (Grandpa) Jacques had already become the imaginary hero before I even started this book, he quickly fell off his pedestal as more stories came in.

Figure 5.4: Jacques and Mannes in the coffee gardens, 1928. *Source: Laurine Francken-Hollander*

Most of the accounts about him I did not want to hear. My mother and all her siblings have memories of his rage, which would quickly culminate in a slap in the face, or worse, a fistfight. My mother has a recollection of her oldest sister Tineke and him rolling down the stairs as they argued about an inappropriate word she had used. Both my mother's oldest brother and youngest sister further remember running away to hide behind a sandbox and under a table to avoid a spanking. My aunt Tineke remembers how, after my great-grandfather died, her father took her into the room, grabbed her hand, and held it up to the dead man's ashen face: "Feel how cold he is," he said to her, as if it were a chamber of horrors rather than the scene where a loved one had just died. "The only bodily contact we had with him," my mother wrote in an e-mail, "was when he drew a little cross on our foreheads before we went to sleep."

Jacques Francken, like most fathers of his day and age, was not necessarily the warm and fuzzy figure that the fathers of my generation have become to their children. He was distant and cold, but he provided for his family, and that was of course the main requirement for fathers in the first half of the twentieth century. Had this something to do with how he was raised by his mother? Was Coba emotionally available if all she did was rely on babus? Rob Nieuwenhuys says that during his entire life he could remember the scent of his babu better than that of his mother. Was this the case for Jacques Francken as well, and did it influence his relationship with his own children?

Whatever the reason for my grandfather's questionable parenting, he faded out like an underexposed movie clip the more unsympathetic he became. Kali Jompo, on the other hand, came into full view. Kali Jompo (see fig. 5.5) was rather high up in the mountains. The nearest town, Jember, lies in a valley of fertile soil and good rainfall in eastern Java, south of Bondowoso and west of Banjuwangi. In the seventeenth and eighteenth centuries the Dutch competed for the land with the French and the English. In the colonial period Jember was a sugar, coffee, tobacco, and rubber town, but after independence the Indonesian government nationalized the Dutch tobacco

Figure 5.5: Kali Jompo in 1929. *Source: Jack Francken*

plantations, which turned Jember into a big tobacco town. In 1957 the University of Jember was founded.

When I pulled up an old town map from 1922 (courtesy of the online map archive of the Koninklijk Instituut voor de Tropen in the Netherlands), I saw the Jompo River (after which the family estate was named),which runs through the town. I noticed that there was a Dutch school, an Indies school, and a Chinese school. The Chinese school was located in the Chinese quarter, far away from all the Dutch administrative buildings and the soos.

Peddy Francken succeeded Mannes and Kitty and has one surviving son, Harry. I decided to ask my mother how I could reach him. The resistance I had felt earlier when asking about my family's past resurfaced when my mother told me I should not contact Harry because he "might have been too traumatized" by the deaths of his father and sisters during the war.

"So what happened to his father?" I asked my mother on the phone.

"He died of dysentery in a Japanese prison," my mother said.

"He was executed," my aunt Tineke told me, "his head chopped off by a Japanese sword."

I also got different versions of how Harry's sisters were killed by Indonesian rebels.

"So don't contact him" was the message I got from Tineke as well. She suspected Harry did not even know the truth. I let this sit for about a day and then talked about it with my husband over dinner.

"Do you mean to say," Jonathan said, "that everybody in your family knows something but that Harry himself may know nothing?"

"Yes," I admitted, sipping wine as if trying to hide my own uneasiness. After Coba and Jacques, I realized that the narrative focus had shifted and the real crux of this book might be what happened to Peddy and his daughters, Joke and Willy. I decided to write to Harry (he did not have e-mail at that point), and I received a warm letter back. We decided to meet when I was next in Holland.

When I met Harry, I immediately noticed his slight Indies accent, which gets stronger when he is emotional. He seemed very animated, was warm, had a sense of humor, and was not afraid to open up to me, not even at our first meeting. While his father's story was a mystery to him, the story of his sisters' murder is the stuff of movies, and from that moment it would haunt me through the writing of this book. I will return to these stories in the chapters that lie ahead. First it is necessary to write down Harry's memories of Kali Jompo.

Harry clearly remembers the steep road that led up to the plantation. On arriving at the estate, one saw a large oval lawn and, to the left, a shallow stone swimming pool for the children. As the movie showed, the house itself was not very big; it had a large room with a dining room in the back, but also the characteristic porches for ventilation, a spare room, and the *kamar scolah* where Kitty taught the kids. A pantry (*gudang* in Malay) was used as a time-out room when the kids were naughty.

According to Harry, the rubber factory lay lower than the house and you had to descend stairs to get there. Down there one saw a square lawn with a flagpole, and always close by, the lure of the jungle. The factory got its power from the *kali* (river) through hydraulics and a generator, which also gave the house its electricity. This had been built under Peddy's supervision. Mannes and Kitty would have had no electricity in the house and probably used oil, kerosene, or gas lamps. The terrain was steep, and at the bottom ran the river with a bridge, where the children played with the children of the village nearby. Most of the plantation's workers also came from that village.

Talking, writing, and, later, e-mailing with Harry, I am surprised that so few letters and documents remain. The Franckens must have written letters home, if only to inform the rest of the family whether the family business was prospering or not. When I wrote my uncle Jack, the oldest brother of my mother, he answered, "One can speculate and talk about Kali Jompo, but we have few actual facts. The property was thought of as some Valhalla here in Holland, and certainly it did bring in a great deal of money for my grandfather and your great-grandfather. But we have virtually no records of that time or any sort of personal history which Hella Haasse recreated in her family novel *Heren van de thee.* Apparently she had an extensive company and family archive." I lacked such an archive, and I was beginning to believe that I had only been scratching the surface.

I asked my mother for pictures. Did she not have a single picture of my grandfather's childhood in the Indies? She remembered only one—a picture in which he is seen as a pudgy little boy dressed in his Holy Communion suit. Later I was able to find this picture through my uncle Jack (see fig. 5.6). My grandfather does look a bit chubby. He stands behind a chair on which Peddy Francken, the youngest brother, sits. Peddy has long, curly locks and wears a dress and dainty black boots. I wondered whether this was the fashion of the time or whether it was Coba's frustration that her lastborn was yet another boy. The picture was taken in a studio with a Surabaya address, and I thought it striking that of all the pictures, this one should survive. In a later chapter I will return to Peddy and Jacques and their particularly strained relationship regarding Kali Jompo. My mother wrote later in an e-mail: "I also vaguely remember a forbidden photo album with naked Balinese women. It was hidden and kept away from us." So the Kali Jompo film with Mannes and his children was the best I had, which brought me back to Mannes.

Figure 5.6: Jacques and Peddy Francken as children in the Indies. *Source: Jack Francken*

Mannes had learned about rubber from Jos Everard, Laurine's husband. In 1920 Mannes and Kitty moved into Kali Jompo. Five of their six children would be born there. It was a lonely life, Marjolein told me. Because the children received their education at home, they did not "go down" into Jember much. The soos they hardly frequented at all. A family friend, Huib Wiedenhoff, who grew up in the area at about the same time, remembers how at night the planters raced to the club, leaving clouds of dust in the air. There was a lot of partying going on, people drank too much, and the singing could be heard in town. "If there were ladies at the club, they were usually white," Huib told me. Momentarily I wondered whether Mannes shunned the club because of the (possibly racist) white elite, which might not look favorably on a mixed marriage like his own.

After the club closed for the night, some of the planters would take off for the kampung. Huib writes: "Mother told me that those men were naughty, and Aunt Aaf told me years later in Holland that that was how many planters contracted 'shrimp poisoning' (syphilis)." As in the colonial novels of the time, the kampung was the locale of illicit sex. Huib assured me that the Franckens did not hang out with the soos crowd, but he also remembered that there was another friend of the family who did frequent the soos, and "mother told us not to kiss her on the mouth (which we regretted because we thought she was such a sweet and cute woman!)."

The club or soos was a welcome change from the monotony of life in the gardens, for both men and women. In *Rubber* Lulofs explains that the evenings at the club were the "only gleams of brightness." Besides plenty of alcohol, there was good food, like fresh ham (most ham and cheese in the Indies came in cans), and "sometimes there was a new wife. Then they all stared themselves blind looking at her fresh pink cheeks and her bright eyes and her new fashioned clothes. She would bring the latest news, the latest melodies and a whiff of the old land after which they all hungered."[20]

The emerging cultural force of America is very prominent in the soos life of Lulofs's *Rubber*. The Americans were the big rubber buyers, after all. After Great Britain's rubber quota restrictions in the 1920s, a treaty that the Dutch never joined, rubber was shipped straight to the West Coast of the United States (rather than being transported via London or Amsterdam). In Lulofs's book the Americans not only personify the new face of capitalism, big business, and big money, but are also the more decadent, fun-loving and sexually daring characters, in contrast to the more reserved Old World Dutch characters.

When Louis Couperus revisited the Indies in 1921, he noticed that Westernization had taken place, a change that seemed entirely at odds with the more authentic Indies world that he remembered from his childhood: "The tired European bathes, dresses himself, and has afternoon tea. He even goes to the cinema because there are cinemas! There is a dinner, there is bridge. The European tries to forget everything that reminds him of the Indies, while he is here."[21]

Because the Franckens kept to themselves, not partaking in teas, games of bridge, or the twenties revelry of Lulofs's club life, their behavior was, according to Willem Walraven, somewhat "suspect." One had to mingle and hobnob or one would pay for it careerwise. Most promotions were not made at work but on the tennis court and in the soos. But Mannes and Peddy did not need to be promoted— they were the administrators of their own family business. Nonetheless, I do believe that they would have joined the others at the club to celebrate the Dutch holidays, like *Sinterklaas* (the Dutch Santa Claus) on December 5. Huib Wiedenhoff, who was a child at the time, fondly remembers these evenings at the Jember soos: "There were delicious pastries and marzipan from Hellendoorn, the pastry chef in town. My father was *Sinterklaas* for many years. Upon his arrival the presents stood piled up in the windowsills of the *soos*."

Willem Walraven objected to the stubborn celebration of Dutch holidays because they seemed so out of place in the blistering heat in the tropics: "How can one celebrate Christmas with green trees and tropical heat?"[22] C. M. Vissering comments likewise. After being inside, singing Sinterklaas songs, she walks outside. "Is this really Dutch?" she asks herself. "Is there anything in the Indies that is really Dutch? What is real is the lighting up of the fireflies, the rustling of the *cemara,* and the noise of the volcano. Everything that is original to the Indies is real! But what we call real [like *Sinterklaas* in the tropics] is fake, unreal!"[23]

What was fake and unreal in another sense, too, was the social hierarchy in the Indies. Whereas in Holland there was a social stratification that was determined by class distinctions and/or family heritage, in the Indies the distinctions were much more blurred. Success and status were defined by the amount of money one made rather than by family or class. Rob Nieuwenhuys notes, "The man from the small burgher milieu would socialize with the man from the prominent burgher family, just like the man whose noble family tree went back centuries would have a drink with the man who was the son of a sugar baron and his *nyai*."[24]

Lulofs brings this contrast to life in *Rubber:* the chief manager and most important people in town are Stoops and his wife, who have a special table at the club, which Du Perron calls the *duizend gulden tafeltje* (thousand guilders table), reserved for people with big incomes. In *Rubber,* the Stoopses have forgotten "the days when she worked in a café in the Rembrandt Plein at Amsterdam [Mrs. Stoops is a former prostitute], and Stoops was a cigar maker's apprentice."[25]

While based on money and career success, people's fate was also dependent on varying harvests, weather, and the unpredictable rise and fall of prices on the world market. Some would say it was mere luck and that farming in the Indies was a form of gambling. "And what was life in the plantations except a game of chance?" Lulofs writes. "An illiterate might go home with half a million guilders, and a man with brains might return empty-handed."[26]

This was also the big difference between Mannes's and Peddy's tenure at Kali Jompo. Whereas Mannes would experience golden years in rubber, Peddy's time would coincide with the Great Depression of the 1930s. But before this changing of the guards occurred, there were other signs showing that times were changing forever.

Chapter 6

1929, TURNING POINT

In 1929 the big man, my great-grandfather, J. M. W. Francken, died in the big house that he had bought and maintained with the big money from sugar, coffee, and rubber. 1929 was also the year in which my mother was born, having been conceived shortly after my grandparents' grand tour of the Dutch East Indies in 1928. This tour coincided with the inauguration of the new Catholic church in Jember, to which the Franckens had donated a large altarpiece. This raises a question: was this a Francken gesture to put back into the local community what the family had taken out, or was it done to reserve a spot for my profiteering great-grandfather in the hereafter?

Of course, 1929 was also the year of the Wall Street Crash and the beginning of a global depression. In Indonesia the late twenties were also the culmination of the political beginnings of Sukarno, who would become Indonesia's first president upon independence in 1949. In 1925 Sukarno had emerged as a public figure for the first time. He founded the Algemeene Studieclub, which worked toward the independence of Indonesia. The club turned into a popular political movement and party, the Perserikatan Nasional Indonesial (PNI), later the Partai Nasional Indonesia. All this could happen because of the more tolerant Ethical Policy. However, Sukarno's push for independence was ultimately too much for the colonial leadership, and in 1929 he and six other leaders were accused of instigating riots and thrown into jail.

Did Mannes and Kitty notice anything of the independence movement or revolts, which were more conspicuous in the big cities, and in western Java and western Sumatra in particular? While newspaper articles and novels of the nineteenth and early twentieth century mention the occasional revenge by a coolie or a spurned *nyai* as ordinary occurrences, some of the Dutch on the plantations began to feel more uneasy as well. One of the planters' wives in *Rubber* is found languishing on the veranda every afternoon, waiting for her husband to come home and sometimes fearing the worst as attacks of coolies on Dutchmen seem to have become more common:

> Then there might be [a] noise, some unusual event in a day of which every sound and every event was familiar. The old anxiety flared up again. One's finger tips ached, and the blood beat in one's head. Then it turned out to be nothing—a pig that had roamed away into the forest and was being rounded up by yelling coolies.... What could happen? ... And then slowly the obsession grew again and one listened to the sounds from the rubber plantations, to the voices and the shouts. It was an obsession that sapped one's vitality. And then again one hushed it, till suddenly like a thunderbolt there came the news that another assistant had been murdered.[1]

Was this paranoia or real? Kitty or Mannes could no longer tell me, but clearly a revolutionary, or rather, a nationalist, sentiment was building, which in turn caused the colonial government to become more repressive. Edgar du Perron wrote about this when he returned to the Indies in the 1930s and heard Dutch comments like these: "Either we colonize, or we don't. If we do, it is better to show the natives sternly that we are always going to be boss. If one does otherwise, one creates confusion and disappointment on both sides."[2]

My grandfather was not in favor of the Ethical Policy either. But what did he know? He had left the Indies as a little boy and was far removed from the circumstances in which the Javanese lived. For one, the Dutch East Indies were no longer the setting of *tempo dulu* and the laid-back time of the *oudgasten* his parents had been. On the contrary, the planters' lives of Mannes, Kitty, and later Peddy and Fré involved hard work until it was time to repatriate to Holland. Guides to colonial living in the 1920s and 1930s "extolled the energetic and engaged activities of the new breed of husband and wife. Prone to neurasthenia, anemia and depression, women were exhorted to involve themselves in household management and child care and divert themselves with botanical collections and 'good works.'"[3] The general belief was that to work harder meant to leave sooner, or that the goal of living in the Indies was "to make money and leave." In his autobiographical novel *Country of Origin,* Du Perron mentions time and again that Europe always lay on the horizon as the final destination, and fellow author Busken Huet wrote in a letter to his friend, E. J. Potgieter: "All the people want is to go to Holland. Almost every European lived between two worlds."[4] At the same time, it also became evident that more and more Europeans stayed permanently, as living conditions, with better hygiene, medical care, and refrigeration had improved so much over the years.

Jacques Francken and his wife, Anny Huijsser, left for the Indies in 1928, not only to revisit the scenes of Jacques's childhood but also to see up close how things stood at Kali Jompo. In the late twenties the Indies still had a reputation for the accumulation of easy wealth and fast fortunes. In truth, few Dutch people actually made it big in the Indies: "The big careers became known, but the many failures are forgotten. Next to Indies glory there was also Indies decline: the weeds, the moldy walls, the disintegrating floors, decaying glass, and the stereotype of a disillusioned, cynical human being."[5]

What was my grandfather's trip like? How did he feel about returning to his country of origin, and how did my grandmother, who had never been to the tropics, experience the trip? The trip itself cannot have been a hardship, as the boats on which people traveled were very luxurious and comfortable. To travel to the Indies, one had two options in the late 1920s: one could either take the boat train from Amsterdam to Genoa and from there take the boat to Egypt, or one could take the boat directly from IJmuiden to Southampton and from there to the Mediterranean via Gibraltar. The boat train was far from shabby: the compartments had a maximum of six seats and the beds were to be found in separate *wagon-lits*. The restaurant on the boat train was the epitome of chic: leather chairs, intimate lamps, and cooks and waiters in white aprons.[6]

Due to a very succinct itinerary that my grandmother left behind, I know that my grandparents left on October 1, 1928, from Haarlem to Amsterdam by car to take the noon train to Utrecht. "Dined at Cologne and retired to the sleeping car at Frankfurt at five in the afternoon," my grandmother writes with businesslike conciseness. The next day they woke up in Basel, had lunch at Lugano, and arrived at Genoa at seven that evening. At Genoa they stayed at the Miramare: built in 1903, it was one of the first posh grand hotels on the Italian Riviera. When I looked it up on the Internet I saw an ornate white building that looked more like a gigantic wedding cake than a five-star resort. It must have been an exclusive address because Laurence Olivier and Vivian Leigh honeymooned there in 1949.

On October 13 my grandparents boarded the *Pieter Cornelis Hooft*. While passing Stromboli and Sicily, my grandfather did not miss Catholic Mass in the music salon on board the ship. Port Said and Suez are hardly mentioned, and about life on board my grandmother merely lists the names of the people she dined with and the fact that there were only two Englishmen and one American on board. However, the photo album that comes with my grandmother's restrained travel journal tells me more about the luxury on the ship. I marveled at how well dressed Anny and Jacques were for this trip: my grandmother walked around in Charleston dresses and Jacques wore a three-piece or a white tropical suit. These kinds of trips could only be financed by people who had money or people (civil servants and the like) who were sponsored by the state or their employer.

Louis Couperus gives the reader a rare glimpse behind the scenes on these large ships. When visiting the kitchens and refrigerated rooms, the author was overwhelmed by the many cans and bags of food, in addition to "hundreds of cheeses, fowl," and "endless grapes." "The wine cellars," Couperus writes, "glisten with rows and rows of bottles."[7]

If my grandparents had gone shopping in Port Said, they would have been disappointed, as the city had changed for the worse. Back in the 1900s, when my grandfather and Couperus had seen it last, it was alive with an appealing and exotic local color: "Arab neighborhoods and markets, horrifically dirty but picturesque—especially the fruit stalls were beautiful, colorful spreads . . . there was an Arab busy-ness, white *gandourahs* [shirts], red *tarbouches* [hats] and the fellah-women walked around in their black gowns and veil." "But now," Couperus writes, disheartened, "all I see is hundreds of begging children with sick eyes with droves of flies."[8] Was Anny, upon seeing these children, reminded of her two children, Tineke and Jack, whom she had left behind in Haarlem with two German nannies? She probably did not have much time to dwell on this, because the Suez Canal was waiting.

The Suez Canal was a significant shortcut to the Far East. Sailing around the Cape of Good Hope was much longer and not always safe because of the treacherous winds and currents, and crossing the desert from Egypt to the Red Sea could be grueling as well. The canal, 120 meters wide and 170 kilometers long, was a considerable improvement and greatly increased traffic to Asia from the Middle East and Europe.

After the Suez Canal came the murderous heat of the Red Sea. The Dutch author A. Alberts believed that those six days in the Red Sea were a good preparation for someone who went to the Indies; the boiling city of Batavia would be child's play after the Red Sea.[9]

Bas Veth, whose cynical *Het leven in Nederlands-Indië* (1900) caused a stir in Holland, wrote that the Red Sea was the beginning of the tropics: "It is getting really hot. The bathrooms are being used more often. The Indies women walk across deck in *sarong* and *kabaya* and the *oudgasten* change into their white suits. The *totoks* (Dutch) are observing this but keep walking around in their European garb for a few more days."[10] Couperus comments that on this leg of the journey one would rather walk around in the nude or never leave one's bathtub. Yet the atmosphere on board was almost festive. Couperus explains that the trip to the Indies was for most filled with anticipations and dreams, whereas on the way back these dreams had usually been shattered by a loss of fortune or health.[11]

After the Red Sea one reached the Indian Ocean, which often looked more like a lake than a stormy sea. Ceylon (present-day Sri Lanka) was a welcome change for those who began to experience cabin fever. Ceylon, with its capital Colombo, was a somewhat decadent place in the 1920s. The English colonials danced the tango by moonlight, drank, played tennis, gambled, and gossiped—Colombo was thus a perfect introduction to the life and colonial milieu of Batavia.

What did my grandparents do while they were in Colombo? Did they, like Couperus, shop and eat English curry with chutney? Or did they visit the Dutch churchyard with the seventeenth- and eighteenth-century graves of sailors and soldiers? Thanks to the journal entry of January 28, 1928, I know that Jacques and Anny visited the botanical gardens and stayed at the Mount Lavinia Hotel. This was another grand colonial hotel overlooking a beach with swaying palm trees. No doubt it was a welcome diversion from life on the ship and the cramped quarters of my grandparents' cabin.

The first port in the Dutch East Indies was Sabang in Pulau Weh. Nothing is mentioned of Sabang or the arrival in the Sumatran port of Belawan Deli on February 1. The next day the ship made a stop at Singapore, where my grandparents stayed at the Hotel Europe. I could not find any record of this hotel, but undoubtedly it was another prime location with fabulous views.

After Singapore there were the heat and crowds of Batavia. This port, which Bas Veth condescendingly describes as a "bite out of a swamp," was full of crocodiles, while inside the harbor one could see the old warehouses, some of which dated back to the days of Jan Pieterszoon Coen. The scent of the tropics immediately entered one's nostrils. "It's not a stench necessarily," Veth writes, "more like a vapor, the scent and exhalation of rotting leaves, flowers, fruits mixed with odors coming out of the soil."[12]

How did my grandfather feel the moment he walked off the boat? Was it a sweet homecoming for him as it was for Du Perron in the

1930s? "My earliest memory of returning goes back to Priok (i.e., Batavia harbor). As the boat moored, I saw two of my oldest friends and heard the voices of the coolies: 'Tuan! Ini ude ketemu, tuan! Ini die ni!' Oh the delicious, generous, bragging noisiness of that Batavian voice! I no longer thought of the battle between the races or classes, I walked down the gangplank under that scorching sun which I welcomed like an old acquaintance."[13]

From the port, the journey went to the train station, where the swarming crowd might have been overwhelming for a woman like my grandmother. Here one saw the perspiring half-dressed bodies of coolies, Dutchmen with handlebar moustaches and white helmets, soldiers, Javanese women breastfeeding their infants in public, *warung* (roadside eateries), and, on the station floor, big red stains. "These are not blood stains," Veth writes, but "spit of the sirih-chewing natives."[14]

While driving through Batavia I imagine that the first impressions of my grandfather and grandmother might have been worlds apart. Du Perron had that experience with his wife, who had never been to Java either. As he leaned out of the car to take in and recognize as many colonial rooflines and verandas while getting excited about the dark and spacious shadows between the verandas' columns, his wife believed that the same places were unattractive and dark. "First misconception between a European gaze and an Indies reality," Du Perron writes, "the dark which for me means coolness, peace and coming home represents to her dirt and melancholy."[15]

Where Du Perron found his first ride through Batavia thrilling, Couperus was plagued by melancholy because the old colonial and elegant homes that his ancestors built were now hotels that were peeling and falling apart. Where there used to be carriages with horses, he saw cars that left in their trail big clouds of dust and dirt. Where Couperus longed for *tempo dulu* in 1921, ten years later Du Perron accepted the pastness of the past and realized that one can't go home again. Du Perron would also realize that the Dutch had to get out of Indonesia: "When I sit in the train and see that red soil again, I intuitively feel that this is where I belong; here alone I have the feeling of homecoming even though I no longer have a home here. Unfortunately this does not mean I should stay in the Indies. . . . To be on the right side, one has to be Indonesian. . . . I cannot justify my stay here. People like me have to get out of here."[16]

My grandparents stayed in the fancy Des Indes Hotel in Batavia (which would be demolished in 1971). Even though they visited *Weltevreden,* the European upper city, built by Daendels, my grandmother cannot have enjoyed this outing much as she was coming down with a sinus infection that put her in bed for no less than ten days. On February 13 Jacques and Anny left for Bandung, where they had a beautiful evening walk in the much cooler city. In Bandung, nicknamed the Paris of Java, they stayed at the Preanger Hotel, one of the two five-star Art Deco hotels in the center of town, along with the Savoy. If we are to believe the cantankerous comments of the hard-to-please Bas Veth, Indies hotels were nothing to write home about. The second-rate addresses he stayed at had dirty walls, moist floors, and big cracks that in Holland one could only find in cellars and sheds, he wrote. The ceilings were painted a dirty yellow: "A simple farmer in Holland would not even use that color to paint his outhouse."[17] Clearly, my grandparents (see fig. 6.1) were sheltered from this kind of reality.

From Bandung my grandparents' grand tour went to Yogyakarta, with another grand hotel and Javanese dances during dinner. On February 15 they went by car to the Borobudur, where they met up with Willy and Lily Francken. These two women must have been descendants of one of JMW's brothers who had gone to the Indies in the late nineteenth century.

The next day Jacques and Anny took the train to Surabaya, where they stayed at the Oranje Hotel, a location that would play a critical part in the Indonesian Revolution seventeen years later. On February 18 my grandmother writes, "Tour of Surabaya. Jacques had business meetings." Did these meetings have anything to do with what was left of the Kervel sugar fortune? The night after that, my grandparents dined at the renowned and elitist Simpang Club, which, like the Oranje Hotel, would become a highly charged symbol during the Indonesian Revolution of 1945.[18]

Figure 6.1: Anny and Jacques Francken during their grand tour of the Indies, 1928. *Source: Laurine Francken-Hollander*

Noticing the places they visited, I wish my grandmother had kept a travel journal. Or did Anny, whose father was one of Holland's first photographers, consider this album her journal? She seems to have been the one who took all, or nearly all, of the pictures. Because of this there are fewer pictures of her, except one where she is seen sitting on one of the small native horses. The poor animal seems to sag under her weight (see fig. 6.2). Images do not lie. Memories do, and the misplaced nostalgia I seem to have for my family past is even more untrustworthy.

Figure 6.2: Anny Francken on one of the native horses. *Source: Laurine Francken-Hollander*

Finally, on February 20, my grandparents traveled by train from Surabaya to Jember, where Mannes was waiting at the station with his car and his kids. From there they drove up to Kali Jompo, following the steep mountain road. My grandmother took several snapshots of my grandfather and Mannes posing among the coffee trees at Kali Jompo. Mannes is relaxed, tanned, showing off his open shirt and the planter's way of putting one's socks over one's pants legs to avoid leeches (if one did not walk around like that, Couperus says somewhere, one might be accused of being a mere "salon planter"). Mannes seems in his element, at ease and happy. My grandfather is standing next to him, awkwardly dressed in a three-piece suit and a heavy hat, the kind one would wear on a cold and rainy day in Holland. Jacques was younger than Mannes but looks older and much more serious, like a bookkeeper who has come out to the fields to remind the workers that profits are down. He would continue to play that role with Peddy too, while not always showing an understanding of weather and/or soil conditions, plant diseases, and the whims of the market.

There is almost not a single picture that shows my grandfather smiling. His charisma, if one can speak in those terms, is dark and somber. He seems such a solemn man (see fig. 6.3), a man who carried the crushing weight of the world on his shoulders. To me he looks like someone who was difficult for others and most difficult for himself. A man of continuous introspection and self-analysis—someone who would internalize things. I write this almost with a certain fondness, as it is a trait I recognize and share. There is one particular picture that intrigues me. I see my grandfather, dressed in a dark kimono, sitting on a veranda in Surabaya. It is the only picture where there is a hint of a smile, a speck of emotion. Nevertheless, I suspect that my grandfather was perhaps a very emotional man, and it is this curious combination of masked intensity that draws me in and gives me a sense of kinship.

My mother's youngest sister, Enny, validates some of the guesswork I have done regarding the grandfather I never knew. She also tells me,

Figure 6.3: Jacques at Kali Jompo, 1928.

I think my father was very fond of me; maybe this was because I was born nine years after your mother and it was nice to still have such a little one about the house. He called me "Enneke" or "Prikoog" [Sharp-eye] because I always knew where to find things when they fell down or got lost. My father was very Catholic and fulfilled his religious duties as he ought to. Every Friday evening he went to Mass to pray for a peaceful death because he did not want a long sickbed at the end of his life.

The devout Catholicism of the Franckens also comes out in my grandmother's album. There are several pictures of the church in Jember the day (March 11, 1928) the new altar was being shown to the flock. It was certainly the final high point of the Francken dynasty because before the stock market crash the rubber market was already in decline. When the rubber restriction quotas were lifted in April 1928, the New York price of rubber fell from over a dollar to about twenty cents. After the Wall Street Crash in 1929, the price of rubber went from twenty cents to three cents. The price would not rise, and then only by a few cents at a time, until mid-1934.[19]

On the day of the church celebration in 1928 the future rubber bust was far removed from the Franckens' minds (see fig. 6.4). After

Figure 6.4: "Family reunion" on the steps of Kali Jompo, 1928: the two children are Mannes's. Mannes sits to the right of them. Jacques stands to the left of the priest. The two people on the far right are Fré and Peddy. *Source: Laurine Francken-Hollander*

church they took off for one of the beautiful beaches in the Jember area. My grandmother notes that on March 15 Dr. Jens Gandrup visited Kali Jompo. At first I assumed he was a medical doctor but when I did a search for his name I found out he was a Danish botanist who was the director of Jember's Besuki Research Station from 1925 to 1930. Apparently he used the Kali Jompo gardens to collect specimens for his rubber-related research. Gandrup would die in the war, in Malang, in 1943.

On March 17 it was time for Anny and Jacques to leave the family estate and travel to Malang, where they stayed at the Hotel Splendid. To my surprise and amusement (after reading about all the sumptuous hotels my grandparents stayed in), I found that Hotel Splendid, an old colonial villa with large rooms and high ceilings, still exists as the Splendid Inn Hotel and is used by hotel guests who want to indulge in the recreational use of marijuana.[20]

In Malang my grandparents visited the Stuckys as well as the aunt who had no legs. The next day they went by car to Tosari. Not a word is spent on André, Jacques's younger sibling who had died of diphtheria so many years earlier, but I am positive that Tosari must have elicited vivid memories in Jacques's mind. Maybe he did not want to dwell on these dark memories, because the next day they were back in the Oranje Hotel in Surabaya, where they danced late into the night and where my grandmother contracted food poisoning before they took off for Bali. In Bali they visited Kintamani, a mountain district famous for its Sanghyang trance dance. They took a number of car trips, saw a bat cave, and visited Den Pasar, but ultimately they seemed in a hurry to return to Surabaya for more late-night dances by moonlight.

On March 30 they boarded the *Plancius Semarang* and sailed back to Batavia, where once again they stayed at the Des Indes the next day. The dancing at the hotel was interrupted by a visit to Buitenzorg (now Bogor). My grandparents had a fast pace to their itinerary, for the following week they stopped by ship at Singapore and Medan, which was known as the Paris of Sumatra. In Medan they stayed at Hotel de Boer (built in 1898 and currently the Hotel Dharma Deli), made famous by the stay of Mata Hari, the Dutch oriental dancer and double agent in the First World War. The hotel was one of the first to have a "mosquito-free room." Rather than having mosquito netting around the bed, this room had wire gauze windows, a novelty for its day. Madelon Lulofs used the hotel in her novel *Rubber*, as it was also a party hotel for planters who would come down to Medan to drink.[21]

From Medan my grandparents were homeward bound. On April 4 they were back at Colombo and on April 22 at Suez, from where they traveled all night by car through the desert to Cairo. At seven in the morning they had breakfast at the famous Swiss Shepherd Hotel. From there they went by camel to visit the pyramids, making it back in time to have lunch and tea at the Shepherd Hotel again. At the end of April, almost four months after they had left Haarlem, they arrived back home. There is not a word in Anny's travel notes about missing her children or emotions they felt among the many and unusual sights, sounds, and scents of the tropics. This must not have been an ordinary trip for my grandparents, and I wish I knew what Jacques felt and thought visiting the country of his birth. The silent pictures of the album show a seemingly contented Jacques at times, but there is not a single picture that hints at true happiness, at being reconnected with the place where he was born. Maybe it was more of a business trip than a sentimental journey.

In 1930 Mannes is still mentioned as the administrator of Kali Jompo in the address books of *Kleian* (the Dutch East Indies). Peddy is mentioned as well, as an "employee" of Kali Jompo. Peddy's wife Fré had already joined him in 1927. Because Peddy was in the Indies, she had been married "with the glove" in the Netherlands, a common custom to speed up the arrival of Dutch brides. What was that like—to marry a man in absentia, take the boat to Batavia, and exchange one's first kiss in the new country?[22]

Bas Veth overhears a fellow passenger say, "We travel with 'two gloves.'" Veth believes it is vulgar to get married that way and mentions that "one of the gloves" is startled when she sees the pale face and wrinkled suit of her new husband waiting for her in Batavia harbor.[23]

How was the first kiss for Peddy and his new wife in the hustle and bustle of the humid harbor? Were they nervous? Did they have a romantic first wedding night under the big mosquito net in their Des Indes hotel room? According to a document that Harry sent me, they did have a formal wedding ceremony on November 29, 1927, in Jember. Three years later they would have their first child, a daughter named Wilhelmina (nicknamed Willeke and Willy) Jacoba Louise Francken. In 1932 her sister, Johanna (Joke) Laurina Maria Francken, would be born.

Marjolein tells me that her father, Mannes, wanted to leave the Indies in 1934 because his oldest son, Ferdinand (another Peddy), had to go to secondary school. There were probably no quality secondary schools nearby, so Holland was the only option—and besides, Mannes and Kitty had been in the Indies for almost twenty years, the average time one spent there, after which repatriation or a leave more or less automatically followed. Mannes decided to drive back (!) in their big Studebaker. The Studebaker is proof that Mannes had done very well in rubber. It was the ultimate planter's car, bought when business was good, much like the Cadillac Escalade, the trophy car of the dotcom generation of the late 1990s in San Francisco.

So off went Mannes and his family in their big Studebaker, all the way through Java. They took the boat to Sumatra, drove through the tropical rainforest, and swam in Lake Toba, Indonesia's biggest crater lake. From Sumatra they took the *Christiaan Huygens* through the Suez Canal and across the Mediterranean to Genoa. In the streets of Italy the Fascist rhetoric of Benito Mussolini was a sinister indication that Europe had been changing rapidly. In Holland Fascism began to rear its ugly head, too, even though the Dutch naively believed that they could remain neutral and avoid another war. They would be mistaken, underestimating both the German and Japanese threat in Europe and Asia.

Chapter 7

KALI JOMPO DURING THE GREAT DEPRESSION

When Mannes left in his Studebaker, he took the good economic times with him, or so it seemed. Peddy, the new administrator, was eager to prove he was a worthy successor, but the Depression created the most difficult of economic circumstances.

After my request for letters or other family documents, Peddy's son Harry found some letters by his father and sent them to me. When I opened the envelope and saw the "Cultuuronderneming, Kali Jompo" letterhead, I felt for the first time that Kali Jompo was not some figment of my imagination but a real place with real people and real crops.

The letters date back to when Peddy had just taken over from Mannes. From a long, confidential letter of June 17, 1934, to Henri, the oldest Francken brother, it is clear that Mannes had put in a good word for Peddy, as Jacques, who was the director of the company in Holland, seemed to have had his reservations about Peddy's administrative qualities. Peddy became the administrator anyway, but the letter also reveals that Peddy believed Mannes had mismanaged both the coffee and rubber cultivation, resulting in a declining yield. In a funny way the long letter to Henri seems a way of covering for himself, as if he were afraid that Jacques might turn around and blame any potential losses on Peddy (which seemed to have happened anyway in the end, regardless of the poor economic times).

Jacob van der Zwaag confirms the grim picture of the early 1930s: "As an export country, the Dutch East Indies received the full blow in 1930–1933. The price of rubber fell from forty-one percent in 1930 to a mere seven and three quarters of a percent in December of 1932. . . . All the plantations were suffering and there were no profits or dividend payments. . . . The export value of rubber fell from eighty-three and a half million guilders (1929) to forty-three million (1930), and finally to sixteen and a third of a million in 1931." Unemployment was rampant (that is, among Europeans, ten thousand of whom lost their jobs in three years), beggars were to be seen in the streets of the big cities, and hotels and restaurants closed down.[1]

The dividend payments of Kali Jompo reflected the downward trend—with a slight recovery at the end of the 1930s. In 1930 and 1931 no dividend payments were made at all. In 1932, 1933, and 1934 they were at 3 percent, but in 1935 they were again back to nothing. In 1936 and 1937 they rose from 6 to 10 percent.

The only annual report I have from the 1930s is for 1935, reviewing the previous year.[2] Unlike the reports from the twenties and forties, which were printed by a professional printer, the 1935 report seemed to have been typed by my grandfather in what seems like an effort to save money wherever possible. 1934 was far below par, with disappointing rubber and coffee harvests. The rubber harvest reached 78,000 kilos (compare to 130,000 kilos in 1926, the last available report in the 1920s), and the coffee beans were no more than 1,891 picols (compared to 2049 picols in 1926; the picol or pikul is about 61.76 kilos). All of this meant that 1934 was a year of loss, amounting to 2,215.21 guilders (which is about 26,199 U.S. dollars in today's terms). In spite of this loss, and possibly to placate investors, my grandfather suggested covering the loss by dipping into cash reserves in order to pay out a dividend of 3 percent, or 30 guilders per share (there were 170 shares in total).

Rather than blaming the poor economic times or the global market, Peddy painstakingly returned in his letters to matters of soil, planting, insects, and weather. "There used to be three layers of soil here at Kali Jompo," he wrote to Henri. "The topsoil is beautiful and loose and is in fact the dark top layer that Dad used to talk about: in some places this layer was so deep that you could stick an entire walking cane into it. Under this there is a claylike, dark red second tier followed by a layer that has the color of bricks. This layer sits on rocks and *padas*. You should realize that the deeper we go, the less structured the soil becomes."

The letter fragment seems an apt metaphor for the situation Peddy was in: by the time he took over the estate, most of the three fertile layers had been washed away and Peddy had hit rock bottom, quite literally. What was Peddy to do? "The Great Depression," Humphrey de la Croix comments in *Indië herinnerd en beschouwd,* "meant the disappearance of the demand for consumption goods in the West, and because of that there was a sharp decline in the demand for raw materials. Whereas the value of export products from the Indies was 1,577,0260,000 guilders in 1928, in 1935 this had shrunk to 470,479,000 guilders."[3]

Since the early twenties unemployment among Europeans in Indonesia had been growing, and many were repatriated by the Dutch government. In the 1930s "white pauperism, like the depression itself, was of crisis proportions," Stoler explains, and "in 1931 of the 240,000 Europeans in the Indies, some ten percent were unemployed."[4] In the thirties it became more difficult to be repatriated, as the Great Depression was just as much a fact of life in Europe. So some of these Europeans got stuck in the Indies and became impoverished, a fate Willem Walraven dreaded for his Indo grandchildren: "In one or two generations there will be Walravens in the *kampung*! No one walks underneath the palm trees unpunished."[5] The Dutch colonial government was not happy with the large group of impoverished whites, as it undermined the status position of the ruling elite. This fed more Indonesian nationalism, or so the Dutch believed. This in turn triggered Dutch nationalism, which expressed itself in the Nationaal-Socialistische Beweging (NSB), the Dutch Fascist party. Du Perron, who had left Europe in the 1930s because he had loathed the rapid spread of Fascism, was in for a surprise when he found a similar Fascist movement in the Indies.

Due to growing nationalism, the thirst for independence among the Indonesians, and the ever more aggressive nationalism and imperialism of the Japanese, many Dutch colonials felt vulnerable, trapped, distrustful, fearful, and pitted against a once-submissive group that now wanted to throw off the shackles of colonialism. Indonesian nationalism flared up, was repressed, and flared up even more until the nationalist leaders Sukarno, Hatta, and Sjahrir were banned to the islands of Flores and Boven-Digul in 1933. To resist nationalism the Dutch wanted a more authoritarian regime, and the NSB seemed to strive for the same goal. Dutch NSB leader Mussert visited the Indies in 1935.

The fear of losing the Indies, which had been expressed in the famous saying "Indië verloren, rampspoed geboren" (the loss of the Indies is the birth of disaster), seemed to turn into an alarming prophecy. The phrase, first used in a 1914 pamphlet by C. G. S. Sandberg to refer to the disappointment with the gradual constitutional separation of the Dutch East Indies, was later taken up "as a slogan, especially during the Indonesian Revolution, by those in the Netherlands who believed that Dutch prosperity depended on continuing colonial rule of Indonesia. They pointed especially to the return on Dutch investments in Indonesia, to Dutch markets there and to the supply of materials for Dutch industry as well as to the calculations of 1938 that the colonies [in spite of the Depression] contributed 13.7 percent of the Dutch national income."[6]

Many colonials, especially those who had grown up in the Indies and those who had an invested interest in its business, were vehemently opposed to Indonesian independence. Louis Couperus writes in 1921: "With unbreakable ties we are attached to the Indies; it would be a disaster for both Holland and the Indies if this tie were to be broken. . . . The Indies are our glory and our love."[7]

Ten years later Du Perron was more pragmatic than Couperus. Indonesian independence was inevitable, in his view, even though he also acknowledged that European colonials had few choices in the polarizing times and prewar years of the 1930s: as a European "you were for the colonial regime or against it. If you opted for neither you would hover between the fake parties such as the Indo-Europeesch Verbond [the Indo-European Bond], the Vaderlandsche Club [the Fatherland Club], and even the NSB, for nine out of ten NSB members were malcontents who have been calling forever for a new Coen or a new Daendels." According to his biographer Kees Snoek, Du Perron was a visionary in that he did foresee "a kind of final battle between the Dutch and the Indonesians, but he did not want to be there when it happened."[8]

Toward the end of his life Willem Walraven, who died in a Japanese internment camp, felt that the climate had changed forever. He sensed that the old mellow atmosphere was gone since the "Indo" had "joined politics." The women, he thought, were the worst; the hatred in their eyes made him "bitter."[9]

Kali Jompo was far removed from the political turmoil and changing climate in the cities. In the countryside, the Dutch had a more intimate and better relationship with the local people than the colonial crowd that danced under the crystal chandeliers of Buitenzorg. Roel de Neve and Vincent Houben write that the social position of the land owners differed enormously from the social position of the civil servants, soldiers, and the merchants in Java's cities. In the country the indigenous world was in close proximity and landowners had good and friendly relationships with the locals.[10]

If I am to guess where Peddy stood politically, he would probably be less enlightened than Du Perron but in Couperus's camp. The NSB was not an option as the Franckens were vehemently anti-NSB. Politics are not even mentioned in any of Peddy's letters: all he writes and obsesses about is how he can keep his head above water and make the improvements that the land requires in order to produce a more profitable harvest.

Unlike my grandfather, who loved theory and learning, Peddy was a practical man. After his schooling with the Jesuits in Holland, he left almost immediately for the Indies with Laurine in 1914 and became a traveling businessman. Before that he had worked at Kali Jompo but left because of a fight. After his short business career in Java, he joined another planter and learned more about the cultivation of rubber and coffee. In the late twenties he was back at Kali Jompo with a wife, two daughters, and a son.

When Mannes left in 1934, it seemed only natural that Peddy become the company's administrator, even though, as mentioned earlier, Peddy foresaw problems and did not want to get blamed. In rank, the administrator was inferior to the director (and shareholders) in Holland, and when there was no profit, all fingers were pointed at him.

When Peddy (see fig. 7.1) took over the gardens, Mannes had been planting coffee separately from rubber, which according to Peddy had

Figure 7.1: A young Peddy, possibly taken right before he left for the Indies. *Source: Harry Francken*

harmed the coffee trees and stunted their growth. He proposed to reorganize and plant rubber trees next to coffee trees. Because of his experience with the steep terrain of Kali Jompo, Peddy also recommended the cheap *awiran* system, which retained the natural humus layer better than *groenbemesting* (green fertilization), advised by the widely recognized *Proefstation* (Research Station).[11] Both Mannes and Jacques seemed to trust the agricultural reports of this station. Conversely, Peddy claimed that these researchers were "idealists" who belonged on the Mookerheide (the Dutch equivalent of the Yorkshire moors), "where they should pen countless books in a little hut. With those kinds of people," Peddy writes, "one can only catch monkeys. They belong to the stratosphere rather than here among these coffee plants."

Peddy's fiery temperament comes to the surface in the diligently typed letters. He was passionate, energetic, dynamic, but also stubborn and a trifle hot-tempered. After Mannes sent an older colleague to Peddy's, presumably to check up on him and recommend *groenbemesting* again, as well as using tractors for the land, Peddy almost ended up fighting and triumphantly showed the colleague the steep terrain (see fig. 7.2) to prove his point about the uselessness of tractors.

Figure 7.2: The steep terrain at Kali Jompo. *Source: Harry Francken*

In another part of the letter, apparently written after my grandfather hinted that Peddy ought to do better with the "divine" land he had come to oversee, Peddy cries out: "The results here at Kali Jompo are anything but good advertising for a good system. On the contrary, when strangers visit us, I am embarrassed about how things are planted around here. Maybe those people even think: what kind of planter lives here, for God's sake. In the meantime, they don't know that I have not at all contributed to this mess . . . , so to say that I'm lucky is based on a misunderstanding." (Unfortunately, I do not have my grandfather's letters to Peddy, so I can only infer, from Peddy's answers, what my grandfather might have written back).

Peddy further tells Henri in a thirteen-page letter that Kali Jompo's direction and its shareholders should realize that because of Mannes's mismanagement, "the direction should not make demands or pose certain conditions or play HVA." (Handels Vereniging Amsterdam, or HVA, was a big corporation owning many plantations in Java. It was known for its autocratic management style.) Peddy continues: "It befits us to be very humble concerning Kali Jompo and to beg for God's blessing so that we may opt for the right cultivation system. . . . I therefore intend to dedicate my family and this land to the Holy Heart of Jesus, not because I am so devout but because we need God's blessing so much—and also because 'enlightened' Mankind (who is laughing?) does not seem to need religion anymore!" My uncle, Peddy, did not mince his words, but whether Mannes really messed up is open to debate.

The same letter mentions the thriving coffee trees, which were yellow and dying when Peddy arrived. He announces that he brought them back to life because he followed his own instincts rather than sticking to the advice of the Proefstation. That my own grandfather Jacques Francken (an apparent proponent of tough love) was unpleasant in his letters seems apparent when Peddy writes, embittered,

> Based on the infighting, to appoint me as the next administrator and the worries about my capacities as well as the unpleasant tone of the letters, conditions, and demands of the director in particular, Fré

[Peddy's wife] noticed that it almost seemed as if you were anticipating that the company was going to be run by a crook who needed to be monitored because he might burden the company with back taxes. We get the impression that you, concerning Kali Jompo, still sit on a high horse in Haarlem and that you seem to believe that Kali Jompo is a valuable possession, yes, a goldmine, and that I should thank the Lord on my bare knees because I was so lucky to oversee this beautiful piece of land.

Peddy's frustrations were deep, as they must have been for many administrators. Pressured by directors and shareholders in Holland, they sometimes had to apply more modern and more expensive methods that were not always suitable for the land. "As far as that 'going along' with the agricultural fashion goes," Peddy complains, "modernity has not always paid off in the last few years at Kali Jompo. . . . I have calculated," Peddy continues, "that it has cost us 90,000 guilders [in the past ten years]." This comes to 9,000 guilders a year, or 750 guilders a month (about $6,000 today).

My great-uncle was a man of principle, and by being stubborn and trusting his own methods he risked confrontation with his family. He also missed the wisdom of his father: "It's a pity Dad is no longer around, for with him these insanities would not have happened." I think of the painting of my great-grandfather, the one in which he wears a pince-nez (see fig. 7.3). He looks like an owl, and apparently this image was emblematic of the great agricultural wisdom he was known to possess.

But it was also a battle of wills between a younger and older brother. Peddy did have to prove himself, of course, and his inferiority complex comes to the surface when he says things like: "I warn you in this letter because by now you probably still have very little confidence in me and I will possibly be cornered with the question: how long has that little arrogant fellow worked in agriculture? What does he know?"

Both Rob Nieuwenhuys and Madelon Lulofs have observed that Indies society was very individualistic: everyone was basically on his

Figure 7.3: Jacques Marinus Wilhelmus Francken. *Source: Jack Francken*

own (much like the first pioneers of America). But this forced pattern of self-reliance also made people in the Indies question authority more easily, and in particular they questioned the authority, governance, and rules that were coming out of The Hague. While The Hague and Jacques seemed to embody the rational ego, prescribing laws from afar, Java and Peddy seemed to represent the rebellious, impulsive, and more emotional id.

Was Jacques out of touch, and did he idealize life in Java? He had been there last as a tourist, staying in fancy hotels and burning the midnight oil with late-night dinners and dances. Or maybe he still had the *tempo dulu* life of his parents in mind. This was the life as P. A. Daum had portrayed it in some of his Indies novels: "Life is about ease and pleasure. That is the only ideal that counts. Indies people know what the good life is. Lazing about in a luxurious environment, beautiful women, a good cuisine, nice drinks, and no more exercise than is good for one's digestion."[12] But Peddy knew nothing of this kind of *tempo dulu* lifestyle. He probably worked from sunrise till late at night with perhaps a one-hour siesta during the hottest part of the day. And still it was not enough, because the Depression widened and deepened.

In part Dutch policy was to blame. The Dutch had a so-called open-door policy: they did not levy high duties on imports, and most immigrants immediately received the same economic rights and status as every one else. This was advantageous to Japan. Not only did Japanese immigrants begin to compete aggressively with the Dutch in the Indies, but "immediately after 1930 Japan began to flood the Indies as well as the rest of the world with its products and at the same time build up, wherever it could, an agricultural production in competition with that of the Indies. Before the Depression the Japanese imported only ten items; in 1934, these imports exceeded Indies exports to Japan by seventy-four million guilders; 31 percent of the imports came from Japan and only five percent of the Indies exports went to that country."[13] In other words, Japan was monopolizing the Indies market while protecting its own.

In 1937 the Dutch government tried to intervene by balancing imports and exports through the promotion and support of small businesses in the Indies and the protection of Indies trade, an effort that succeeded in balancing trade but angered the Japanese. Whether this government measure was of any use to the Franckens' business remains to be questioned, although the dividend payments, which had been nil in the previous years, did seem to come back, however modest. At least Peddy managed to stay afloat, whereas many rubber gardens, as large as or larger than Kali Jompo went bankrupt or lay fallow.

At the same time, Kali Jompo's survival may have had to do with its diversification in crops (coffee) as well as the fact, that despite the slump, the demand for rubber increased as it moved into the home: everything from electrical insulation, shoe soles, waterproof boots, refrigerators, vacuum cleaners, rain gear, and birth control required rubber. "Many 'Victorian' sports and games," Henry Hobhouse explains, "derive from a time when vulcanized rubber became available: lawn tennis, football, even billiards. Rubber became essential in hoses and seals of every kind, in suspension of all sorts, in sound-proofing, heat insulation and carpeting. Aircraft were stuffed with rubber, more so even than were cars."[14] My great-grandfather had made a good gamble in planting his first rubber trees at Kali Jompo. It made a small fortune, but in the end the family could not hold onto it.

Chapter 8

LAST BIRDS OF PARADISE

Peddy's letters bring a dose of reality: about the Depression, about backbreaking labor, about trying hard but not succeeding, about loss of face, about being humbled, and about the brewing threat of Japanese competition and hegemony.

I got a completely different picture when I started asking Harry about his childhood at Kali Jompo. He and his sisters were the last birds of paradise, the last generation of Dutch children who were born in the Indies to experience a childhood as marvelous and exotic as the Indies childhood of Peddy and Jacques. While Peddy was banging away on his typewriter late at night, Willy, Joke, and Harry were in bed under their mosquito netting, dreaming of the adventures they had had in the *kali,* the kites they flew with the kids of the village nearby, and the orchids they took care of in their mother's flower garden.

It was an idyllic childhood (see fig. 8.1). Huib Wiedenhoff, a childhood friend, reminisces in an e-mail: "It was fun to walk with your bare feet through the shallow, clear creek and catch the tropical fish.[1] Later in Holland, I had to pay a small fortune for the same aquarium fish!" He uses the Malay word *kaki* for feet—there are many Malay words in Dutch, as there are many Dutch words in Malay and Indonesian, but the postcolonial generations of Dutch and Indonesian speakers know little about the strange marriage of these two languages. When a Dutch person uses the word *kakkerlak*

Figure 8.1: Fré, Willy, and Joke Francken on the steps of Kali Jompo. *Source: Harry Francken*

(cockroach) or an Indonesian person talks about his *kantor* (office), they may think these words are as old and as original as their own languages: our shared colonial heritage is hidden in more ways than one.

What else does Huib remember? The birds, all sorts of tropical birds, he writes: "At home in Kebon Sari we would try and find their nests and raise some of the birds ourselves." Nature, in its entire colorful variety, was right outside one's doorstep, and the adults enjoyed their natural environment too, especially when they went hunting for wild boar. One could also meet bears and tigers in the jungle, and of course the monkeys were always there swinging from tree to tree and screeching wildly during the heavy monsoon rains.

At one point Huib chanced upon an indigenous wedding at one of the plantations. He was not allowed to go there but was drawn in by the delicious food. At the same time he noticed a cow that was pulled down and fell to the floor suddenly. Its legs and head were tied to bamboo poles.

> There was a lot of music and singing and some men with ornate platters approached. They were accompanied by a man who wore beautiful clothes. He started praying out loud, took a little knife, and started cutting into the neck of the cow. Time and again he would stop to pray until the cow pushed and pulled, upon which more blood flowed. Small pieces were cut from the cow's neck and put on the platters. At

that point I left. I did not want to wait for the slaughter of the goats.
I did not sleep very well that night.

Huib also tells me about some of the plantations he knew. When
he mentions Kali Jompo, I perk up: "Kali Jompo was the estate of
the Franckens. We loved this place because we played a lot with
Willy and Joke. Harry was known as Herrieke." It is an Indies custom to nickname children: Laurine was Iesje and Lorretje, Jacques
was Jacquie, Henri was Harry, Herman was Mannes, Ferdinand was
Peddy, Willeke was Willy, and Johanna was Joke.

Huib remembers my great-uncle Peddy with telling detail: "He
sometimes wore snake-leather shoes with a lot of white in it. That
was too effeminate for my taste. In his office there were a lot of bottles of booze." The Franckens did not like the club, but they did
enjoy parties with friends. Huib mentions that Peddy made illegal
gin in his office, together with another planter. "He had big glass
containers that used to hold [the very poisonous] formic acid."

In my mind I wandered with Huib through the house, and leaving Peddy's office with the bottles and tired typewriter, I imagined
the big library with the encyclopedia in which Huib's mother discovered that she had the first symptoms of leukemia. There was a dark
living room with a *celeng* (boar) head on the wall. By way of the big
front room, one ended up on the front porch with the steps that led
to the lawn, the garden path with gravel, and Fré's flower borders.

For Dutch people the mountain climate of Jember was much
easier to tolerate than the stifling heat of the big cities. Willem Walraven (whom I have quoted several times now because he is such a
wonderful chronicler of the daily life that the Franckens knew) loved
the mountains because one could sleep under blankets, be free of mosquitoes, and create vegetable gardens and cultivate roses.[2] For the
Javanese the mountains were sometimes too cool, and to warm up
they would sit cross-legged on the hot asphalt, or so Harry tells me.

Did Willy, Joke, and Harry sleep without blankets? The nights
could be cool—their bedroom windows did have steel bars to protect them from wild animals. At night, one could sometimes hear

the breathing and heavy paws of a panther or tiger walking on the open verandas.

In the morning the children would be awakened by the first noises the servants made. Pamela Pattynama, who has written about daily life in the Indies, says: "Even before the sun was up, while it was still cool, one could hear the morning noises of the animals. The *kebon* [*sic*] swept the grounds and the *babu* was over by the well, splashing with water. Between the trees there was the smoke and smell of little charcoal fires."[3]

At Kali Jompo you could "shower" with cold water or wait till the tiled tub, which had to be filled with water first, was full and sufficiently warmed up. In that tub, you could sprinkle yourself with a *gayung,* a cup on a stick. The well had a wall around it so the *babus* and *koki* had a little bit of privacy when bathing. Huib tells me that he and his brother sometimes peeped over the wall to spy on the women; if the women discovered them, they would scream and, as Huib says, "we would be in trouble!"

After the *mandi* (bath), it was time for breakfast with oatmeal, bread, and butter. Jam and cheese came in tins. Ma Eh, the cook, took care of most of the meals. Mina ironed with an iron that was heated by charcoal. There were several women to help with laundry and cleaning the house. The Franckens also had a chauffeur, Kassidin, but when Fré discovered he slept so much during the day, she trained him to be a butler as well. Harry remembers how Kassidin waited at the table in white. Kassidin also bossed around the babus.

After breakfast Kassidin took the girls down to the Dutch school in Jember (see fig. 8.2). Harry rode along as soon as he was ready for kindergarten, but because he was naughty and spent more time in the *gudang* (the school's pantry), his mother took him out of school and let him run wild with the boys of the nearby village: "They were my equals—we played as equals," Harry tells me. "I had a car with pedals and we all took turns, but I slowly began to notice that they did give me the special treatment; after all, I was the *orang belanda.* Nonetheless, I always went to the *kongsi* [the plantation grounds; *kongsi* really means firm or partnership] and the women

Figure 8.2: Joke and Willy with Kassidin in the background. *Source: Harry Francken*

always spoiled me because they seemed to like such a little white boy. Maybe this is why I love women so much."

Life at Kali Jompo was lonely because it was in such a remote area. According to Harry, this was no problem for his mother because she was a real homebody. She enjoyed working with the staff and did the bookkeeping. She sewed all the clothes for the children and provided first aid for people in the village (hence the medical library of the Franckens). She also tended to her flower garden, where she grew orchids, and a vegetable garden.

At noon the children came home and had lunch, after which it was time for a nap. Usually the adults slept and the kids played. Huib remembers going down to the factory:

In the factory a lot of water was needed for the peeling of the coffee beans and there was a big water engine. Outside there was an enormous gutter—this one started high in the mountain and the water came down with tremendous speed. "Do not come near the gutter!" the adults had warned us, but my older brother Joop wanted to impress the girls and decided to hang over it while touching the water with his feet. He liked to brag . . . or was it hormones? Anyhow, the force of the water almost dragged him down!

Figure 8.3: Kali Jompo in the 1930s. *Source: Harry Francken*

In the coffee rooms there were "big bags of coffee beans which were emptied in big concrete water containers," Huib says. "The beans," he continues,

> would be rotting in there for quite a while. I guess they call it fermentation. After that, they opened the doors and all the beans came pouring out and they were then crushed and washed in between what looked like a press. The peels were washed away and the white-greenish beans ended up on big iron grates. The workers would be shoveling beans all day in the scorching sun. When the beans were almost dry it was great to climb up and run through the beans on your *kaki* and roll your whole body in them. . . . Uncle Peddy was in the office or in the fields but he never sent us away! It was lovely!"

The fermentation Huib refers to was required to separate the green beans from the berries. According to Hobhouse, there are "two methods of fermentation, wet and dry, both involving large tanks of water. . . . In the so-called 'dry' method, the pulp is removed from the tanks when semi-dry, semi-wet. In the 'wet' method, the pulp remains in the tanks until naturally separated from the beans.

In both cases, the beans, now separated from the pulp are dried, either by being spread over a large area subject to Sun and Wind or in a mechanical dryer like a grain dryer. The first method is more labour intensive than the second."[4]

One may wonder why, during the rubber boom of the 1920s, Kali Jompo did not become an all-out rubber farm. The reason to hold onto coffee had to do with diversification—in farming, as well as in the stock market, one should never bet on one horse, and coffee had always been a great money maker for the Dutch in general and the Franckens in particular. What's more, "the more demanding the growing conditions, the higher the quality of the [coffee]."[5] The higher altitude and the cooler nights made Kali Jompo beans stand out from the varietals that were grown and harvested in Brazil. Because these higher-altitude and higher-quality coffee beans were much rarer on the world market, they were sold at higher prices.

The Dutch were masters at running the coffee trade, a monopoly they took over from the Arabs in the eighteenth century. The first substantial coffee cargo arrived in Amsterdam in 1712, and by 1725 the coffee trade of Amsterdam amounted to nearly a thousand long tons a year. "By 1750 Java was the trade name for coffee from any of the Dutch East Indian islands," and even though the empire was on its last legs in the eighteenth century, Holland remained a key player because of increased production in the East Indies and the country's strategic midway point between coffee-consuming Germany and Scandinavia. But the Dutch liked their coffee, too, "being the greatest consumers per head of liquid coffee for two centuries after 1700."[6] The power of coffee should never be underestimated, for even today, "coffee is worth six to eight times as much as crude oil when oil is at $60 a barrel—about $480 a long ton. . . . Coffee has always made some men rich; others have gambled at the wrong time or in the wrong direction and have depleted their wealth. This is still true in the futures market." So in retrospect the Franckens were right (in spite of the success of rubber) to hold onto coffee cultivation, especially because the Kali Jompo bean was high in quality and always in demand on the world market.

Harry remembers the coffee rooms as vividly as Huib. At night he and his sisters would sometimes sneak out of the house and walk down to the coffee shed to lie down in the warm coffee beans: "Sometimes the *mandur* [chief, foreman] would still be shoveling coffee, but the moment he saw us, he would put away his shovel and tell us the most amazing stories. It was great."

During the coffee harvest the children had to stay indoors because of the danger of snakes and scorpions. The Javanese women and workers, however, did bring their children. The little ones would be wrapped in a *slendang* (a sort of sling), and those that could walk would accompany their mother carrying little tins and baskets in which they collected something that they picked up from the ground. Huib explains: "Willy and Joke told me that they collected the droppings of the *luwak*." The *luak,* or coffee rat, resembles a small mongoose. It has a good nose for the tastiest and ripest coffee beans, which it eats. In its droppings one can find the undigested beans, which are used to make the very expensive but very delicious luak coffee. Huib writes: "We looked inside those baskets and we thought the whole idea revolting, but we did not drink coffee anyway."

Although the children were not allowed to go outside during the harvest, Harry and his sisters often slipped out anyway. "The atmosphere was wonderful," Harry remembers. "The roadside would be lined with *warung* [eateries] because the workers snacked all day long. In the background was the constant pounding of a bamboo drummer who played a rhythm that was supposed to stimulate the workers and speed up the picking. My mother told us we could not eat from the *warung* because it was not considered hygienic." (Hygiene might have been one of the reasons, but another one surely was that Dutch children were kept away as much as possible from the local foods and *warung* because Dutch mothers believed that the eating of local food led to "Indianization.")[7] Thus, the local food became forbidden fruit and all the more desirable. "We helped with the harvest," Harry remembers, "and brought our beans to the *mandur* at the factory, who would pay us. With this money we went to the *warung* and bought all our favorite foods."

Neither Huib nor Harry talked about the rubber or latex sheds. Could the smell have kept them out? Lulofs writes in her novel *Rubber* that rubber smelled like "rotten eggs combined with Lysol" and "some coolies never got rid of the smell: when they wanted a woman they had to pay double."[8] Louis Couperus visited a rubber plantation in 1921 and thought the hevea rubber gardens boring to behold, just rows and rows of unexceptional trees producing a white milk in which Couperus had no interest whatsoever. Let us not forget that Louis Couperus, the Dutch Henry James, was a sophisticated man from the city. His roots lay in Batavia and The Hague, where his ancestors had resided in stately homes and offices, pushing paper rather than harvesting coffee or rubber.[9]

Although rubber might have seemed a much less attractive and less sensational crop than coffee, it would become vital to Indonesia's growth as an independent nation. Without rubber, "Indonesia might have found it impossible to survive as a sovereign state and would have broken into component islands," while at the same time it "remains a commodity at least as valuable and vital as oil, and unlike oil, natural rubber came to be grown instead of only being extracted."[10]

While Harry hardly mentions the rubber in his dad's gardens, he does have fond memories of the monsoons: "We always went out to have fun in the rain. We made slippery paths down the slope and while sitting on our butts, we slid down on the slick clay. I'd come home black with mud. I usually had lost my shorts during the sliding, and mother pretended she was mad, but I don't think she was for real."

Kite flying was another pastime: "The kids from the village helped me make a kite," Harry tells me in a letter. "The kite's rope would be dipped in glue and put through a fine kind of glass powder. Then we dried them. Flying the kites, the kids would compete by a meeting of the ropes: they would 'saw' each other's ropes and the kite that survived would move on to the next kite. The men made big kites which they decorated with little whistles and buzzers so they made a lot of noise when they were high up in the sky."

Figure 8.4: Willy, Joke, and *babu* in the Jompo river.
Source: Harry Francken

The famous Dutch historian Lou de Jong also grew up in the Indies and has this to say about the interbellum period:

> Everything in the Indies still looked stable. . . . There were no strikes, demonstrations, riots or revolts. . . . The Great Depression did not make a big impression on our personal lives: there were home, school, parties, the pool, and vacations in the mountains. It was a privileged time, carefree because of the sun and glorious Nature. Our memories of being a child in the Indies always have a magical aura: there is no other place in the world that satisfies the inner fantasy world of children, a world that is full of secrets, adventures, and thrilling phenomena.[11]

De Jong and the Francken children were part of a privileged world indeed, a world that perhaps lived inside its own bubble, because contrary to De Jong's childhood impressions, political turmoil was certainly perceptible in the cities and the recession was felt everywhere: the once-prosperous land had turned into a wasteland, and the "per capita availability of foodstuffs declined from 1930 to 1934. . . . Undoubtedly for many Indonesians times were very hard indeed on the eve of the Japanese conquest."[12]

Among the Dutch in the big cities the pinch was felt too. Some had no money to pay for repatriation. They would have to rely on local charities and soup kitchens, which grew in number. Walraven mentions that the police in the cities of Batavia and Surabaya offered night shelters for Europeans, which was, in his view, an unprecedented situation.[13] Yet the last generation of colonial children experienced a sheltered childhood and noticed little. But while Harry was flying kites and listening to the whistling and buzzing in the air, dark clouds were gathering over Java. Japan was looming on the horizon like an eagle watching its prey. The Japanese occupation would be the catalyst for the decolonization of the Dutch East Indies.

Chapter 9

THE JAPANESE INVASION

> The Germans had already made the concept of "lightning
> war" their own. But never in military history has lightning
> struck in so many places with such devastating results as
> it did in Asia and the Pacific between the beginning of
> December 1941 and the end of April 1942. Moreover, the
> distances involved were vastly greater than those being
> covered simultaneously by the Germans in Europe. At its
> maximum extent, the Japanese Empire stretched 6,400
> miles from west to east and 5,300 miles from north to
> south; its circumference was a staggering 14,200 miles.
>
> Niall Ferguson, *The War of the World: Twentieth-
> Century Conflict and the Descent of the West* (2006)

Long before Japan's territorial expansion, Honda Toshiaki (1744–1821),
whom some called the Japanese Benjamin Franklin, had already
proclaimed that in order to become an empire like that of the Dutch
or the British, Japan needed "four things: gunpowder, metals, shipping and colonization."[1]

The first Japanese "acquisitions" consisted of Chinese Formosa
(now Taiwan) in 1894, Korea in 1910, and, after the First World War,
the former German possessions of Kiaochao in China and the Mari-
ana, Caroline, and Marshall Islands in the Pacific as a reward for
having been an ally of Great Britain. As the Japanese made the transition from "foreign orientals" to "honorary Europeans," the white
man's burden became a Japanese one, as Japan felt its culture to be
naturally superior to that of the Taiwanese, the Koreans, and the
Indonesians, whom they called mere "islanders."[2] Rather stealthily,

Japan had also moved its army deeper into Manchuria while Europe was preoccupied with the Great War. Prior to Japanese military imperialism, the Japanese had already tried to penetrate the Indonesian archipelago with Japanese migrants and trade. As a result, the first Japanese consulate in Batavia was opened in 1919, and a year later the *Java Daily* was started, the first Japanese-language newspaper in the Indies.[3]

Propelled by the "Great Asianism" ideology, which prophesied that it was Japan's "predestined mission" to "liberate" the entire Asian region from Western rule, the Japanese had conquered all of Manchuria by 1932, which was also "the crucial moment at which Japan's estrangement from Western democracies began."[4] The League of Nations, predecessor to the United Nations, condemned Japan's Manchurian conquest, which inflamed Japanese sentiment against the West further, and the Japanese bowed out of the League of Nations in 1933.

The Japanese hid their imperial ambitions behind the "liberation of Asia" rhetoric, which appealed to the young, including young nationalists abroad, like Sukarno. Apparently, Sukarno foresaw Japan's role and dominance before the war and embraced it as a potential means to an end—independence for Indonesia.[5]

But in order to "liberate Asia," the imperial army had to grow significantly, which it did. To control the expansion of Japan's military, order and discipline were strictly enforced by physical violence, including face slapping, blows with the fist, hitting with bamboo sticks or canes, kicking with army boots, as well as shaming. The army became the soldier's "family" and "towering over the whole familial-hierarchical structure was the all-powerful god-figure of the emperor himself.... Every day recruits would bow in the direction of the Imperial Palace to show respect; each order they were given was issued 'in the name of the emperor'; every beating they received was meted out because the emperor would have wished it."[6] This culture of violence in honor of the emperor would have disastrous consequences for the POWs and the civilians who were to surrender to the Japanese in the following years. In fact, Rees believes that the bullying and violence in the Japanese army during the 1930s made the violence of the Nanking massacres (1937) possible, violence that was further exacerbated by the fact that Japanese soldiers were brainwashed to believe that the Chinese were subhuman, "like animals and bugs."[7] In a similar fashion, the Germans dehumanized the Jews, a mechanism that, in both cases, opened the door to genocide.

The similarities to Nazi Germany are worth pointing out: both countries had "turned their backs on democracy," both were rearming rapidly, both saw communism and the Soviet Union as enemies, and both had bold ambitions to expand territorially. To underline these commonalities, Japan signed an "anti-Comintern Pact" (an anticommunism treaty) with Germany in 1936, "thus demonstrating to the world that her strongest friends in the West were the new fascist nations of Germany and Italy."[8]

Niall Ferguson comments that the economic volatility of the 1930s had "weakened existing empires" while stimulating the growth of new imperial states such as Germany and Japan. "It had been economic volatility that had inspired a new and ruthless imperialism based on the seductive notion of living space—of economic recovery through territorial expansion."[9]

For the Western Allies the war with Japan did not begin with Manchuria or Nanking but with Pearl Harbor. After Nanking (and prior to Pearl Harbor) the next opportune moment for the Japanese lay in Europe, with the Germans' swift annexation of Poland in 1939 and invasion of the Netherlands, Belgium, and France in 1940. In September of 1940 the Japanese moved their troops into northern Indochina (now Vietnam), thereby gaining easy access to British Malaya and the Dutch East Indies. After announcing an oil embargo, the United States also threatened an iron and steel embargo, which convinced the Japanese that they had no choice but to control the Dutch East Indies because of the latter's plentiful resources, which were required to fuel the war machine. But the Japanese did not strike immediately.

On July 2, 1941, the Japanese initiated the so-called Co-Prosperity Sphere, a pseudocollaborative pact between Asian nations that was

Japan's way of legitimizing future conquests. This triggered the American freezing of all Japanese assets in the States, plus a complete oil embargo. Britain and Holland followed suit with similar sanctions against Japan, while "Japanese newspapers, in their usual tone of victimhood, reported that Japan's lifeline was being strangled by the ABCD powers: American, British, Chinese, and Dutch."[10]

Needless to say, the Dutch colonial government began to get very nervous. With the pressure building, the Dutch in the Indies had not forgotten the words of Hachiro Arita, the Japanese Minister of Foreign Affairs, who had implied that the Indies would be appropriated by Japan if Holland resisted the Germans. Ironically, rather than focusing on their own defense against a potential Japanese invasion, people in the Indies raised taxes and encouraged civil contributions (which would buy more than one hundred and twenty Spitfires and thirty bombers) to support the Allied war effort in Europe. With hindsight, the money would have been better spent on the reinforcement of the KNIL, the Dutch colonial army.[11] Incidentally, the Indonesians themselves had offered to reinforce the colonial army in exchange for representation in local, regional, and national government. But afraid to give up their own privileged position, the Dutch declined the offer, excusing themselves by saying that they could not make such a decision without a free Dutch Parliament, which was no longer in existence under the Germans.[12]

When the Japanese "invited" the Dutch colonial government to join the Co-Prosperity Sphere, Batavia declined, whereas French Indochina (or rather the Vichy government in France) agreed. This opened the floodgates to the Japanese occupation of the rest of Southeast Asia. From the tip of southern Indochina it was but a small skip and a jump to the British cities of Hong Kong and Singapore. From there, the Dutch East Indies were also within easy reach. Contrary to popular belief, Nicholas Tarling writes, the Japanese advance into Southeast Asia was "the product of growing fear and unthinking optimism. It followed a long period in which Japan had sought to achieve its aims by pressure rather than invasion. It was not in fact prepared for the task of occupation. In the case of the Indies, it still hoped to avoid armed force, and it did not declare war" until the Dutch did, after the attack on Pearl Harbor.[13]

After the Dutch East Indies refused to join the Co-Prosperity Pact because of the unreasonable conditions stipulated by Japan, Japan started building up its troops in southern Indochina and told its nationals to leave the Indies and Dutch women and children living in Japan to leave Japan.[14] Significantly, the colonial government of Batavia was a firm ally of the United States, which meant that, after the Japanese embargoes, all the rubber that was produced at a 120 percent rate of the normal quota was delivered straight to the United States. This is worthy of note because at this point all communication between Peddy and Jacques seems to have been interrupted because of the war in Europe and the impending war in Asia.[15] After all the years of economic hardship and toil, 1941 must have finally been a good year financially for Peddy and his family. The last dividend payment of that period that I have managed to find was conservatively determined at 5 percent. In the annual reports for 1940 and 1941, drawn up by my grandfather as late as 1948, I read that because of the war the directorate of Kali Jompo was transferred to Peddy in Java. In the same report I saw that 1940 and 1941 were good years indeed, with profits totaling 26,588.96 guilders, which did not quite rival the boom numbers of 200,000 guilders of the 1920s but still amounts to more than 240,000 U.S. dollars in today's terms.

Peddy's sudden windfall could not continue under the Japanese. As noted in the annual report for 1948, when the plantation was confiscated by the Japanese in 1943, "coffee was still harvested but rubber was no longer tapped." This seems contradictory because it was rubber especially that the Japanese hoped to get out of the Indies. The report also mentions that in 1945, when local food shortages became particularly bad, 252 acres were cleared to plant food crops for the local population.

Although the Dutch colonial army had been preparing for war in 1941, it had not modernized and was lacking modern fighter planes and arms. On November 30, 1941, the Dutch navy placed itself in position, and on December 2 and 6 the Dutch colonial army was mobilized while Australian troops were allowed to enter Java. But still the Japanese did not move, or rather, did not move in the direction of the Indies. This was because the Japanese knew full well that if they attacked Singapore and the Indies, the U.S. fleet in Hawaii would come to the rescue. One of the reasons why Japan carried out a preemptive strike against Pearl Harbor was so that it could have unhindered access to the resources of the Indies.

The attack on Pearl Harbor took place on December 8, 1941, at three in the morning, Japanese time, 6 a.m. December 7 Pearl Harbor time. A Japanese delegation in Washington, DC, was still engaged in diplomatic talks with the U.S. government when it happened. Almost immediately the Indies declared war on Japan, and Queen Wilhelmina, who had escaped to London, where she acted as the head of the Dutch government in exile, announced that "a bomb on Pearl Harbor" was the equivalent of a "bomb on Java." Just five hours after the strike on Pearl Harbor, the British colony of Hong Kong was attacked; the British, like the Dutch and the Americans, had completely underestimated the Japanese military might and the crazed commitment of the kamikaze suicide missions.[16]

On December 12, the People's Council of the Dutch East Indies prepared the people to resist the Japanese in case of an attack. Peddy would take his own measures, something I will return to in the next chapter. After the devastating loss of Pearl Harbor, Hong Kong, the Philippines, and Singapore were easy prey for the Japanese troops. After Singapore, the Indies were next.

Bernard Vlekke writes that "before a single Japanese set foot on Indonesian soil, 50 percent of the Dutch planes had already been lost, submarines had been sunk, and the remaining aircraft were in bad condition, supplies low."[17] The Japanese charged ahead, and while some of the Dutch troops fought bitterly, there was a general impression that the Dutch army was as incapacitated as it had been in the Netherlands. The German and Japanese invasions were decided in days and weeks rather than months. On January 10 the first Japanese troops landed in Java, on February 20 and 22 Bali and

Timor were taken, and on March 5, Batavia, which was defended by the Dutch, British, Australian, and American Allies, surrendered.

Vlekke, writing in 1946, believed that as soon as the Japanese threat became tangible in the Dutch East Indies, all the former strife and talk of independence disappeared and sixty million Indonesians were immediately loyal to the Dutch/Allied cause. Vlekke underestimated the force of the independence movement and did not anticipate that the Japanese occupation would speed up independence for the Indonesians after the war.

Also, as is typical of his generation, Vlekke was very much mistaken in his rather colonial assessment of the supposed loyalty of the Indonesians. In a recent article Elly Touwen-Bouwsma has argued that there was an underground nationalist movement that went aboveground as soon as the Japanese invaded. While the nationalist leaders Sukarno, Hatta, and Sjahrir had been jailed by the Dutch at Bengkulen, the nationalists supported the Japanese because they believed they could not overthrow the Dutch on their own and they would never share full autonomy and equality with the Dutch. Another motive for joining the nationalists and supporting the Japanese invasion was that many Indonesians feared the rumored scorched-earth policy of the Dutch.

Thus, between the moment of invasion and capitulation in early March of 1942, "local nationalists seized the opportunity to set up so-called *Merdeka* [Freedom] committees. They instructed people to greet the Japanese with cries of 'Banzai' and to carry a handkerchief in the likeness of the Japanese flag with them." At the same time, they stirred up anti-Dutch feelings. In Jombang, where my grandfather was born, the Dutch police reported that nationalist propaganda proclaimed that "the natives must have no sympathy for the Dutch. They had tyrannized and exploited the Indonesian people. The Indonesians should help the Japanese to murder the Dutch." This caused social unrest and looting, of which the main targets were the Dutch, Eurasian civil servants, and the Chinese.

Even though the Merdeka committees, political rallies, and the waving of the Indonesian flag were quickly outlawed by the Japanese,

Touwen-Bouwsma believed that this was the "first social revolution" in Java and as such, "a forerunner of the large-scale social revolution which erupted directly after the capitulation in August of 1945."[18]

Sukarno's role and actions during and after the Japanese occupation are still a point of contention among Dutch historians. Condemning Sukarno for his collaboration with the Japanese (as Jacob Zwaan has done) is akin to identifying oneself as an imperialist and generally "not done" in context of the Dutch postcolonial discourse.[19]

Petra Groen criticizes Zwaan for calling Sukarno a "Japanese puppet," an "opportunist," and a "megalomaniac."[20] She argues that Sukarno used the Japanese occupation as a viable road to independence, through defeat of the Dutch, and, as such, the only means to an end. She adds that Sukarno disagreed with the political convictions and goals of the Japanese and may have used the Japanese as much as the Japanese used him.

Groen concludes that the final contribution and role of Sukarno should be determined by the Indonesians, not by the Dutch. While there is some merit to such an argument, it also raises questions, for does this mean that Germans would also be precluded from writing about the Second World War or the Holocaust? As I discussed in my introduction, this kind of self-imposed censorship that some Dutch historians engage in seems to derive from recurring Calvinist guilt regarding past colonial abuses and crimes committed by the Dutch.

This politicized polarization between a more colonial and anticolonial point of view is not only typical of the postcolonial historical debate in the Netherlands, but also characteristic of the warring voices within postcolonial literatures. As Pamela Pattynama has argued in a recent article: "In the Dutch collective memory the Indies have become an ambivalent and controversial place. On the one hand the Indies are still associated with the continuing colonial rhetoric of an idyllic, exotic, and adventurous past (which was already being demythologized during the colonial period). On the other hand, the postcolonial vision is filled with shame and guilt regarding Dutch racism/orientalism, exploitation, and war crimes."[21] Both interpretations may be called extreme, tending toward stereotypes that may not reflect the actual colonial and postcolonial experience at all.

When Remco Raben organized a NIOD exhibit in 1999 entitled Representing the Japanese Occupation of Indonesia: Personal Testimonies and Public Images in Indonesia, Japan and the Netherlands," which also appeared in book form, the public could see some of the same extremes in the reactions of people who visited the exhibit. All parties involved in the war (the Dutch, Japanese, and Indonesians) who visited the exhibit were focusing on their own memories of victimhood and therefore found their own experiences underrepresented in the show.[22] While the Dutch have always maligned the Japanese for uprooting, interning, terrorizing, and starving them, Japanese veterans remember the horrors of the atomic bombs and their "unfair" treatment during postwar military tribunals. Indonesians who visited the show, Raben writes, were remarkably quiet: "Memories of the Japanese period are ambiguous and tend to be overshadowed by the subsequent struggle for independence and the horrors of civil unrest during the 1950s and 1960s. For Indonesians, the complicity of their own intellectuals and politicians during the Japanese period makes a simple crystallization of memory impossible."[23]

Raben's findings show that the different perspectives on the war in Indonesia are biased to such a degree that one cannot speak of an objective historical discourse as long as survivors and witnesses keep pushing their version of the war. This needs to be noted because I too have been influenced by the constant stereotyping of villainous Germans and Japanese soldiers.

It is probable that the Franckens did not notice the real impact of the invasion until Surabaya was invaded. From Elly Touwen-Bouwsma's article we know that a Merdeka committee was formed in Jember and that thousands of people in Jember greeted the Japanese army with "Banzai!" chants. Harry remembers that his mother told him the Japanese were preparing a possible invasion by using undercover Japanese agents: "Jember's most popular hairdresser turned out to be an undercover agent who was also a very senior officer with the Kempeitai (the Japanese military police)," Harry writes me in an e-mail. Were the "Banzai!" cries loud enough to travel up the mountain to Kali Jompo and be heard by the Franckens? If they were, how did the family feel and how did they view the Indonesians who believed that the Jayabaya prophecy, which predicted that the Indonesians would be liberated by an Asian people, had finally come true?

After Java, Sumatra was "liberated," and in June 1942 the Moluccas were taken. One could argue that the Indies were the last sacrificial lamb. While some American troops helped defend the Indies, it was too little, too late for the Indonesian archipelago, which had always been a difficult place to defend because it was so spread out. Nonetheless, the Americans were in time to help defend Australia, which would form a vital base for the counterattack on the Japanese in 1945. Although the initial victory went to the Japanese, they would be "faced with a war of attrition with the greatest industrial power among all the belligerents—a type of war she could not win."[24] The Japanese feared that if the Allies attacked, it would come from the Australian corner, which made eastern Java especially susceptible to guerrilla fighting and fifth-column activities, a realm that Peddy was pulled into as well. On March 8, 1942, the colonial government surrendered to the Japanese. The Dutch did not know it then, but they had already lost their colony forever.

Chapter 10

PEDDY'S FATE

Yes, the dead do speak, but in their own way and at their own time.

Pramoedya Ananta Toer, *The Mute's Soliloquy* (1999)

It's not just that Japan has doled out less than one percent of the amount that Germany has paid in war reparations to its victims. It is not just that, unlike most Nazis, who, if not incarcerated for their crimes were at least forced from public life, many Japanese war criminals continued to occupy powerful positions in industry and government after the war. And it is not just the fact that while Germans have made repeated apologies to their Holocaust victims, the Japanese have enshrined their war criminals in Tokyo—an act that one American wartime victim of the Japanese has labeled politically equivalent to "erecting a cathedral for Hitler in the middle of Berlin."

Iris Chang, *The Rape of Nanking* (1997)

The original scenario was that Mannes and Kitty would return to Kali Jompo in the late thirties or early forties so that Peddy and his family could go on a well-deserved leave, but with the outbreak of the war in the Netherlands, this obviously had to be postponed. People in the Indies had a false sense of security—many thought it was better to be in the Indies than in German-occupied Holland, not knowing that two years later they would lose their homes and property and be interned in camps where men were separated from women and where torture, disease, starvation, and death broke the numbing routine of lining up for roll call at noon and bowing to the emperor. Others, like most of the POWs and Dutch male civilians, were worked to death on the Burma railway line. Still others ended up in the so-called death marches through the jungle until they dropped dead and were left behind to be devoured by ants.

In the Netherlands it is taboo to compare the suffering of Holocaust victims to the hardships of Europeans, Eurasians, and Indonesians who fell victim to the Japanese. In my search for more information about the Birnies, an old planter family in Jember who lived close to the Franckens, I got in touch with a Birnie descendant who also happens to be a well-known Dutch author by the name of Alfred Birney. "Whoever dares juxtapose the Jewish and Indies episodes from the Second World War in whatever way," he tells me in an e-mail, "will not be heard in the Netherlands. . . . Indies people and Indos in particular receive no sympathy whatsoever. To be colonial and to have been colonized at the same time is something that people in Holland never understood and will never comprehend." There is no yardstick for all the suffering in the Second World War, but it is equally counterproductive to sweep the war in Asia under the rug just because it did not take place in Europe or has not been adequately portrayed in Hollywood movies.

As mentioned earlier, I had several versions of Peddy's death: "Peddy died in prison, where he was executed by the Japanese because he would not bow his head to the Japanese emperor," one version goes. Another version was that he was in fact decapitated, and yet another was that he died as a result of dysentery. My most direct link with Peddy was Harry, his only son.

Harry exhibited the typical tropics nostalgia when he spoke of his childhood in our first face-to-face meeting. His father was a colorful figure in these reminiscences, a man who played soccer with him on the lawn. He would take Harry down to the plantation as well, which must have given the little boy a sense of importance. Harry also remembers how Peddy played chess with Fré and how he would distract her and push over the chessboard when he noticed he was losing. Peddy was too skinny, and Fré tried to fatten him up with oatmeal,

Figure 10.1: Fré, Harry (as a baby), and Peddy at Kali Jompo in the 1930s. *Source: Harry Francken*

which he would secretly feed to Harry instead. My great-uncle was a prankster, a man with a naughty sense of humor, but above all a man who loved his family. At the same time, Peddy was combative. Harry remembers vicious fights between his father and mother. No doubt stress caused by the Great Depression, the demands of the plantation, and the raising of young children played into this.

From the few letters Peddy left behind, I also know that he was a hard worker and a worrier. He was passionate and driven when it came to doing the best thing for Kali Jompo. When I asked Harry about his father's death, he told me that he died of dysentery in Sukamiskin Prison. He said it rather matter-of-factly but added that he did not even know where his father was buried. "How should we know?" Harry writes me in a letter. "As one of the many people who died under the Japanese," he explains, "my father must have been dumped into an unmarked grave. Why after all, would the Japanese have bothered to give him a proper burial?" His straightforwardness is at once startling and understandable, as, throughout his life, Harry has been trying to distance himself from the war trauma that befell his family.

However, I was not willing to leave it at that. The unmarked-grave theory and the many versions of Peddy's death indicated that there was something fishy going on here, or rather, that something went terribly wrong with the providing of information to relatives of the deceased after the war. This may have had to do with the general state of chaos and disarray Java was in after the capitulation in 1945, but it may also be rooted in the fact that no one in my family ever asked the right questions relating to Peddy's whereabouts and death. Why has my family not been more curious? Did they ever even question why Peddy died in Sukamiskin Prison rather than in an internment camp? Most Dutch citizens ended up in these camps, whereas prisons were reserved for people who resisted the Japanese regime. Given Peddy's resistance to his authoritarian older brother, it is somewhat likely that he also would have rebelled against the dictatorial Japanese. Even so, the people who were in prison were there because they awaited trial or execution. Acting up or rebelling in the internment camps was punished with torture, isolation, or the withholding of food and water. In order to end up in a prison, one had to have done more than merely act up.

The Japanese used Sukamiskin Prison in Bandung for the internment of VIPs of the colonial administration and later on, when Peddy was there, for political prisoners. Was Peddy a political prisoner? Andrew van Dyke seems to indicate that he might have been. In his listing of Japanese jails in Java, he writes that they contained not only "criminals held by the Dutch before the surrender" but also "members of clandestine newspapers, resistance group members, and persons who hid or otherwise aided escaped Allied servicemen. These unfortunates would be tortured by the Kempeitai and later disposed of. Examples of these facilities were Struiswijk, Glodok and Sukamiskin."[1] Obviously, Peddy would have belonged to the latter group of unfortunates who were either resistance fighters or men who helped resistance and/or Allied fighters. At the same time, all this was somewhat speculative, as I had no concrete proof that Peddy actually died in Sukamiskin. To find out, I decided to write the Red Cross in the Netherlands.

Within a month I received a letter from the Red Cross confirming that Ferdinand Adriaan Marie Francken, born in Malang on October 8, 1897, died in Sukamiskin Prison in Bandung on March 15, 1945, almost exactly five months before the Japanese surrender in August of 1945. "On the basis of our information," the letter tells me rather coldly, "the cause of death cannot be determined." This, the Dutch historian Winnie Rinzema-Admiraal tells me later, is "because the Japanese never recorded cause of death," not least because the cause of death might been brought on by the Japanese themselves, through torture, for example.

More importantly, while Harry said he had no information about where his father was buried, the Red Cross told me Peddy was buried at an *Ereveld,* the equivalent of a military cemetery, usually reserved only for soldiers and resistance fighters. If Peddy had died and been buried at Sukamiskin he would have been exhumed and reburied at the Ereveld after the war. Whatever his heroism amounted to that would warrant the Ereveld honor, in the Red Cross letter he has been reduced to a bunch of numerals and numbers that indicate his burial place in the cemetery: "Dutch Ereveld Pandu, Bandung, section IV, 101." With the date and location of his death confirmed, I tried to find out what happened to Peddy between the beginning of the invasion and his death in Bandung. What had he done to end up in Sukamiskin and the Pandu cemetery? To give a little more background and context, I have to go back to the moment when the Japanese invaded Java.

All accounts of the Japanese invasion written by civilians convey a sense of complete shock and surprise. Hein Matthijs was ten when he heard the famous radio broadcast with the national anthem, the "Wilhelmus," being played for the last time: "The next morning the Japanese entered B., on foot or by bike; they looked like a shabby and, in my view, not so dangerous army. I could not understand that our soldiers had lost the war against this army. It was eerily quiet in the street—here and there there were a few Indonesians waving little flags. My brother and I peeked through the cracks of the closed curtains. My mother and sister were in the back room . . . my father sat in his chair, staring quietly into space, completely defeated."[2]

Carel van Benthem, who worked for the colonial government in the unidentified town of T. and whose notes Hein Matthijs used to tell his story "Een kwestie van karma" (A Question of Karma), remembered the invasion as follows:

> On March 1 the Japanese landed near T. A few days later they stood in front of the office of the assistant resident in T. I can still see the face of d.W. when Suripto, the head *mantri,* entered the room after a short knock on the door: "There are visitors for you. They are Japanese soldiers!" Slowly d.W. hoisted himself out of the chair and mumbling goddammit he walked out. I followed him and saw about twenty-five Japanese soldiers by the front porch; they had placed their bicycles neatly against the building's pillars. A man with a star on his collar stepped forward and said in bad English: 'You boss here? We now occupy this city. We shoot you when there is trouble! More soldiers coming! All European males must assemble here tomorrow for registration! . . . You two responsible! No going home tomorrow, you two must stay here!" D.W. was nodding with quivering lips; he was not very brave anymore, but had become a fearful, older man.
>
> And this is how the Japanese on their little bikes, dressed in shabby uniforms and canvas shoes, occupied T. They moved into the BB office and at the elementary school and other strategic places they placed guards to prevent "rampok" (plunder) parties. As soon as the Japanese appeared in T., the town became a rumor mill about the Japanese who went around on their bikes or in stolen cars. "They rape women and girls, they did that in China and Malaya too," was the gossip, but I don't think anything like that happened in T.[3]

Although incidents of rape were rare, possibly because the Japanese considered the Europeans superior to the Chinese, the many Chinese who lived in Java were subjected to some of the Nanking cruelties the Japanese were now infamous for. The fact that we do not have an accurate or complete record is no proof of less violence. All the war records are incomplete from the moment the Japanese took over the command from the Dutch. Henry Hobhouse acknowledges that the "Japanese enjoyed humiliating whites, but unknown thousands of Chinese were murdered in the East Indies in massacres of often paranoiac cruelty."[4]

Though better off than the Chinese, the Europeans noticed almost immediately that life was to change dramatically. To reinforce the Japanese slogan "Asia for the Asians," everything that had to do with Holland or the Dutch was being isolated, confiscated, and interned. The Dutch language was forbidden, and Malay became the official language. All Dutch holidays and the Dutch calendar were abolished and replaced with their Japanese counterparts.

By March, most banks were closed, which meant that all financial traffic with Europe stopped. Consequently, many of the Dutch colonials lost their income. Some tried to withdraw their money from the banks before they closed. Many would lose everything in the years to come: capital, pension, home, household effects, and the most valuable of all: their lives. Poverty among Europeans grew rapidly, and soup kitchens with long lines became a common sight. And yet these were blessed circumstances compared to the later circumstances in the camps and prisons.

In his letters home Walraven noticed how the situation for Europeans became more dire every day. In May and April of 1942 all Dutch civil servants, physicians, teachers, and lawyers were rounded up, while all the others were told to register by swearing an oath of loyalty to the Japanese Army. People would then receive an ID card (*pendaftaran*), for which men paid 150 guilders and women, 80 guilders. Many could not pay the full amount at once, in which case they had to pay in installments.[5]

In September 1942 the first European men were interned in camps. Within less than a year all the *belandas* were behind barbed wire, which was barricaded with *gedèg* (a bamboo fence). Because of the fence the inmates lost their view of and contact with the outside world, deepening their feelings of isolation and over time, a sense that the outside world had forgotten them. Men were separated from women and fathers separated from their children. The children stayed with their mothers, but as soon as the male children reached puberty they were taken away from their mothers and put into all-male camps. A few tried to go under cover. The Indonesian writer Pramoedya Ananta Toer remembers seeing a Dutch family climb a riverbank:

"The father's skin is burnt and he's dressed not in European clothing but in Javanese traditional dress. His wife and children are similarly attired. They're all barefoot. All eyes turn toward them and walk beside the family with sympathy—imagine the desperation and fear holding them in a viselike grip!—but no one dares to offer them a place to hide."[6]

The tables had turned: the Dutch who once behaved as lords of the manor were now on the run, and although the Indonesians would live outside the camps, they too would be affected by the Japanese reign of terror which involved forced labor, forced prostitution and rape, injustice, poverty, and starvation. Soon after the invasion the local population was forced to hand over its rice to the Japanese officers, and slowly but surely there was a lack of food, clothing, medicine, and medical care. "People in the *kampung* walked around in rags [and] along the *kali*, sick, emaciated, and starving people lay down to die."[7] Hundreds of thousands of Javanese farmers were forced into labor (*romusha*) and died in the jungles of Burma, Thailand, and Sumatra.[8]

What was happening to Peddy and Fré in these dark days? What did Peddy do besides harvesting coffee and rubber, and where did he get the money to keep the plantation running? I had no information whatsoever relating to this crucial period. There were no letters, no journals, nothing. All Harry could remember was that he was flying his kite with the village boys. Once the kite got stuck in a tree, Harry went home: "It was about three or four o'clock in the afternoon. I wanted to chat about my kite adventures, but when I walked in I saw my father, mother, and sisters sitting in the living room. They were silent and looked depressed. It turned out that the Kempeitai had been by and announced that my father would be interned."

Who were the Kempeitai (KPT)? Some have called this army division Japan's secret service, while others have described it as the military police and Japan's torture squad. Everyone agrees on one thing: their interrogation techniques were gruesome. The Kempeitai were already renowned before the war for murdering some pro-Western advisors of the emperor. After this they gained in popularity and thus consolidated their hold on the Japanese army.[9]

I found several black-and-white pictures of Kempeitai officers. They looked like forbidding little boys with ballooning riding pants, tall and heavy boots, Boy Scout hats, and fat leather belts, which were also used as torture implements. When I heard that Peddy was picked up by the Kempeitai, I momentarily saw this as evidence that my great-uncle was involved with the Allied/Dutch resistance. After all, if someone was picked up by the Gestapo in the Netherlands, the suspicion was that the victim was somehow associated with the resistance. "Not so," Winnie Rinzema-Admiraal explained to me in an e-mail. "In eastern Java the Kempeitai had more authority than elsewhere and while most men in Java were loaded onto trucks, in eastern Java, the Kempeitai were especially authorized to round up men."

It is nonetheless disturbing that Peddy was picked up by the Kempeitai, considering its reputation. The historian Laurence Rees, who managed to interview a member of the Kempeitai after the war, writes this about standard Kempeitai procedure:

> Most interrogations would begin by beating the suspect with fists or a stick, "but beating exhausts us, so we move on to torture," says [former KPT officer Tshuchiya]. . . . "The iron bar was brought in and it was all red with heat and it was hard to stay in the room because human flesh is burned and smells bad." Alternatively the KPT might use the "hanging" torture, in which a large stone was tied to the suspect's body and the victim was suspended in a position of excruciating agony for hours at a time.
>
> But according to Tshuchiya, . . . "beating or hanging people upside down is not so effective as water torture: you tie them face up, lying on a long bench," says Tsuchiya, "and then you put a cloth on their face and then you pour water onto the cloth so the person can't help but drinking it. You push their stomach out with water—blow it right up." When the stomach was distended the KPT would beat their victim hard on the belly with a stick so that the water was vomited back up. Then they would repeat the procedure again and again. "During the torture some

people are killed," says Tsuchiya. "Those people who aren't expert at it kill them because if water goes into the bronchial tubes and the lungs, they die. You tell by the colour of the face and the colour of the nails. If it's a bloodless face, like a dying face, that's the moment we have to stop. We try not to kill them—but take them to the verge of being killed."[10]

Victims who had not confessed would receive no medical help or food afterward.

I do not know whether Peddy was at the receiving end of all this, although Theo van Elzen writes that the smallest crimes would result in the biggest punishments. Van Elzen explains that the Japanese were extremely paranoid, and their paranoia was aggravated by the language barrier and cultural differences: "The slightest suspicious behavior was interpreted as the undermining of authority, sabotage, or conspiracy."[11] In this way many innocent people fell into the hands of the KPT, and some of these, after coerced confessions, were tried and executed. Peddy might have been innocent: as Robert van Maaren and Herman Eijgelshoven emphasize: "Almost everyone who was suspected of resistance activities was arrested by the KPT [but] the arrested people were not always resistance fighters or participants. Through torture, however, they were nonetheless identified as such."[12] Van Maaren and Eijgelshoven also note that by June 1943, when Peddy was still under suspicion, "all organized resistance had ended."

Fortunately, when Peddy was picked up, neither Fré nor Peddy knew what lay in store for him. What were their last twenty-four hours together like? How did they spend the night: asleep or awake and worried? Did they make love or simply hold onto each other until daybreak? How was the final embrace, the last kiss, the good-bye with the children? Did they have time to say what needed to be said while the Kempeitai officers were waiting in the car, the engine running? What were those final words? "I love you, I will see you, I will write, be brave, I will miss you . . . ?"

As a woman I find it easier to identify with Fré, the lonely wife who stayed behind with her three children, the servants, the house, and the gardens. I can even imagine the car driving away on the gravel road, down to the valley. I see the last glance, the final wave, and the hand-blown kiss. Would Fré see her husband again? She would, she might have decided, for only hope gave way to life and her life she had to live because of her children.

That first week after Peddy's departure must have been the most difficult. Fré may have avoided the empty office with its liquor cabinet. She may have imagined the sound of Peddy's footsteps in the house—nothing but a bittersweet illusion. She must have missed his presence, his talks with the *mandur,* and the light coming from his study late at night. She must have missed his warm body in bed, and she may have felt a reluctance to wash the sheets, for fear of losing his scent forever. The children would have asked for daddy that first week, but these questions may have lessened as their mother soon found a routine, a system, and a mindset that made it possible to carry on and survive. Fré and members of her generation did not allow themselves to dwell on things too much: *Niet klagen maar dragen* (Don't complain, carry your burden) was the Dutch mantra. But life could not have been easy. Fré may have run out of money, the gardens lay fallow, and the servants had to be sent home. I know from one of Marjolein's letters that some of the servants stayed out of loyalty: "Nyonya Pranken (Mrs. Francken), we stay regardless . . ."

Life for the children would change dramatically, too. The two girls stopped going to school, although Harry continued to play with his friends in the village. The Dutch novelist Jeroen Brouwers, who was a little younger than Harry, remembered the changes of the war very distinctly: adults disappearing, the pantry emptying, the animals vanishing, the air-raid alarms screaming, and finally the soldiers appearing in the house to take him and his family to the camp.[13]

While the Francken children still had each other and their familiar surroundings, Fré had to weather the changes and Peddy's absence on her own. As a woman living in a remote part of the country, she was also vulnerable, which gives rise to the question of how the Japanese treated the growing number of Dutch women who were forced to say good-bye to their husbands and older sons. Although there was great concern after the news that trickled in from Nanking five years earlier, according to Brugmans et al. only a few Japanese officers raped European women. Nonetheless, Brugmans includes a journal entry of a Dutch woman who, walking home late at night, was startled by two Japanese officers who jumped in front of her from behind a tree. She managed to escape them, and at home she found that her two girlfriends had locked themselves in the bedroom because earlier that night five Japanese soldiers had knocked on the door. The houseboys opened the door, and asked whether there were any pretty ladies in the house, they replied: "There are no pretty ladies here—they're all old!" The Japanese then walked around the house but finally abandoned their venture.[14] While rape cases were few and far between, the potential threat and fear was there, as the following story from Marjolein Francken evinces as well.

In one of her letters she tells me that shortly after Peddy was arrested, Fré was seen by a few Japanese soldiers who had come up the mountain to find the lady of the house. In an act of solidarity, the servants formed a human chain around the house. This gesture of loyalty and silent protest was evidently respected by the Japanese, who turned around and left. Throughout the occupation, the Indonesians would play an ambiguous role: at times they were the protectors of their former employers, but there are also incidents where they became the accomplices of the Japanese, participating in the disciplining and torturing of Europeans and Eurasians.

In the meantime, I struggled to find more facts about Peddy. Where did the Kempeitai take him, and how was he treated? My initial attempts to contact the Dutch War Archive in Amsterdam (NIOD) were fruitless. I had my suspicions, but I needed hard evidence, preferably in writing. One of my assumptions had to do with the fact that after the Dutch surrender became imminent, about two hundred Allied and KNIL (colonial army) soldiers took off for the jungle, to escape but also to set up a guerrilla force. This happened less in the more densely populated western part of Java than around Malang, middle Java, and eastern Java. It is plausible that planters like Peddy who were living near the jungle may have helped with these efforts. Once these soldiers were caught and interrogated, they may have mentioned Peddy's and other planters' names.

My hope for hard evidence fizzled when I learn that not only are Japanese war documents scarce and incomplete but many of them were apparently destroyed after the Japanese surrendered in 1945. I also realized that if Japanese documents on Peddy exist, there is a high chance that they carry false information. If he confessed to anything at all during torture sessions, the confession would have been coerced and therefore useless. The Japanese who witnessed and kept up these records were the enemy interrogators and executioners and therefore not reliable or neutral sources. The victims, on the other hand, were often forced to give false statements, and once they had talked, they were silenced forever by the executioner's sword, gun, or noose.

Imagining Peddy's fate seems overwhelming and depressing. If he was held by the KPT the entire time, his ordeal must have been horrific. Arrested in April or May of 1943 and dying in March of 1945, he spent almost two years in excruciating circumstances. Maybe my failure to find the nasty details of his circumstances was a blessing in disguise.

I almost gave up on Peddy's case. Of course there could be worthwhile war archives in Indonesia too, but a student of mine who has been to some of those archives discouraged me: the archives are unorganized, she said, and to find anything of use, you have to spend months if not years in Java. I did not have that kind of time or money, and instead I read another book on the war in Java. I was almost beginning to despair. Was I reading more books as a way of postponing my writing? How many more books would I have to read to find even the smallest detail that could possibly crack Peddy's case? Was I wasting my time? And what or how did it matter if I found anything at all? How could Peddy's story be relevant to Kali Jompo's story as a whole?

Pondering these issues, I vented my frustration by loudly shutting the book I was reading. However, with a last peripheral glance at the page in front of me, I realized I was seeing something worth noting. It was an article by the Dutch historian Winnie Rinzema-

Admiraal, whom I mentioned earlier.[15] My heart skipped a beat and I immediately opened the book again in search of the page. This could be it: the needle in the haystack that I thought I would never find. Did this article contain the missing link?

Almost immediately the article pulled me in. The author demystified the romanticism a reader might associate with planters' lives in eastern Java. Examples of imperialism, pioneering, and paternalism that novelists like Hella Haasse describe in their novels did not apply, Rinzema-Admiraal writes, to the planters in the Jember area. I sat up straight and read on. For one thing, Rinzema-Admiraal comments, the personnel on these plantations was very mixed. Many Indo-Europeans had positions of power, and egalitarianism, if one could speak of that, was much more prevalent in eastern Java than in the hoity-toity society circles of Buitenzorg and Batavia. However, during the Depression much of the land lay fallow, which caused unemployment and poverty, even among planters.

As if reading my mind, she then describes the terrain of this particular corner of Java: "The plantations lay like enclaves between the agricultural areas of the people and the dessahs." Because most of these plantations were so isolated and because the Dutch colonial government feared the Japanese would invade from the east, the government relied on the planters to maintain law and order by serving as a kind of militia, and handed out guns to them. When the Kempeitai arrived in eastern Java and found the planters armed, they were immediately a suspect group. The planters did resist—a resistance that was not necessarily serious or secret—their defiance ranging from hiding weapons to helping soldiers who were hiding after the Dutch surrendered. These actions may seem relatively innocent to us, but to the KPT they were serious infractions.

Rinzema-Admiraal writes: "In the eastern part of Java there were heavy penalties: employees at plantations in Besuki, Jember, the area of Kali Baru, and Banyuwangi, all belonged to the suspects." The first wave of arrests took place from April 1942 to the middle of 1943. One of the detainees was administrator J. H. Treur of the plantation Sumber Wadung. He had offered shelter to soldiers and had hidden weapons, a very serious crime in the eyes of the Kempeitai. The article continues: "Most of the arrested planters in the Banyuwangi affair survived the extensive torture, after which the matter was referred to the court-martial in Batavia. Apparently the accused complained two times that they had made false statements during their torture sessions. Their complaints were of no use and may in fact have aggravated their situation and final verdict."

The group was then transported to Sukamiskin in Bandung. It was Japanese custom, Rinzema-Admiraal told me later in an e-mail, to imprison people far away from where the crime had been committed. In Sukamiskin the living conditions and the little food they got were abominable. Add to that the "aggressive treatment of the Indonesian mantris (overseers)" and it may come as no surprise that "thirty men died within a few months from dysentery and edema." The remaining twenty were liberated in September of 1945. Was Peddy one of the thirty dead men? And if so, what was life in Sukamiskin like? What was Peddy thinking as he was driven through Bandung, a city that Couperus had praised for its big, white, modern buildings that reminded him of The Hague's seaside town, Scheveningen?

Maybe his arrival was similar to that of Governor-General A. W. L. Tjarda van Starkenborgh, who arrived there with other Dutch civil servants on April 6, 1942. After the men entered the prison, all belts, shoelaces, and neckties were taken to prevent the prisoners from hanging themselves. Then the group had to line up against a wall in the darkness. The men thought they were about to be executed, but it was a mock execution, a well-known scare tactic that the Indonesian independence fighters would later copy from the Japanese. After this, the men were taken to tiled cells, which were very cold at night. It was a lonely life, and to chase away boredom the men communicated by knocking on the walls. Starkenborgh and his men were finally transported to the Struyswijckprison before Peddy would arrive at Sukamiskin.

Then, out of the blue, I received an e-mail from my mother: "I was talking to Tineke," she writes, "and she suddenly remembered that Peddy, before the war, had built a hut in the jungle in which he was stockpiling weapons." My aunt Tineke has an indestructible memory, and I was inclined to believe this story, as it matched the details of the planters' conspiracy. But it was still no proof, so I wrote the War Archive in Amsterdam again with the details of Rinzema-Admiraal's article. The collections in which I was most likely to find information about Peddy have restricted and very restricted access, and it was very frustrating that I could not travel to Amsterdam and look for myself. My query was at the mercy of whoever responded to the info@e-mail addresses at the War Archive and the National Archive.

Around the same time, I received a letter from my uncle Jack, my mother's oldest brother. He was a volunteer after the war and was sent to Java with the Dutch army when the government tried to re-colonize the Indies. This turned into the police actions, which really only helped the Indonesian independence further along: the United States finally threatened to withdraw Holland's Marshall aid if the Dutch did not pull out of the Indies. Thus Jack ended up at Kali Jompo, trying to save the plantation from going under altogether.

Jack sent me a picture of a young Peddy, which comes from a publication by HFC, the Franckens' soccer club in Haarlem. The text that goes with the picture explains that Peddy was the "little brother" of Mannes and Jacques and that Peddy would accompany his older brothers and walk around on the field in the big shoes of his brothers. When I took a careful look at Peddy's picture, I recognized family traits in his handsome, regular, long face. He has a long nose, the Francken almond-shaped eyes, and a beautiful, sensuous mouth. Like my own son, he has a little masculine dent in his chin. He was smiling at me, I thought, and for a moment it seemed we connected—it was as if he was giving me permission to proceed.

My uncle Jack had little extra information on Peddy. "Back in Jember, I did speak to an administrator by the name of Treur—I believe he ran the plantation, Sumber Wadung. He was in the group of prisoners with Peddy and he sang his praises. Treur called Peddy a courageous man, the kind who would talk back to the Japanese, which always resulted in Peddy getting beaten up."

Initially I read this passage without making any connections, but the name Treur lingered in my mind. When I went back to my notes, I found Rinzema-Admiraal's article again and I was floored. She mentions Treur and Sumber Wadung in one sentence, and Jack's information was the long-lost evidence and link I was looking for. This finally confirmed that Peddy *was* part of the planters' group that was accused of hiding weapons and helping Allied soldiers. Jack further writes that Treur also told him that toward the end of Peddy's life, when they were handing out Red Cross packages with food at Sukamiskin, Peddy told the others to take the package away and give it to someone else because he, "wasted to a shadow and deathly ill," would have no use for it anymore, as he believed death was near.

I am trying to imagine what Peddy's last few nights were like: he must have been bitterly cold and possibly fading in and out of consciousness. His realization of his approaching death would echo the last words of his daughter Joke, half a year later. For a moment I contemplated writing the Red Cross again to find out when exactly those Red Cross packages were delivered at the prison but I refrained from doing so. What did it matter when ultimately Peddy would die alone, starved, sick, and hallucinating about happier days with his family at that pretty plantation high in the mountains of eastern Java?

Weeks after my letter to the NIOD in Amsterdam I was surprised by an e-mail from Jeroen Kemperman of the NIOD. My assumptions were right. According to Kemperman there were two planters' conspiracies and waves of arrests in eastern Java. Peddy was taken in for questioning during the first wave: "A small group of Dutch planters [Peddy among them] and about ten Ambonese were seized, and were suspected of making preparations for a possible Allied landing." On the day when Peddy said good-bye to his wife and kids, he ended up in a cell with the planters W. G. J. Wilbrink, Correljé (no initials given), and H. P. Goudriaan. That same night eleven more people were brought in. The non-Europeans (most likely the Ambonese men) were interrogated brutally by the Kempeitai until the next afternoon. A few days later, on April 27, 1943, the three planters were released because of lack of evidence.

Peddy must have returned home before he was picked up again in June, to be interned at the all-male camp of Sekar Putih near Bondowoso, a small town in eastern Java. When I asked Harry to verify this, he told me he could remember that his dad returned for a number of weeks and then was picked up again, which brought about another tearful good-bye.

In September 1943 Sekar Putih was cleared out and Peddy and his fellow inmates were transported in a boarded-up train to arrive at the Tangerang prison. To cite from Goudriaan's report, which Kemperman shared with me: "The fourth-class wagons were overcrowded, the ventilation was nil, and this journey lasted for about sixty hours." "The details of such a trip are known to everybody," Huib Wiedenhoff comments. "What it means to stand among dying people in a hermetically closed and hot train car, without food, water, or sanitation, is something we all know!"

Rob Cassuto writes on his Web site (http://robcassuto.com) that he was only three when he made such a train trip, but he remembers it vividly: "It was primitive and degrading. The overcrowded train cars would come to a stop and stand there for hours in the scorching sun or freezing cold." Kept inside during the entire journey, Cassuto remembers the hunger, thirst, and crying children. There were no toilets on the train.

In the course of the war, overall conditions of internees (who were sometimes moved from one camp to another) deteriorated. This was also the case for Peddy. Tangerang, twenty kilometers outside of Batavia, was a terrible place. The food was bad and tasteless and the Japanese were quick to beat people up if they did not abide by the rules.

From Tangerang the inmates were moved to the juvenile prison, Tanahtinggi, in the middle of October: "The total number of people," Goudriaan says, "amounted to about fifteen hundred people who were split up into four groups: *totoks,* NSB people, Indos, and the so-called ball boys." They were called ball boys because they wore a white patch on their sleeves with one, two, or three red balls. In effect they were the camp spies, who reported to the Japanese about inmates who violated rules. Goudriaan explains that the Dutch language was forbidden and that Peddy was reported for speaking Dutch and then severely manhandled by the Japanese. There is also a report of Peddy being hit so hard in the face that one of his decaying teeth abscessed. Peddy then received some medical care from the Franckens' former physician, who was also held at the camp.

In the meantime, back in Jember, the Kempeitai did a house search at the Kotta Blater plantation, where they found weapons and ammunition. This led to more KPT paranoia, and they arrested around ninety people in September of 1943 (during the second wave of arrests). One or more of these people must have mentioned Peddy Francken and others during their interrogations, for in January of 1944 the KPT started picking up former Jember planters and employees who were held at the different camps. On or around January 12, 1944, Peddy, G. Birnie, R. W. Vink, W. G. J. Wilbrink, J. W. Erkelens, H. P. Goudriaan, and some others from Jember were picked up by the Jember KPT. They were transported to the Kempeitai in Batavia, where they "got free lodging," according to Goudriaan. The next afternoon they were brought to the kota station, where they were handcuffed and transported by night back to Jember.

What was it like for Peddy to arrive back home at the Jember railway station? Coming from the railway station, still in handcuffs, he must have momentarily inhaled the familiar mountain air after hot Batavia. The car that took them from the station to the jail went by the old *soos,* then took a right past the old Imports Building, the Bureau Openbare Werken (BOW) Office (Office for Public Works) and the salt warehouse. The Jember prison was next to the bank where Peddy may have had his bank account or may have taken out a loan for Kali Jompo. Maybe Peddy's cell inside the jail looked out on the hotel where my grandparents had stayed during much happier days in 1928. Or maybe he could see the roof of the European school where his Willy and Joke had been driven by Kassidin. Or maybe he saw the *alun-alun,* the town square where his children had played while he was at the post office to mail his letters to Henri and Jacques. And maybe he could hear the occasional splashing of the Jompo River at night, when the air was not poisoned by the gut-wrenching screams of his fellow torture victims, because Goudriaan says that some of the worst torture took place at the Jember jail. The men, whether guilty or not, were indicted for their resistance or fifth-column activities, which, in the view of the Japanese, amounted to preparations to assist the Americans in case they landed in eastern Java.

Aside from the regular torture sessions and the chronic lack of food, the inmates were also abused by some anti-Dutch *mantris* (Indonesian guards), who whipped the inmates with long rotan whips when things did not go their way. For almost a year Peddy survived this hell, and then in December of 1944 he and some others were handcuffed again in the middle of the night and transported to Batavia, where the Japanese court martial was held in a building that used to house the French Consulate. In what state of mind did Peddy arrive back in Batavia? An old map of Batavia that I have shows the station where Peddy must have gotten out. From there he was loaded onto a truck that went past all the familiar sights: down the Molenvliet, past the Prinsenlaan, the famous Des Indes Hotel, and the Hotel Des Galleries, where he might have stayed with Fré when she first arrived.

After the war, the French Consulate building, which is near the Koningsplein, was turned into the Public Relations building, where journalists from all over the world gathered to report on Indonesia's struggle for independence. Johan Fabricius, a Dutch novelist and war correspondent for the BBC, arrived in Java in September of 1945. He says this about the building where Peddy was tortured once again: "The Japanese had used this building as a war tribunal. . . . Inside there was a big room with a high part where the Japanese military judge was seated. By his side was a bare-chested formidable man who held a whip in his hand to remind the accused and witnesses to tell all. As far as Tanah Abang, on the other side of the *kali* one had to cover one's ears because of the heartbreaking screaming of the interrogated men and women."[16] Goudriaan remembered their imprisonment in Batavia as follows: "The food was okay but mentally this was the toughest period." In January of 1945 Peddy and others appeared before the "fake court and in spite of vehement denial" of what they had stated while being tortured, their sentence was read: ten years of penal servitude.

With this sentence and suffering the damage of months of torture and malnutrition, Peddy arrived at Sukamiskin in Bandung. In March Peddy started throwing up and became dehydrated. He died of dysentery on March 15, 1945. Maybe I should phrase this differently: Peddy did not die of natural causes but was very slowly tortured, maimed, starved, and killed by the Japanese for building a grass hut and hiding some weapons in the jungle. Kemperman writes: "From Goudriaan's statements it can indeed be inferred that F. A. M. Francken was sentenced for participating in the planters' conspiracy." But Kemperman concludes: "However, it is highly probable that most of the men who were sentenced were never actively involved with resistance activities."

Peddy was forty-eight years old when he died in a cold prison cell in Bandung. His only surviving son, Harry, had to wait sixty years before the War Archive in Amsterdam could finally tell us what had happened to his father. The Japanese soldiers who tortured Peddy and others have not all been prosecuted, and for all we know they may be spending a happy old age in a retirement home in Kyoto or Tokyo.[17] And yet this does not close Peddy's case forever. In a copy of a letter from Jack to Marjolein, the two Francken cousins seem to have discussed a puzzling fact, brought to the surface by a priest named Hutten who served at the Jember Catholic Church in the 1990s. Hutten wrote Marjolein that he had found a record in the church archive mentioning that Peddy was brought to Kali Jompo to die after he had been extensively tortured by the Japanese. Jack notes: "This is news to me, because I was told he died in Sukamiskin in Bandung." But maybe, he continues, this is a doctoring of the facts "to soften them and spare the family from the terrible reality that must have taken place at Kali Jompo, as Father Hutten suspects."

I tried to get in touch with the church and the Carmelite Order that works at St. Joseph's, the Catholic church in Jember. I received no replies, and I doubted whether the church archives are intact, for in the last decade churches all over Indonesia have been burned down and ransacked. Even though Father Hutten must have had the paperwork to back this up, the story seemed to run counter to the Red Cross and NIOD records, as well as the testimony of witnesses like Goudriaan and Treur who had seen Peddy at Sukamiskin. I checked anyway with Radboud University in Nijmegen, the Netherlands, to see if duplicates of the files of the church in Jember exist (for this one needs to contact the Catholic Documentation Center at http://www .ru.nl/kdc).[18] I also checked with the Carmelite Order in the Netherlands, who referred me to the Carmelites in Indonesia. They told me that I could no longer verify the story with Father Hutten, as he died in Malang in August of 2003, one year before I started the research for this book. People often live long lives, but when you do research like this your window of opportunity is small. Peddy's trail ended there, and Hutten's mysterious letter was one of the many questions remaining regarding Peddy's disappearance and death. The full facts, the final details, we may never know.

Chapter 11

THE PLANTERS' DOSSIERS
FROM THE SECRET ARCHIVES

That a book is never finished is evidenced by the making of this chapter. While relatively early on I found Rinzema-Admiraal's article on the planters' conspiracy, other clues and leads were harder to come by. The matching of the name Treur was pure coincidence, and the final e-mail of NIOD, confirming my great-uncle's involvement, took months to reach me. When I tried to request more information from NIOD, I was told that all had been said on the matter and that both the involvement of my great-uncle and the topic itself had been exhausted.

Likewise, when I wrote the Dutch Ministerie van Buitenlandse Zaken (Ministry of Foreign Affairs) to request the dossiers that Rinzema-Admiraal had consulted for her piece, a reorganization of the archives made the dossiers harder to retrace and significantly delayed the process. When I finally did receive the dossiers in the mail, I was in the finishing stages of this book and felt lukewarm about studying the new material, being under the impression that I would not find anything new or interesting that had not been explored already or was worth adding to this book. In addition, the archivist who sent me the material had noted that Peddy was mentioned only once in the dossiers and that therefore they might be of little use. But when I started reading the dossiers, new facts came to light that have not been sufficiently highlighted before.

The dossiers all contain depositions of the various planters (Treur among them) who survived the KPT interrogations and prison sentencing.[1] Their statements about their POW experiences were made shortly after the war, in 1946, taken down by NEFIS officers in Batavia. The files fell under the category "War Criminals." Because of the still-sensitive nature of this material I will use initials (K. and W.) for the names of two planters who seem to have played a very disturbing role in the fabrication of a conspiracy or espionage story, thereby buttressing the already existing paranoia of the Japanese KPT. In addition to raising suspicion regarding their colleagues' prewar and postsurrender activities, one planter actively helped with rounding up his fellow planters (he also helped out at the interrogations, during which he did not refrain from hitting people himself), while the other was an undercover fellow prisoner who during, but especially after, torture sessions was mixed in with the victims to persuade them to confess to false stories and sign false statements.

Although Rinzema-Admiraal was correct in pointing out that the planters were a suspect group to the KPT because they were carrying weapons to perform their duties as *Landwacht* officers (a prewar measure of the Dutch government), while also helping out in the capacity of the *hulp politie,* she does not altogether seem to rule out an actual conspiracy, and she hardly mentions the dubious role of planter K., who is named in almost every single deposition by the planters. The presence of a spy ring or resistance network that allegedly was to prepare and aid the American landings in eastern Java seems to have been a trumped-up story and may even be in need of some demythologization, as the impression may have been raised that these planters could not have been so seriously tortured and punished had they been truly innocent.

The only incriminating evidence that I have been able to distil from the case is that Treur admitted that in March of 1942 he and other planters were told by Assistant Resident K. L. T. Crince Le Roy to offer shelter to roaming soldiers. Treur housed twenty soldiers for about a week. When the soldiers left, they wanted to leave their weapons and other gear at the plantation but Treur told them to take it with them. However, when a mantri came to inspect, he found a motorcycle on the grounds (Treur did not even know it was there). This was immediately cause for suspicion, and Treur was tortured for hours in September of 1942, during which he was hit on his bare back with a piece of wood. After that he was let go, to be arrested again during the second wave. During the later interrogations, Treur stated in his deposition that they were "talked into" fifth-column activities with the Americans. In my mind, the majority of the planters were above suspicion. In fact, they themselves heard of the so-called planters' conspiracy for the first time when KPT officers, but also K. and W., told them about it during their first torture sessions.

There were indeed two waves of planters' arrests. The first group involved *Landwacht* officers residing east of the Tunnel Merawan, west of Banyuwangi and south of the railway line (I will refer to them as the Banyuwangi planters). The second (Peddy's) group consisted of Jember planters in the remaining parts of Besuki (I will refer to them as the Jember planters). The first group was called up in March of 1943 by the Bondowoso KPT. Among them was planter K., who immediately started collaborating with the Japanese after the KPT found weapons, cameras, *Landwacht* uniforms, and other suspicious materials at his plantation. To avoid torture and death, K. told the Japanese that there was a planters' conspiracy, instigated at a large local meeting in March of 1942 at the plantation Kali Baru (several planters later confirmed that this meeting did take place, but they denied that it was a forum for resistance activities or the beginnings of an underground network). K. was released shortly after his arrest and would be seen during the war driving a Japanese car and living in a big house. It was no secret that he was collaborating with the Japanese, and rumor had it that "he had betrayed the Banyuwangi planters."

As for the alleged suspicious meeting at Kali Baru, it was preceded by the Japanese finding twenty thousand guilders in the safe of Administrator Isaska. It was not unusual for the plantations, especially the more remote ones, to have large amounts in their safes, but whatever the reason for the money being there, it looked fishy to the Japanese because they had gotten wind of the story that Governor H. C. Hartevelt, after the Dutch surrender, had given Assistant

Resident Crince Le Roy and Assistant Resident A. C. M. Jansen fifty thousand guilders. Besuki Minister Siebold van der Linde, an important leader figure in the group who was arrested during the second wave, stated that this money was not intended for anti-Japanese activities but was earmarked to keep the plantations in the eastern corner of Java running until liberation by the Allies. As money became scarcer and banks closed this seems a plausible story, although one can also see that it could be easily misconstrued as money intended for fifth-column initiatives. Rinzema-Admiraal casts doubt on Hartevelt's donation as a "plantation subsidy," as she believes that most plantations were holding enough cash to survive the war. Does this also mean that Rinzema-Admiraal believes the money might have been used for initial underground activities? The answer is not clear from her article.

Isaska, his wife, one other woman, twenty-seven Banyuwangi planters, and a number of Ambonese were arrested and tortured in a tobacco barn also known as the *sinc gudang* at the Birnie estate. After two planters, J. T. A. Man and P. M. Mulder, were beaten to death, a physician, Dr. H. Nijk, who was also imprisoned, communicated with the others through a bathroom window and proposed "to make something up" to escape the fate of Man and Mulder. Apparently, this made-up story became the basis for the final sentence, whereupon the group had to appear before a Japanese war tribunal in the land council building of Jember. The KPT officers encouraged the victims to confirm their testimonies in front of the tribunal, as the case would be closed after that and they would be sent back to the internment camps.

After the tribunal in Jember the Banyuwangi group apparently heaved a sigh of relief, presuming the ordeal was over, but the next morning the death sentence was made known, to the great disillusionment of the group. Siebold van der Linde saw the three trucks with the condemned men drive by on the day of their execution: "They were all bare-chested. Whether they were handcuffed I could not see. I did hear that they had exited the prison in handcuffs and were chased onto the trucks with beatings and blows." The execution took place at the end of May or the beginning June of 1943 in a forest about thirty miles south of Jember. The bodies were dumped into a mass grave. The widows of the dead men were summoned to the Jember police station by the end of June, where they could pick up the clothes and belongings of their husbands: they were told that their husbands were still alive but had been sent to Batavia. It was not until after the war that these women heard from the Red Cross that their spouses had been killed years before.

The planters of the first wave were killed on the basis of exaggerated and most likely made-up charges. Although they seemed to have died in vain, their death was a clear warning for the second group of planters, as a number of Ambonese who had been present at the trial and the execution warned them, through Siebold van der Linde, not to confess to anything while being coerced, since false confessions were used as a valid ground for guilt, conviction, and a death sentence.

During Peddy's first arrest in April of 1943, he and Goudriaan entered the Jember police station and saw two women as well as potentially other prisoners of the Banyuwangi conspiracy. Goudriaan denies having been tortured during that first encounter with the Jember KPT, but the Ambonese who were arrested with them were tortured that night. To see the other planters of the first group was an eerie coincidence, as Peddy and Goudriaan would be subjected to the same charges and treatment as the first group. In June of 1943 Goudriaan was arrested again but released and interned at Tangerang, where Peddy was also interned.

In January of 1944 he and Peddy were picked up with other planters/*Landwachters* and taken to the Jember KPT, where he was tortured by Nagamatsu (nicknamed Aurora because of his golden teeth) after arrival at the station. Nagamatsu beat and kicked his victims with wooden sticks. An Indonesian, Saleh mantri, also liked to hit the prisoners with sticks and whips. R. W. Vink, the administrator of Kalisanen, who had been arrested with Peddy, was hit over the head with a chair and would die in Jember Hospital of dysentery. W. G. J. Wilbrink, who was in the group with Peddy, Vink, and Goudriaan, was tortured extensively and would die, like Peddy, in

Sukamiskin in May or June of 1945. When I sent Peddy's son, Harry, a list of the planters' names, he wrote me that he could only remember Wilbrink's plantation Keputeran: "We were there once and stayed over for the night. It was a beautiful estate."

Other planters declared that those first torture sessions consisted of being beaten and kicked while they were forced to sit outside, during the hottest part of the day. The more senior people and alleged ringleaders of the group, like Governor H. C. Hartevelt, Resident A. C. Tobi, Assistant Resident K. L. T. Crince Le Roy, and Assistant Resident van Arcken (no initials given), were treated more severely and waterboarded several times. Hartevelt died during these sessions on June 1, 1944. Resident Tobi tried to commit suicide by cutting his wrists the night after he was waterboarded. This suicide attempt failed, and he was taken to the hospital in Jember, which meant not only a temporary reprieve from torture, but extra food supplied by Mrs. Stadt, "Mamma Erkelens," and Miss Lies Schweizer.

Crince Le Roy was also tortured extensively, and Van der Linde was waterboarded five times. Through it all, K. and W. were on hand to make the planters confess. Van der Linde even says in his statement that "everything gave" him "the impression that W. played the same role as K." Van der Linde and most of the planters finally did "confess." These confessions were drawn up in Japanese, translated in Malay and then given to the victims to read. Van der Linde refused to sign the confession, which led to more abuse, so Van der Linde and the others finally did sign. Tobi and Crince Le Roy never did make or sign any confessions.

At this juncture in Van der Linde's deposition, he apologizes but acknowledges that he was "wasted" and that his "only wish was to end it and die." Nonetheless, he was reproached by Tobi when the men were let out in the courtyard together. "Wrong, wrong," Tobi said, "that you all have signed." No doubt the memory of the fate of the Banyuwangi group was still fresh in Tobi's mind. W. apparently was cursed at by the Japanese because the two most senior people in the group had not signed, which made the case against the planters weaker, if not a failure. It did not pay off in the end for W. On May 5,

1944, he appeared before the tribunal in Jember and was sentenced to death. He had been under the impression (as he had told Van der Linde) that he would escape execution because of his collaboration with the Japanese, but he was hanged, together with Isaska, on November 11, 1944, in a prison in Surabaya.

On September 24, 1944, Van der Linde was taken to the Jember jail, where he, with the other planters, had to work in a rope yard.

On December 14, 1944, the entire group, heads shaven, was taken to Batavia to appear before the Japanese tribunal. Van der Linde states:

> There were about fifty of us, with among us the accused Ambonese and the Menadonese. We were all shackled together, barefoot, and only wore a Malay jacket and some shorts. Immediately after our arrival in Batavia we were taken to the tribunal in the French Consulate. . . . I was the first one who was called in. Only then I heard that I had been declared guilty of the Tobi conspiracy, which consisted of the blowing up of bridges, the destruction and sabotaging of telephone lines and railway lines as soon as the Americans were to land in eastern Java, and that I, together with the Ambonese and Menadonese, would aid the Americans in supplying food for the landing forces and that I, together with the physicians of the Red Cross, would take care of the wounded and burying of the dead; and that the Dutch church and Dutch administration had ordered me to carry out this conspiracy.

The long list of charges seemed preposterous, but almost everyone was charged with such a list, to which all protested, following Van der Linde's lead. "We realized," Van der Linde argues, "that we were dead men walking regardless, yet we did not want to die being charged with a lie."

The protest and retraction of statements had no torture consequences for Van der Linde, but Goudriaan reported that one of the more cruel Japanese guards "tortured Mr. Francken extensively by hitting him on the head with a saber." There it is. The only mention of Peddy Francken, yet the third or fourth known incident where he was at the receiving end of major blows. Jacob Stadt said that the time at the French Consulate was "hell: we were beaten without cause or reason. The Japanese acted like animals and they were constantly looking for reasons and excuses to hit us." This all came to an end on January 11, 1945, when all the men were read their sentence. Van der Linde claims that they were divided into three groups with sentences of fifteen, ten, and eight years. "Yet the plot," Van der Linde continues, "to get Resident Tobi convicted had failed." On January 13, 1945, the men were taken to Tjipinang, from where they were transported to Bantjeu Prison in Bandung on January 24. The next day they were all taken to Sukamiskin: "We were fifty men total," Van der Linde sums up, "but three months later thirty of us had died as a result of malnutrition. The remaining twenty were liberated in September of 1945." Stadt states that there was not enough food or adequate health care. It would be the end of Peddy Francken, a case that was based on Dutch betrayal, Japanese paranoia, and the unfortunate role planters had played as *Landwachters*.

When I looked at the few annual reports I have of Kali Jompo, I felt an almost smug satisfaction reading what my grandfather writes in the report of 1948: "After the war the *awiran* system, which had been proposed by the former administrator to prevent loss of soil through drainage and to improve the humus layer, was introduced." In the same report Jacques Francken writes: "With profound regret, we announce that our European personnel, to wit administrator Mr. F. A. M. Francken and employee Mr. J. G. van Mil, became victims of the Japanese occupation. With Mr. Francken we lose one of the best administrators we have ever had. He will stay in our memory for a very long time." Neither Jacques nor Peddy's wife, Fré, would ever know what living hell Peddy Francken had gone through. For Peddy's son, Harry, the truth would come out more than sixty years later, after repeated requests at the address of the War Archive in Amsterdam and the Ministry of Foreign Affairs in The Hague. I wonder how many people like Harry there are who are waiting for and may never find out the kind of detailed information these victims need in order to heal and move on with their lives.

Chapter 12

WALLPAPER PASTE
AND DOG SAMBAL

> Fear.
>
> Years of fear.
>
> Fear of a meaningless, unexpected event.
>
> Everything was absurd. Everything was uncertain.
>
> Life was a negation of life.
>
> That fear did not manifest itself until later, after the liberation. At night. Especially at night. Then you are on your own, facing yourself, the self that comes out of your subconscious, kicking, weeping, and screaming.
>
> Lydia Chagoll, *Buigen in Jappenkampen* (1995)

While Peddy was under arrest and being tortured, Fré was living without a husband, without money, and with a sense of increased danger—not only were roaming Japanese soldiers a fact of life, but the Dutch communities also became increasingly vulnerable to *rampokkers* (plunderers), mostly Javanese gangs who went from underground to aboveground when they started supporting the nationalist movement. Historian Robert Cribb explains: "Gangsters are an ancient feature of the social landscape on Java. . . . It was typically in time of war, rebellion or economic crisis, when the state was under threat, that brigands conducted their activities with the greatest boldness, plundering not just individual travelers but whole villages."[1] An added complication was that in May of 1942 the Japanese issued

Regulation Number 17, which meant that all private estates like Kali Jompo became Japanese property and the planters were obliged, until they too were interned, to run the estate, increase production, and hand over all proceeds to the Japanese occupiers.[2]

The men were interned before the women. Because of this the call for internment in December of 1942 was to some women and children a relief. Without money and husbands, the prospect of the camp and a new life in the company of other Dutch women may well have seemed a less vulnerable situation than being at home alone.[3] Little did these women know that the Japanese camps (320 in total) held their own hardships.

What needs to be emphasized is that even though the Japanese singled out the non-Asian races in their ethnic policy, the camps, while hardly four-star resorts, were never intended as extermination camps, like the Nazi death camps. The Japanese claimed there were three reasons for having internment camps. First, they were retaliation for the Allies, the Americans foremost among them, who had interned Japanese and Japanese American citizens in camps after Pearl Harbor. Second, the Japanese argued that they had to protect the non-Asians, and especially the Dutch, from the wrath of the Indonesians; this might have been the case in the big cities but was less of a factor in the more rural parts of Java. And third, because of the closed-down banks and the lack of cash flow from Holland, many Dutch nationals were down and out and needed to be taken care of. Ironically, the Japanese ignored "the fact that the impoverishment was a direct consequence of their own Japanese invasion and measures."[4] At the same time, these arguments, while there is some truth to them, should also be seen as propaganda to whitewash the entire operation. As other historians have pointed out, the hidden and real reason for having the camps was to end Western influence in Asia.[5] The goal and justification were *Asia Raya,* an indivisible greater Asia in which Westerners had no place.

How did the Franckens experience their departure from Kali Jompo? They were allowed to bring only a small suitcase and a small bag that should contain two to three plates, a spoon, a fork, a knife, and one or two cups per person. What did Fré bring? Objects of the utmost practicality that would help them survive? Valuables? Or objects that had sentimental value? What does one take when one's house is on fire? In hindsight, it may have been a blessing that Fré would never return to the family estate: after the Dutch abandoned their homes, the Japanese (as the Germans did with abandoned Jewish homes) moved in, emptied out everything, and shipped most of the valuables to Tokyo. Some Dutch families buried their valuables, family silver, jewelry, and other valuables or hid them in deep wells. In an e-mail Harry told me that a deep hole was dug between the garage and the spare bedroom. All valuables, locked inside chests, were lowered down in there. "You wonder whatever happened to the stuff," Harry writes. "I assume that as soon as we were gone, everything was dug up again and distributed among the locals."

The Franckens were not taken to a camp at first. Instead they were transported to the city of Malang, where they lived in a district that was cordoned off with barbed wire by the Japanese. It was called De Vrouwenwijk (the Women's Quarter), as well as De Wijk, the Bergenbuurt, and Guntur. Because the Japanese had so many internees at once, they did not immediately have ready-made camps for them, so they grouped internees together in neighborhoods. Sometimes there would be many people in one house, but conditions were still tolerable.[6]

Aside from the barbed wire, life took on a semblance of normality. Families carried on as usual, albeit without husbands, brothers, and older sons. Food was still available. For some women like Fré, who had spent some time alone, the company of the other women in the house may even have been comforting in these uncertain and unpredictable times. By the beginning of 1943 all the so-called protected neighborhoods were so congested that the Japanese started moving the women into camps. The Franckens still had some relatively carefree months in De Vrouwenwijk. Harry remembers celebrating his sixth birthday there—he received a bag of marbles from his friends Beppie and Kiki.

The Franckens were probably moved in February of 1944. According to Voorneman, a large group of European women and children from eastern Java arrived in Ambarawa (middle Java) in the middle of that month. In the course of 1944 all interned women still in eastern Java were transported to middle Java, farther inland and thus more hidden from the outside world.[7] Mrs. De Koning writes that she was picked up on Sunday, February 13, 1944. It may well be that the Franckens were part of this transport as well,[8] the first horrific transport of many to come. The women and children were loaded onto open trucks and dropped off at the railway station in Malang. Since the internees were never informed about the destination, the women did not know whether they would be on the train for four hours or forty-eight hours. "It was the first time I saw a train locomotive up close," Harry tells me in an e-mail. "I remember the noise and a profound sense of panic."

The women and children were squeezed together in fourth-class cars, which were mostly boarded shut and hot. There was a little window, but every time they tried to open it a bit further for ventilation or light, the Japanese soldier who rode along on the roof hit the window with his saber and yelled: "Tutup!" (Close!). At nightfall the train came to a stop, but the women were not let out. They did not get food or water either. There were no toilets in the wagons, a particular nuisance for people who had come down with dysentery. "The train journey was endless," Harry remembers. "When we stopped at night, I managed to peep through one of the holes in the wagon and marveled at the fireflies I saw outside. It was both pretty and unreal."

After a journey of about twenty-two hours without food or drink, the train reached the station of a town in middle Java named Ambarawa. The trip had been exhausting due to the heat, thirst, lack of hygiene, and cramped conditions. Many of the children were cranky because they were tired and were suffering from whooping cough. It became clear that the women could not get out immediately, which they were eager to do. Japanese soldiers, as if driving back animals, started throwing stones when the women tried to leave the train. Finally, after a long wait, they were allowed to come out.

Located in a valley at a high altitude, Ambarawa is known for its cold, blustery winds. The women and children were shivering in their thin clothes. From the station, the internees were pushed into buses to be taken to what looked like an army base. But a sign saying "Rumah Penjara" (prison) shocked them. After their tolerable period in De Wijk, a prison was not something they had counted on.

The prison had been built under Daendels in 1810. According to Du Chattel, it was "surrounded by fat stone walls and bordered some swampy lakes, which counteracted the cooler climate because of the incidence of malaria. The old and declining prison had dark gates and rooms, broken kitchens, and a newly built cell block. Behind the prison, called Camp X, were Banyubiru XI and XII, which were fenced in with barbed wire and bamboo."[9]

The camp period, however intolerable, had an important educational value. Esther Captain, who studied camp memoirs, came to the conclusion that the camp had a certain emancipatory effect: "The women had to make do without their husbands but learned to make the best of it because of their children."[10] Captain quotes one of these women: "We spoiled ladies of the tropics learned to work hard, and so did our children."[11] Most of these women had been used to servants and therefore had not performed any domestic chores in a long time. The circumstances in the camps changed all that, and this was, for some, an opportunity for character building; for others it was confrontational and destructive.

I wonder in what state of mind Fré and her children walked through the prison gates. They were taken to Banyubiru X, also known as De Boei, an extremely stuffy, dirty, and dark building. The sanitation, including toilets, was so bad that the Dutch colonials, who had used De Boei as a prison, had condemned the building. Even before I knew that Fré and the kids had been locked inside there, I had read in David Wehl's book that women at the camp had to dig out their own sewer ditches with their bare hands. The sewer ditches became a necessity because a lack of water meant the toilets could no longer be flushed. Mrs. Hooykaas witnessed this one day: "The other day a group of women was digging out the sewer ditch.

A Japanese soldier stood by, watching, with a piece of cloth in front of his mouth against the bacteria. He would throw stones into the ditch so that the filth splashed into the women's faces; he let them work there an hour longer than was necessary."[12] After the *poepsloot* (shit ditch) was dug out, the fecal matter was carried outside to the surrounding fields, where the women had to push the sewage into the soil, once again with their bare hands, as fertilizer. For this dirty job women were rewarded with some extra food, an extra cup of coffee, and a little bar of soap.[13] That there were always women who volunteered for this job shows how dire circumstances had become and how much hunger began to play a part. Some women avoided the ditch altogether and would relieve themselves in the grass of the camp. Apparently one could smell Banyubiru from a mile away.

Harry remembered De Boei both vividly and reluctantly: "It surely was not a Hilton. Everyone slept in one room on plank beds with mattresses. There were no mosquito nets, so the mosquitoes ate you alive, and the toilets were atrocious." The Francken family must have stayed there for about four months. In that time most of the children suffered from measles, chicken pox, diphtheria, and whooping cough. To top it off, most of the people there were plagued by bedbugs, brown bugs that came out at night to suck people's blood, causing their skin to itch and swell up. In the morning there would be a ritual of squeezing the bedbugs, which apparently produced a faint almond scent.

Through an Internet search I got in touch with Gerard Lemmens, who was a bit younger than Harry when he was at De Boei: "We were eaten by bedbugs," he told me in an e-mail, "in the end, my mother didn't weigh more than sixty-seven pounds, and my aunt Mien (mother of Willem Nijholt, a famous Dutch singer and actor) weighed sixty-three pounds. My sister kept my mother alive by taking a spoonful of food from my and her plate to feed it to my mom." I asked Gerard for more information but did not want to traumatize him. He responded: "I can talk about it, but it depends on how deep you go. You should see the movie *Paradise Road*—I related to that but I cannot see it anymore. They torture a woman in that movie in the same way they tortured my mom. She smuggled in an egg after she had to work outside of the prison. The Jap discovered it, and that is why she was tortured. My sister and I were forced to watch it."

The camp experiences in Europe were given more publicity after the war. That the internees in the Japanese internment were afraid that their stories of their very real suffering would never be taken seriously was recorded soon after the war by the English Major Alan Greenhalgh: "The European and particularly the Dutch POWs and internees have had three and a half years of indescribable humiliation and hardships. Every day now they are hearing for the first time of the death and severe sickness of parents and relatives whom they had hitherto thought safe. . . . They need immense sympathy and understanding and their one fear is that what they have been through may not properly be understood."[14]

The medical statistics gathered by Rehabilitation Prisoners of War and Internees (RAPWI) staff and reproduced in Rinzema-Admiraal's book document the postwar effects of the hardships the internees suffered in the Japanese camps. Of eleven thousand patients, 48 percent suffered from chronic irritability, 42 percent exhibited paranoia, 33 percent were neurasthenic, and 21 percent suffered from insomnia. Some of these survivors suffered from posttraumatic stress, a disorder that an English report attributed to the strained circumstances in the camps due to limited living space and lack of privacy, tensions among fellow internees, forced separation of family members, constant, blind transports to other camps, the humiliating tactics of the Japanese, and a generally low level of health. In Jakarta alone, one-third of the internees were gravely ill when the Japanese surrendered, and on January 8, 1946, four months after the war was over, the mortality of former camp children still amounted to two a day.[15]

But I am running ahead of the story. When people in De Boei had to volunteer to be moved to Banyubiru XI, another location within the camp, Fré did not hesitate for a moment. She reasoned that nothing could be worse than De Boei, and she was correct. A fellow internee remembers when Fré, her kids, and the rest of the group arrived in the evening: "We thought we would get healthy people but what we got was an entire transport of sick people . . . Poor souls! Eight went straight to the sick bay . . . we were working all night to get everyone settled in. People were very brave. No one cried like the Jap had predicted. When the sun came up the new residents saw their new place for the first time and it was a revelation."[16] Mrs. Hooykaas, who already lived there, wrote down some of the reactions: "They are ecstatic, oh, how lovely! Look, children, a closet! Water in abundance! How much daylight there is inside—I have never seen so much light! How clear, how cozy, how clean. Oh, how intimate— look, there are chairs there. When they left De Wijk they brought whatever they could, but as they no longer had buckets and little tubs, they did their laundry in a cooking pot."[17]

Unlike the dirty and dark hole of De Boei, a prison that looked out on a stone wall, Banyubiru XI had no walls or *gedèg* but looked out on the beautiful mountains in the distance, which gave the women hope and inspired them: "Although many did not see the beauty of the Indies mountainscape anymore after all the misery, there were also a great number of women who felt strengthened by the view and understood its symbolism: nature continues, even beyond the highest barbed wire."[18]

One should not underestimate the healing effects of the view. Most camps were hermetically sealed from the outside world. Internees looked out on bamboo fences, and the outlawing of correspondence, radio, and telephone increased the internees' sense of isolation and disorientation. All ties with the outside world were severed, and part of the camp syndrome was a sense of having been forgotten.

From June of 1944 the women and children had to line up in rows twice a day to make their bow to the Japanese emperor. This had to be done at a perfect angle, usually during the hottest part of the day. If women bowed inadequately or made eye contact with the Japanese, they were singled out and would receive three blows in the face and six to eight kicks in the stomach. Glasses and teeth would hit the dust, and noses might be broken during this exercise.

Between bowing to the emperor and general boredom, meals became something the internees looked forward to. In May of 1944 the women received one meal of three hundred grams of rice a day, with perhaps some rotten vegetables. The other two meals consisted of a kind of tapioca pudding that looked and tasted like wallpaper paste. On special days there was meat, that is to say, *babat,* the intestines or genitals of a buffalo. It stank, but prepared with red pepper it turned into a spicy meat dish.

In July of 1944 food supplies began to dwindle, not least because hundreds of starving women from Muntilan arrived in the camp. Women started hunting for rats and mice to supplement their meals. More and more patients came down with beriberi due to a lack of vitamins. Hunger edema, with the typical swelling of the legs, also surfaced. Patients would try to recover by eating snails, worms, and stolen vegetables, but it wasn't enough. Banyubiru became known as one of the worst camps, and its death rate would be one of the highest.[19]

Food and medicine became scarcer and scarcer both inside and outside the camps for a number of reasons, three of which Rinzema-Admiraal lists in her book. First, by April of 1944 the Allies were fighting back more and more successfully and all the Javanese supply lines were being steadily cut off. Second, the Japanese tried, unsuccessfully, to turn Java into a self-sufficient economy without investing in it. As Robert Cribb explains, "The Japanese neglected to maintain the physical economic infrastructure of Java, the roads, railways and irrigation works which had been the pride of the Dutch. This infrastructure had been built for the most part to serve the largely European plantation sector of the economy, but it had become equally essential for the cultivation and transport of food for the Indonesian population."[20] Medicine and food that came in through the Red Cross was used for the soldiers themselves and frequently held back and stored in case the Allies invaded.[21] Finally, due to a growing shortage of wood, the Japanese cut down many of the coffee, rubber, tea, and other shrubs and trees for fuel, while much of the other agricultural land lay fallow, which then caused great food shortages.

When the monsoon started at the end of 1944, another year had gone by with no relief in sight and steadily worsening circumstances. How Fré survived with her children is a mystery to me. Or maybe she persisted *because of* her children. Would Peddy have lived longer if he had known his wife and children were still alive?

The monsoon of 1944 drove the women into the dark and stinking big hall where they all slept. "The storm howls around the block and the rain lashes against the boarded-up windows," Mrs. Hooykaas writes. "It is the kind of weather that is lovely when you come to a warm and cozy home after a brisk walk—the place where you change into some dry clothes and where you can eat a big delicious meal by candlelight." The women's comfortable lives with their servants had become a melancholy memory in the barracks of Banyubiru. All they owned now was the mere space of their plank bed.

When the rains stopped, hunger and roll calls became the regular routine again. Nonetheless, the internees enjoyed the warm evenings of April 1945, which reminded them of the warm summer evenings in Holland, a country that seemed much too distant. Did Fré ever think back on her life in Holland? It is more likely that she revisited remembered scenes of Kali Jompo. And what about the children? Schooling happened in secret, for the Japanese had outlawed any form of education for Europeans. But as hunger increased, the children might have had a hard time concentrating on their lessons anyway. Many children who survived the camps and returned to Holland after the war were faced with three years of missed education. This education gap intensified the feelings of alienation some of these children may have felt in their new (old) country and made the assimilation process that much harder.

In February of 1945 the daily rice portion was reduced to ninety grams per person. To compensate for the rice deficit, the kitchen resorted to a cheaper and inferior kind of flour that was crawling with maggots. Everything that lived within the camp (frogs, rats, mice, and snails) was caught and eaten as if it were the finest delicacy. A physician saved the lives of women by feeding them dead rats: "The rat meat is surprisingly tender and digestible. The flavor is good and resembles that of chicken and rabbit. The very young ones which are still without hair you can eat, skin and all; they are very good. The liver of these rats is sometimes enlarged and full of bladder worms, but I always take those out before feeding the rats to patients."[22]

In March of 1945 hunger became so urgent that the internees killed the camp dog, Bello, and prepared it for dinner: "More than five hundred internees were interested in having dog for dinner!" Richard Voorneman writes.[23] The food situation became somewhat better in the following month, but in May 1945, when in Holland the American, British, and Canadian liberators were ecstatically welcomed by the Dutch waving the orange, red, white and blue, the women in Banyubiru still had very little to eat and had no knowledge that the war in Europe was over. There were more cases of hunger edema and recurring malaria. For the internee physicians who worked in the camp, the lack of medication was a particular frustration. There was no quinine for malaria, and to combat dysentery, patients were given cinnamon and rest. "Surgeries were performed with ordinary saws and knives, and festering wounds that would not heal were simply emptied of their pus with a little spoon."[24] For extra protein, women and girls were sent outside to find snails, which the cooks turned into a kind of snail ragout.

At night the women and children lay on their beds with growling stomachs while the bedbugs and mosquitoes fed off them. Obsessing with food, the women would call out the names of favorite foods. "Steak!" someone would call out, whereupon the entire barracks groaned. "Ham!" someone else would call out, triggering more noise. In February of 1945 Mrs. Hooykaas writes: "Many are languishing on their beds, waiting for mealtimes or talking about food. People are writing recipes like crazy." And in a letter to her husband: "You know what baffles me? We are always talking about food and never about men—in a way that you, the men, are probably talking about women."[25]

For women who worked outside the camp it was very tempting to smuggle some food inside. On September 27, 1944, the Japanese tried to scare the internees by accusing 170 women of smuggling. For punishment the women had to line up and sit on the soles of their feet during the hottest part of the day. The other internees were forced to watch them. Mrs. De Koning writes: "So there we stood, while others kneeled; the children were kept quiet so that a creepy and dreaded silence descended on the camp of more than twelve hundred people. In between the kneeling women walked a 'lion tamer' who took off his belt and hit the women, preferably in the face. No one cried out. . . . After this he put his belt back on but seized a rope with knots, which he pulled through the wet gutter, and then whipped the women once again. Again it was eerily quiet."[26]

Heavy penalties with much physical violence and humiliation were intended to break morale and remind the women that resistance was not an option. What was it like to live this kind of life, day by day, without knowing when it would end? Harry remembers asking his mother when the war would be over. It must have taken great optimism to answer that question positively. Mrs. Hooykaas discloses in her journal how she had learned to cope by enjoying "what is good in the present. There are people who say: I don't want to have memories of the camp because they have been lost years. That is nonsense. Lost years do not exist. These years, too, belong to our lives, just like the ones that came before it and the ones that came after it."[27]

But there were others in Banyubiru who did not share her optimism. Peter Groenevelt, who was about the same age as Harry, remembered how he hovered over the sewage ditch one day to do his business "as a result of never-ending diarrheal episodes." Looking at the brown muck floating by, he was seized by the irony of his fate. After all, *banyu biru* means blue water, which was quite the opposite of what he saw under him: "I was sick, hungry, and lonely. I said to myself, 'Life cannot get more difficult than it is now. If I am to encounter any challenges in the future, I will recall this particular moment.' And I still do. I was only seven then."[28]

In the meantime the lack of food in Banyubiru had become so distressing that more women and children were dying. In August of 1945 about three thousand women and children were on the verge of death in all of Ambarawa. Many just lay down, waiting for the end. Besides the lack of food, there was also a lack of wood, and the women had to switch to bamboo to make the many coffins. But bamboo does not seal the way wood does and is not sturdy enough: "As soon as the corpse was put in the bamboo container, it would fall apart. It also let through moisture. With hunger edema corpses this meant that after death the body would let out water, which would come trickling from the bamboo coffins: for relatives and for the nurses who had been with the patient until death, the dripping coffin was something they would never forget."[29] Relatives could accompany the coffin as far as the camp gate, where it was thrown onto a cart and taken to an unknown destination. I realize that Harry's comment about the potentially unmarked grave of his father must have had to do with his memory of seeing the bamboo coffins disappear into the unknown world beyond the barbed wire.

Even though Banyubiru had one of the worst death rates, one positive thing about this camp was that none of the young Dutch women were selected to serve in the soldiers' brothels of the Japanese. At first, the Japanese only forced Asian (Chinese, Korean, Indonesian) "comfort women" into prostitution, but later in the war they started picking up Dutch women as well. Jan Ruff was one of these women. Her account of her first night at a Japanese brothel, during which soldiers lined up to have a turn, is both harrowing and haunting: "We were all virgins. We were such an innocent generation. We knew nothing about sex. And it seemed as if it went on for ages." After three months, the women were put in a camp again, where they were kept separate from the other women. This ostracized the women further, for the fellow internees assumed they had been whores to gain access to food or other favors. This started a cycle of shame, because even after the war Ruff's priest, husband, and parents listened but could not deal with her story. She finally broke her silence in 1992, "nearly fifty years after the crime had taken place."[30]

Although the women of Banyubiru were spared that humiliation, by the time the Americans dropped their atomic bombs on Japan, most of the women and children were dying. If the war had lasted longer, most of the internees would not have survived. Du Chattel cites a RAPWI major who said in September 1945, "If this war had lasted six more months, one could have erected a big white cross in middle Java for the Last Dutch Woman in the Indies."[31] Harry Francken remembered that after the bombs had been dropped, the Japanese threatened to drown all the women in Rawa Puning, a swamp nearby.

Rinzema-Admiraal has shown in a recent article that, not until sixty years later, Japanese archives released data that reveal there was a liquidation plan in place to kill all POWs and internees by the end of the war. The execution of this plan for mass murder was pre-empted by the atomic bombs and emperor Hirohito's subsequent radio speech on August 15, ordering the Japanese army to cooperate with the Allies.[32]

But life outside the camp was no picnic either, a fact that some early Dutch historians have glossed over too easily. While the Japanese preached their hatred of the West, militarized Indonesia's young people, and brainwashed them in the process (for thinking or expressing oneself otherwise would inevitably lead to a visit with the Kempeitai), the Indonesians suffered just as much if not more than the Europeans and other nationals did. The indigenous population experienced many human losses because of starvation and the Japanese reliance on *romusha* (forced laborers). The total number of romusha has never been definitively established (estimates range between four and ten million), but both Shigeru Sato and Henk Hovinga agree that "only 77,000 survived of the 300,000 romusha who were transported overseas." This means that 74.3 percent died.[33]

While the Dutch internees did not have a clue what had happened in the outside world during their imprisonment, the Indonesians felt betrayed by both the Dutch and the Japanese: the Dutch for not adequately protecting the Indies against the Japanese and the Japanese for mistreating, starving, and murdering the population. In addition, after seeing the cadaverous internees coming out of the camps, the Indonesians could not understand that these were the same people who had dominated the Indies for so long; seeing the Dutch in that state demystified their power and showed how vulnerable they had become. The hatred of the West and Japan's militarization of an Indonesian youth movement, as well as the knowledge that the Allies were on their way (with the Dutch at their heels), formed fertile ground for a revolution.

Chapter 13

LIBERATION?

We had won the war, hadn't we? In doubt I wondered
whether our lives would ever be normal again. What
was to become of us? ... The Indies, our Indies, [were]
completely disturbed and appropriated by a small group of
barbarians who were only after their own interest. [They]
could not be managed by a handful of English troops.
Kampungs and *sawahs* were burned down, defenseless
Chinese citizens and innocent natives fell into the hands of
cowardly murderers. Behind every wall, inside every bush
there could be snipers, ready to kill an innocent person.

And in the filthy camps we were trapped, Indies
Dutch men and women who had been so attached to this
beautiful spot in the tropics, and we were kept in the dark!
When, slowly, the situation became clear to us, we were
entirely unprepared for this changed world. We were
powerless, the battle cry "Merdeka" sounded like a threat,
and while singing the "Indonesia Raja" lawless brigands
attacked unarmed, unsuspecting citizens. The Indonesians
themselves were not always spared; terror was king and
regardless of race or skin color, one killed to kill.

Iens van Doorn, *Geluk is als een vogel* (1981)

Harry and his two older sisters, Willy and Joke, had a great deal of
life experience behind them after two years of internment. Did they
talk about Peddy at all? Did Fré wonder whether her husband
was still alive? Did she fear the worst because she knew that Peddy
was inclined to resist and rebel, just as he had resisted and rebelled
against the naysaying of Jacques Francken? Did she know that Peddy
had spent most of the occupation in the hands of the Kempeitai?

Correspondence was censored, and most women in the camps did not know whether their husbands, sons, and fathers were still alive. Harry does not remember a single letter or message from his father after they had said their final good-bye at Kali Jompo in 1943.

Those final days before the Japanese surrender were some of the hardest: more people were dying and the women in the camps had to produce more bamboo coffins. But Fré had survived. Admittedly, the children had been sick and sometimes had intestinal worms that were so long she had to pull them out of her children's behinds, but they were still alive and intact as a family, and that was more than most families had. Many women had lost the will to live and let go. Others, like Fré perhaps, saw survival as the ultimate way to defy the Japanese.

In Banyubiru XI 1945 had started with a pleasant surprise. The noise of an engine in the sky, first vague and barely audible, then closer by, made the internees scan the skies. When the noise was at its loudest, the shadow of a plane fell across the sweltering heat inside the camp. The Japanese were yelling and readying their anti-aircraft guns. Women and children ran along with the silver plane, and when the internees saw that the plane carried the Union Jack, they started cheering but were soon shouted down by the Japanese guards. That, however, could not dampen the spirit of hope. The plane was the first sign that the Allies were winning the war. It was as if the plane encouraged them to survive a little while longer. One of Fré's friends later wrote, "The plane seemed to say, 'Hang in there, we are on our way.'"[1]

While Holland had already been liberated on May 5, 1945, in Banyubiru May 5 was a day like any other. In August two atomic bombs were dropped, on Hiroshima and Nagasaki. On August 14 the Japanese surrendered, but once again the news was not shared with the internees, for whom the day was just another day filled with hunger, heat, starvation, death, and despair.

Under pressure from young and radical nationalists, Sukarno announced the formal independence (*Proklamasi*) of the *republik* on August 17, 1945. The Proklamasi did not come entirely unexpectedly. The surrender of the Dutch colonial army on March 9, 1942, had represented the end of Dutch colonialism in the eyes of the Indonesians. To the European allies, however, the Dutch government remained the de facto government, as established by the Potsdam Conference of July and August 1945. That agreement had no value to the Indonesians, who had not been included at the conference. Whereas occupied Europe saw the arrival of the Allies as a true liberation, "the colonized people of Asia saw the return of the Allies as a renewed threat of foreign dominance," Willy Meelhuijsen writes.[2]

The Indonesians received Sukarno's Proklamasi with caution. As William Frederick has written, "The common reflex was still hesitation. This caution was mirrored particularly well in the use of the already circulating terms *bersiap* or *siap* (be prepared; be at the ready). Although occupation rhetoric lent this word a challenging ring, in late August 1945 to be *siap* was to be defensively alert but calm."[3]

Meanwhile, back at Banyubiru, the internees did not even know the Proklamasi had taken place. It shows what a forgotten and marginalized group they had become, their sense of which grew after the liberation when the Allies were slow in restoring order and providing security. The real change came on August 23, when two Javanese appeared at Banyubiru's gate. They offered food in exchange for money, clothes, and goods. *Gedèggen*, the smuggling and exchanging of food at the *gedèg* (bamboo fence) with the help of the Javanese on the outside, had happened off and on during the war but carried stiff penalties; for the smuggling of a single egg you were hung by your arms and whipped. So at first no one dared initiate contact with the Javanese at the fence.

Two boys finally broke the tension. They ran to the Javanese and ran back with their hands full of goodies. Diet Kramer, a Dutch author who was also interned at the camp, describes this scene in her autobiographical novel *Thuisvaart* (1948): "Old clothes, handkerchiefs, pieces of fabric, everything that had been kept saved and hidden was now brought out and exchanged for food. Women and children all gathered at the bamboo fence; they pushed and pulled to get to the holes in the fence, and the holes became bigger and bigger. They came back cheering, carrying rice in a *pisang* [banana] leaf, a little piece of meat, a bunch of bananas."[4]

Maria Nieuwenhuys-Lindner, a friend of the Franckens, remembered the same scene: "All of a sudden *gedèggen* was no longer penalized. Women and children walked, pushed their way to the *gedèg* and exchanged little pieces of fabric for a piece of *gula jawa,* a *pisang,* an egg, a *lumpia,* wrapped in a *pisang* leaf. I saw a woman running for the fence with a piece of a torn blanket—on the other side of the fence the Javanese man was already pulling on the blanket while she greedily took a raw egg from him. She then bit the shell, poured the contents into her mouth, and ate the shell as well."

According to Kramer, that same day, August 23, the announcement was made that the Japanese had surrendered, but according to Nieuwenhuys and Voorneman this did not take place until the next day. The women were told to line up and the Japanese camp commander, with the help of an interpreter, announced that the war had ended. He praised the women for their behavior during imprisonment. "Now the women started to protest," Kramer wrote, "as these words came from the same man who had whipped them last week and who had kicked them awake if they had fallen asleep during night duty."[5] After that came instructions that the women were not supposed to leave the camp and were to listen to their camp leaders.

The irony was clear: although Indonesia had been formally liberated, the English had not yet arrived, and to maintain order, the supreme commander of the Pacific, Lord Mountbatten, had ordered maintenance of the status quo, which meant that the Japanese, formerly the enemy, were told to protect the internees. Rinzema-Admiraal explains that initially the liberation of the Indies and the camps was assigned to the Americans, but during the Potsdam Conference the Dutch East Indies ended up under the command of the British.[6] Mountbatten had to administer a territory of one and a half million square miles with 128 million people in it, an impossible task. At the same time, one could argue that the British underestimated the situation on the ground, thinking that the Indonesians would willingly cooperate, whereas in reality many of the Indonesians did not want to be subjected to another colonial regime. Indonesia was ready for independence and on the brink of a revolution. These revolutionary sentiments were seriously misjudged and mostly ignored by both the British and the Dutch.

While some of the Japanese adhered to the status quo order and guarded the camps, others committed *hara-kiri* or surrendered to the Indonesians, handing over all their weapons. A very few others—no more than 0.39 percent—joined the Indonesians in the revolutionary fight.[7] There was also a group that interned itself, awaiting the Allies. These different interpretations of the status quo order would exacerbate the power vacuum and would have disastrous consequences for the POWs, internees, and civilians who needed protection so badly.

In Banyubiru the news of the Japanese surrender was hard to believe. As Kramer writes: "It was as if the people could not process it. There was no cheering, no yelling. There was not even a feeling of revenge. People parted. Some cried, others laughed, and still others expressed their opinions. No one walked up to the gate to look freedom in the face."[8]

Nieuwenhuys-Lindner describes a similar anticlimax but also mentions that the Dutch flag (sewn together from children's shorts) was hoisted and that the national anthem, "Het Wilhelmus," was sung. "And yet," Nieuwenhuys continues, "there was not the same ecstasy as when we saw that silver plane flying over on January 28."

After a few more days of gedèggen, the gates were opened and the Dutch women and children walked out in search of the first *warung.* Many of the internees ate too much: at night the women and children were moaning in their beds because of bloated stomachs. This was also the time when the women and children came in contact with the internees of camps nearby. Mrs. Hooykaas writes about the men from Ambarawa VII: "The old men who were taken from our camp to there have all died. There are stories of how they dragged their sick bodies to a garbage dump, where they tried to kill the roaming and skinny dogs. They also retrieved the undigested food out of the toilets to recook it. I believe it. They went crazy with hunger."[9]

With those first few tentative steps outside, the internees began to slowly comprehend that the Javanese had had a fundamental change of heart. Friendly and cautious at first, the population became more hostile as soon as the agenda of the Dutch government was revealed. Jubilation turned into frustration. Lydia Chagoll, also a former internee, remembered that the natives saw the Dutch, starved, sick, and weak as they were, as the embodiment of renewed colonization. Soon the Javanese were throwing burning torches over the fences of the camps.[10] To give some credit to the Dutch, while they did not want to hear of Indonesian independence before the war, "the question of greater autonomy for the Indies . . . had, however, been raised by Queen Wilhelmina of the Netherlands in a broadcast of 6 December 1942 in which she outlined plans for the creation of a Commonwealth of the Netherlands after the war. The Indies were to form a part of this Commonwealth. Each part, she said, 'will participate, with complete self-reliance and freedom of conduct . . . regarding its internal affairs.'"[11]

As for Ambarawa at the time of the liberation, Brugmans includes the account of a former internee from Banyubiru who, on Queen's Day (August 31), went outside with a piece of orange cloth, symbolizing the Dutch monarchy, pinned to her dress. An old Javanese man noticed this and asked her whether Queen Wilhelmina, who was in London during the war, had returned to Holland. When the woman confirmed this, the man said he hoped everything would turn out right but that he was scared: "Our young people have changed so much; they have all been spoiled by the Japanese and we suffered so much."[12] This comment was rather typical of what the Dutch had consistently inferred, that the Japanese had radicalized the younger generation. I should note, however, that while the occupiers definitely contributed to the organization and support of youth (*pemuda*) movements, Indonesian youths, intellectuals, and nationalists were also skeptical of the Japanese. There was already a revolutionary movement in the making before the Japanese arrived, and Frederick notes that from "early 1945 an emerging group of young leaders gathered a momentum of their own in urban life."[13]

When the Javanese became more reserved and hostile, fewer internees dared leave the camp. Everywhere in Ambarawa the Indonesian flag was hoisted, and the first "Merdeka!" (Freedom!) cries resounded. The Indonesians, Meelhuijsen writes, did not want to be handed over like *barang* ("baggage," according to Meelhuijsen, but it really means "things") to the British and the Dutch.[14] Quickly rumors and stories spread that Europeans were being killed outside the camp and that anyone who went out might not come back. "Death to the Dutch," people in Ambarawa began to chant, and most received the message loud and clear. The women and children retreated into the accursed camp.

For Fré and her children the camp became a curse indeed, because that September was also when the Red Cross death lists came in. Diet Kramer writes about the effect of these lists: "Like rats the men had died . . . people were very supportive of the first ten, twenty women who had to tell their children that their fathers would never return. But when the death lists came in with ten names at a time, it turned into mass mourning."[15]

These lists came from the Red Cross Committee, which had been formed in Batavia on August 23, 1945. "One of their first activities was the collecting of data and the giving out of information. . . . It appeared that a number of women who were interned elsewhere had lost their husbands, sometimes years before. These 'Red Cross widows' . . . received confirmation of the time of their husbands', deaths but they did not find out how and where. [In later years] one kept waiting for these details, which sometimes never arrived, and this delayed and aggravated the mourning process."[16] This would be the case with Fré, too. While Harry remembers the Red Cross list in the camp with his father's name, they would never find out what exactly had happened to Peddy or how he had died.

What must have been particularly jarring was that while Red Cross widows like Fré learned that they would have to raise their children on their own, at the same time men began to arrive in the camp and many happy family reunions took place among the grieving widows. The youngest children could not remember or recognize their fathers, and many associated all men with the Japanese. This happened to Iens van Doorn's youngest daughter, Dorien, who hid behind her mother's legs when she met her father for the first time: "'No, no . . . go away,' she cried, 'dirty Jap, mean man!'"[17] When I read this I understood a bit better Harry's comment that he has always loved women so much. During his early years in the camp there were no trustworthy men or father figures. All he experienced was the tight-knit women's community, and the men he met, the Japanese, were to be distrusted and feared.

Because of all the new developments, the month of August probably went by quickly. On September 8, 1945, seven officers were airlifted into Java to report back on the situation there before the Allies arrived on the HMS *Cumberland* a week later. These officers reported on the growing anti-Dutch sentiment of the population and made special note of the appalling conditions in which the Dutch POWs and internees lived.

In September Fré wanted out. Peddy was dead, Kali Jompo (most likely) plundered, and all of the Indies was tainted with the adversity and starvation of the previous years. In the middle of September Lady Mountbatten, dressed in military uniform, visited Banyubiru. Maria Nieuwenhuys-Lindner remembers the visit in her unpublished memoir: "What were her thoughts when she stood there in front of thousands of emaciated women and children? Women and children who were covered with sores that would not heal? Women and children with bloated bellies and legs because of hunger edema and women and children in rags and bare feet because they had exchanged their last clothes and shoes for food?" One cannot think of a more fitting symbol of the end of the Dutch empire in the Indies, although few people in the camps would have seen that then.

Lady Mountbatten's arrival was accompanied by the Relief Allied Prisoners of War and Internees (RAPWI) committee, who put Fré and her children, as well as Maria Nieuwenhuys-Lindner and her children, on a transport to Surabaya after a health check found them fit enough for travel.[18] The key was to empty out the worst camps, like Banyubiru, as quickly as possible. The women's camps at Ambarawa and Banyubiru were among the biggest, and even though bad infrastructure made them hard to get to, the RAPWI Committee in middle Java decided to do an immediate evacuation of fifteen thousand people to Malang and Surabaya.[19] Widows like Fré received priority over women who still had their husbands. Her outward-bound journey was planned for October 1, 1945: Fré and her children would leave Banyubiru that day to never return. Nonetheless, many internees would revisit their camp days in dreams, nightmares, and unguarded moments.

The Franckens' transport was to be the last of four, because after October 1 the situation on the roads and in the city of Surabaya became too dangerous. Already by the end of September "it became clear that the Japanese command in Java had disintegrated and was no longer capable of maintaining order. The Indonesian resistance against the return of Dutch people grew with the day" and greatly encumbered and paralyzed the relief efforts of such organizations as the RAPWI.[20]

In Surabaya itself, the revolutionary atmosphere was heating up. While early September was still relatively quiet, when the first Dutch and Eurasians started arriving in the city before the Allies had landed, the "reception was one of strained accommodation" and overall much colder than the contact the Dutch had had with the Javanese in the country.[21]

As Meelhuijsen has pointed out, for two years all the Dutch people had disappeared from Java's public life, hidden as they were behind the bamboo fences of the camps. So when the Dutch suddenly reemerged in the streets, the Javanese considered their presence an ominous prelude to recolonization.[22] Han Bing Siong believes that it was around the third week of September, when more Allies landed and Dutch army officers exited their POW camps, that tensions rose as the Dutch also started more openly to challenge the waving of the Indonesian flag and Indonesian independence as proclaimed by Sukarno.[23]

On September 29 the first British troops landed in Batavia. The people of Surabaya, foreseeing the British landing there too, started accumulating weapons. It should be noted, in regard to what followed, that the different accounts of the situation in Surabaya have been politicized as the four parties involved in the conflict, the Japanese, the Indonesians, the British, and the Dutch, have been blaming each other for what went wrong.

The Dutch Captain Huijer, who was dropped in Surabaya to observe the situation on the ground and report back to the British and the Dutch, played a particularly dubious role in the massive arms transfer between the Japanese and the Indonesians. Dutch historians and politicians (the politicians in a 1956 parliamentary enquiry committee) have swept Huijer's mistakes under the rug. Bing Siong, on the other hand, has made a convincing case that Huijer, who was a mere observer and had no authority to give orders as he did, staged a "mock surrender of the East Java [Japanese] army commander [that] resulted in a huge arms surrender by all four battalions subordinate to him." Contrary to the conclusions of the Dutch parliamentary committee that would absolve Huijer, Bing Siong believes that "Huijer's interference" was a decisive factor in "the capture of the huge number of arms by the Indonesians [a total of 21,826 weapons] in East Java, and thus also for the dramatic course of subsequent events."[24]

In contrast, historians like P. J. Drooglever seem eager to blame the Japanese. Drooglever does talk about the arms transfer at the Morokrembangan airfield, but writes that the Japanese surrendered their arms more or less spontaneously as they "gave veiled support to the nationalist movement whenever possible." Later he adds that the takeover of arms by *pemudas* . . . went ahead full speed, even stimulated by the Japanese command."[25] He says not a word about Huijer in his entire article.

Bing Siong believes that without Huijer's intervention "the arms transfer would have taken place much more slowly and on a much slower scale, as in West and Central Java" and thus the Japanese and incoming Allied soldiers would not have been overrun by the armed mobs of the revolution in October of 1945. That the Dutch parliamentary committee nonetheless concluded that "the Dutch role in the disastrous events of Surabaya was of only minor significance" is, according to Bing Siong, "absolutely incomprehensible."[26] Bing Siong's persuasive and well-documented argument is corroborated by Richard McMillan, who blames the extremely well-equipped Indonesian forces in East Java on "an act of folly" by Huijer. "Huijer told Lieutenant-General Nagano, the Commander of the Japanese 16th Army," McMillan writes, "that he had been sent by Mountbatten. This was untrue. The Japanese troops duly paraded on the airfield and laid down their weapons. They also handed over their tanks, artillery, anti-aircraft guns, transport and ammunition and then withdrew to Semarang. No sooner had the weapons been surrendered than a division of the Indonesian TKR descended on the airfield, seized the arms for themselves and imprisoned Captain Huijer."[27] After the war, Yaichiro Shibata, commander of the Japanese Second Southern Fleet in Surabaya, regretted handing over his sword to Huijer as Huijer "was not at all able to restore law and order in Surabaya."[28]

One wonders whether the conclusions of the parliamentary enquiry of 1956 were politically motivated: after all, acknowledging blame and accountability could well have led to claims of reparation and compensation by people who fell victim to the explosive onslaught of violence and massacres that swept through Surabaya in October of 1945. To speak of a parliamentary coverup is somewhat extreme, as Bing Siong also indicates that the parliamentary committee did not fully comprehend or was inattentive to the importance of the Japanese battalions "outside the city and the disastrous effects of their surrender." Yet he condemns Dutch historians as well as the 1956 committee for being "skeptical of the motives of the Japanese army in the post-surrender period" while being "tolerant and credulous with regard to those of their own fellow countrymen."[29] Whether one calls it censorship, silencing, revisionist history, or plain ignorance, the fact that there is not a single Dutch historian who has criticized, let alone questioned, Huijer's actions is more disappointing evidence that Dutch colonial history of the war period is partial and unbalanced at best.

By October 1, the day the Franckens arrived in Surabaya, the Indonesian troops had disarmed most of the Japanese soldiers. (The British troops would not land in Surabaya until October 25.) On that same day the Indonesians took over the city's command from the Japanese, which explains the rowdy and disturbing scenes that accompanied the Franckens' arrival. I will return to that in the next chapter.

Until October 1 the Franckens probably no longer ventured out of the camp because it was becoming increasingly dangerous for Dutch people to do so. Not only the Dutch, but other Europeans, Eurasians, Arabs, and Chinese, had become targets of young revolutionaries. David Wehl writes: "As the [British] Indian troops penetrated to other places, Ambarawa, Semarang, Magelang, conditions were everywhere the same, fighting, murder, kidnapping, looting and a ruthless scramble for weapons of destruction. Jungle law had come to Java."[30]

Willy Meelhuijsen, who wrote a book on the revolution in Surabaya, told me in a letter: "The revolution was triggered by Dutch colonial dominance, by the miserable circumstances during the Japanese occupation, and finally by British meddling and the Dutch intent to recolonize. This movement was led by people with very different backgrounds in life. The general population was very scared of the future and the Indonesians were sick of foreign rule. . . . Like a tornado, the rebellion stormed through the streets of Surabaya. People were pulled along in the wild force of this tornado. Well-intentioned revolutionaries, however, were often dominated by the 'mob,' riff-raff, plunderers, and street terrorists."

It is important to point out here, as Robert Cribb has done, that the mob Meelhuijsen mentions belonged to gangsters, killers, and plunderers who "had no political programme with which to follow up their actions; they were opportunists rather than social revolutionaries."[31] The more generic term that one hears in this context as well is "pemuda," which means "youth." These pemuda usually belonged to Indonesian organizations such as the Tentara Keaman Rakyat (TKR; People's Protection Army). Although the TKR was supposed to, and did, help out the Allies with the protection and evacuation of the POWs and internees, "in some places, notably at Bandung, the TKR openly worked and fought with the extremist belligerents."[32]

Most of the internees had no clue as to what was imminent, and thus Fré and her children may have thought naively that the first assaults and street violence against Europeans and Indos in Ambarawa were random and temporary. If she had known that they were the beginning of something much bigger and uncontrollable, she might not have gone into the lion's den that Surabaya would become. But how could she have known if all she had seen was the gedèg of the camp? The reality outside the camps was grim. As Cribb writes, the last few months of 1945 "were a time of robbery, looting, kidnapping, and random street murders, in which Europeans disappeared, even in the heart of the city, to be found a few days later floating in the canals. The number killed was not as terrifying as the randomness and unpredictability of the killings, and the fact that most Europeans could not distinguish assassins from the general Indonesian population."[33] Many ignored the more dangerous conditions, and even though the internees were expected to return to the camps at nightfall, some four thousand truants left the camps forever.[34]

Iens van Doorn's husband, who shortly after the war crossed Java to find his family in one of the women's camps, said that *bollossing* (truancy) was not an option even though he was a truant himself, trying to reach his wife: "It is very sensible of the Japanese to keep you inside! The English have sent too few troops; they counted on the loyalty of the population and have underestimated the chaos that followed the armistice. There are rebels everywhere."[35] Van Doorn writes, "We were all baffled. From when we were young we had grown up with the population, we had played with them as children, we thought we were their friends. Our lives were interwoven with theirs and we could not imagine a future without them."[36]

Johan Fabricius, who arrived in Java as a BBC correspondent around the same time, was just as perplexed as Van Doorn. He was shocked by the rumors of the "deep hatred" the Javanese were said to harbor against the Dutch: "I was inclined to blame all the current troubles in Java on the general chaos of war, on the aftereffects of our rapid and complete defeat in 1942, and on the Japanese slander and Greater Asia propaganda. If people saw that we intended to relieve the economic slump while not hampering Indonesia's self-government, but, on the contrary, help with the realization of such a government, would and could the old trust not be restored?"[37]

What is interesting is that Fabricius, who was part of the international press corps, felt that the terror and violence that happened on a daily basis was seen as an inevitable, necessary (and therefore maybe more acceptable) part of Indonesia's struggle for independence. World sympathy was with the charismatic Sukarno and independence, Fabricius noticed, and Sukarno, Sjahrir, and Hatta were the "hot news" while the Dutch delegation with the not-so charismatic but hard-working and progressive H. J. van Mook were discarded out of hand as "old stuff."

Furthermore, the nationalist leaders, Fabricius writes, insisted that the Allies and Dutch soldiers had to leave for the violence to stop. Fabricius believed leaving would be irresponsible as the Indonesian leadership did not seem to be able to contain the more extremist factions among the nationalists. When he was writing this, many of the internees were, and until a year after the Japanese surrender still would be, locked away in their former internment camps or the so-called protection camps because the roads were unsafe. To quote Fabricius one last time: "Of course *tempo dulu* should not return. Of course these people have, like any other, the right to govern themselves; the colonial era . . . lies behind us forever. But this transition for which the Dutch have understanding too, does it have to happen at the cost of Java's entire economic prosperity? Does it require a bloody terror against Indonesians, Chinese, Indo-Europeans, and defenseless Dutch women and children?"[38]

Many assumptions have been made regarding the reasons behind the slow evacuation. First and foremost, the lack of a central Allied authority and communication center hindered the coordination of care and evacuation. Second, there was no reliable infrastructure as snipers and mines made the roads unsafe. Some of the roads were in bad shape, means of transport were inadequate, and fuel was hard to come by (trains ran on wood because of the lack of coal). Third, the revolutionaries delayed the Dutch internees' return to their former lives and colonial jobs because that would mean business as usual and a violation of the newly gained independence.[39] Fourth, as hostages, the internees had a function too, for many of the Indonesians feared that once all the internees were evacuated and out of the line of a potential crossfire, the Allies could launch a full-blown attack, seize power, and open the door for the Dutch, who were waiting to come in anyway. Finally, from the beginning of the arrival of the Allies in the Indies, there was a chronic lack of troops to help with the evacuation and protection of the internees. The few troops that did land were faced with an opponent who, since the surrender of the Japanese, consisted of millions of armed freedom fighters.[40]

Fortunately and unfortunately, Fré and her children would not be slowed down in their evacuation and final repatriation to the Netherlands. Her premature departure from Banyubiru was a curse rather than a blessing, the timing of which she must have dwelled on many times in Holland when sleep would not come late at night and her memories took her back to that October of 1945 in Surabaya.

Chapter 14

LAST TRAIN TO SURABAYA

> War is war, no doubt about it—a constant cycle of man's
> evil toward man. A tree's branches don't move of their
> own accord; something has to move them. Likewise, men
> don't simply turn into savages; there has to be something
> that makes them that way.
>
> And men then go on to make weapons to kill their
> enemies because there are enemies everywhere. So very
> few stop to realize that their most important foe is them-
> selves, that therein the seeds of savagery lie.
>
> Pramoedya Ananta Toer, "Revenge"

At the end of September Fré and her three children prepared for
their departure from Banyubiru. They did not have much to pack
because most of their cherished items had been traded for food.
They must have said their good-byes to other women and children
in the camp with whom they had formed a strong bond during all
the deprivation and death.

In Surabaya, their destination, things were heating up when the
first Dutch and Eurasian ex-internees arrived before the Allies did.
The first Allied parachutists, some of them sent as a RAPWI effort,
landed in the outskirts of town on September 18 and stationed themselves in the Oranje Hotel, which was still guarded by the Japanese.
The Red Cross operated out of a building across the street. As their
operation grew and Dutch and Eurasian visitors came and went,
the Indonesians became suspicious—maybe unjustly so, as both the
RAPWI and the Red Cross were humanitarian organizations that
performed relief work exclusively. The Indonesians, however, asso-

ciated them with the Dutch government and saw the flurry of activities around the Oranje Hotel as a sign that the Dutch were trying to enter through the back door, possibly under the cover of these organizations.

When on September 19 a Dutch man was so bold as to hoist the Dutch tricolor over the Oranje Hotel, an Indonesian crowd gathered outside in protest. There are different accounts of this incident, which, because of its symbolic value, has been both exaggerated (by the Indonesians) and underplayed (by the Dutch). The truth probably lies somewhere in the middle. William Frederick describes the incident as an obvious provocation during which Dutch children were orchestrated to walk by the hotel with Dutch flags. This seems somewhat unlikely as most of the Dutch children in town had just come out of the camps, may have been in poor health, and may not have been allowed by their mothers to partake in such an event.

Willy Meelhuijsen does not describe it as a provocation but believes that the ensuing street fight broke out "spontaneously" and that the fistfights were "not planned." Both Frederick and Meelhuijsen agree that the hotel was stormed and that an Indonesian pulled down the flag and tore off the blue stripe, turning it into a tattered red-and-white Indonesian flag instead. The Eurasian lawyer V. W. C. Ploegman, cofounder of the Komite Kontak Sosial (KKS), an organization that helped the Red Cross and former internees, was hit on the head with a pipe and subsequently died. The Indonesians were suspicious of the KKS because it had worked with the Japanese. The flag incident at the Oranje Hotel was a tipping point and the beginning of more violent confrontations to come.[1]

In the following week three more RAPWI teams arrived with the Dutch Captain P. J. G. Huijer, whose role in making weapons available to the Indonesians was discussed in the previous chapter. A navy representative of both the Dutch and British high commands, he was sent ahead to inspect Surabaya Harbor, a mission that could easily have been misconstrued as Dutch espionage. The RAPWI visits and Huijer's presence added to "a ballooning sense of crisis," a fact that did not go unnoticed by Huijer himself, who thought the city was in a "nervous and disquieting state." Because of this, the Japanese commanders, David Wehl writes, agreed to send "an extra 300 Kempeitai to guard the women's camps" (the protection camps, which were in secure neighborhoods within Surabaya). "They were never sent."[2] Wehl may have been mistaken. From the unpublished report by Yaichiro Shibata, the Japanese commander of the Second Southern Fleet (for Java and Borneo), it appears that Shibata had indeed ordered three hundred KPT officers to return to Surabaya by train. When they arrived at the station, which must have been on or around the same day that Fré and her children arrived in Surabaya, the Japanese officers were arrested and imprisoned by *pemuda*. Indonesian sources confirm this incident.[3] As the atmosphere in the city grew more and more tense, some of the ex-internees who were already inside the city were moved to the safer, barricaded Darmo quarter.

"Late in September," Frederick writes, "posters had begun to appear in various city locations declaring October 1st would be 'butchering day for the Japanese dogs.'" There were two protective Indonesian armies or militia: The Pemuda Republik Indonesia (PRI; Youths of the Indonesian Republic), the Badan Keamanan Rakyat (BKR), and later, the Tentara Keamanan Rakyat (TKR), initially commanded by Mustopo, a dentist. According to Japanese commander Shibata, who was sympathetic to Indonesian independence, anti-Japanese sentiment was triggered because the Japanese had to collaborate with the Dutch RAPWI officers.[4]

On October 1, at 8:30 in the morning, the city was "flooded with posters, flags and screaming Indonesians brandishing bamboo spears, swords, and fire arms."[5] The city seemed ready to seize power from the forever-weakening Japanese resident and his troops. Alfred van Sprang, a Netherlander who stayed in the Oranje Hotel, described the atmosphere as follows:

> The apparent peace in Surabaya may change into actual unrest. One can no longer count on the Japanese. Surabaya awakens slowly from its siesta. There is more driving to and fro in the streets. Trucks,

loaded with screaming Indonesians, go back and forth in the center of town. Big red-and-white flags are fluttering in the wind. The paint of the nationalist slogans has not even dried yet. Everywhere on the outskirts of town one sees groups of young Indonesians at street corners. They all wear red and white. Most of them carry bamboo spears. . . . The Europeans hurry home. They feel that something is about to happen. Shops are closing. Hastily shopkeepers board up their shop windows. The streets are abandoned. Just the cry of a many-voiced "Merdeka" echoes against the walls. In the distance there are shots. . . . The capture of the city proceeds quickly. . . . Surabaya is in the hands of the Indonesian Republic.[6]

The coup, in which Japanese officers were disarmed, killed, or imprisoned, culminated the next day (October 2), when, after the capture of the Kempeitai headquarters, the Japanese surrendered to "Sudirman and a few others representing the republican government."[7]

Shibata, the Japanese commander, spoke of "imminent upheaval" and "riotous masses." He disagreed with Huijer, who had ordered him to use armed forces against hostile rioters: if the Japanese forces had followed Huijer's advice, Shibata argued, "the Allied Forces, soldiers and civilians, and particularly the large number of Dutch and Japanese interned in the southern part of the city [where Fré and her children were headed after their arrival in Surabaya], would all be massacred and the entire city would be thrown into complete disorder and chaos."[8] Shibata's instincts were right while Huijer's estimation of the situation was, once again, completely and dangerously wrong.

Coincidentally, on the day the hostilities broke out, October 1, the Franckens and many other women and children arrived at the Surabaya railway station amid much chaos and some bloodshed.[9] Conditions were so hazardous that the transports of former internees from Java's interior were canceled altogether on October 2. The Franckens had essentially caught the last train to Surabaya.

For an account of the transport to Surabaya, I rely on the memoir of Maria Nieuwenhuys-Lindner:

We were loaded onto a truck to go to the station in Ambarawa. The train that was to take us to Surabaya was already there. It was October 1, 1945. There were already many people and children at the station, and at a given moment in time and a certain command we were all being pushed into the train. Japanese guards accompanied us on the train. It was a terrible trip; the children lay on the floors between the benches and the aisles. Now and then they slept . . . the cars were immensely crowded and boarded up so that the heat became intolerable.

At the train station in Surabaya revolutionaries were waiting for the transports to come in. Upon arrival the doors remained closed and the women could hear a gunfight between the Japanese guards on the train and the Indonesians on the platform. The women waited in fear until the shooting stopped. A number of them fainted from heat and anxiety. Others were dehydrated. Because Nieuwenhuys-Lindner lost consciousness as well, I also rely on the account of Eliza Thomson, who was on the same transport: "How could this happen? We were stormed by a group of natives. Aggressively they pointed their sharp bamboo spears at us. Enraged, they screamed: 'Merdeka! Merdeka! Merdeka!' They were dressed in rags. Their dark eyes had a wild and terrifying expression."[10]

The women and children were chased onto trucks by pemuda who were in charge. They were then transported to the Gubeng quarter. U. L. U. ten Broek, who accompanied her mother on this transport, remembered that "when the fighting stopped, we were transported to the Celebes Street, on trucks with natives and red-and-white flags."[11] What the ex-internees saw outside was at once shocking and grotesque: they were driving by the "dancing" chopped-off heads of Japanese soldiers, which had been impaled and propped onto bamboo spears.[12] The Indonesians on the trucks were hardly comforting when they bragged that they had killed more than fifty Japanese officers in cold blood. People were dancing in the streets, and, as ten Broek remembered, as soon as they got to the Celebes Street, a bullet came whistling past the truck.

Due to the vilification of Japanese soldiers in general in the various Dutch war and postwar accounts, the sometimes heroic role Japanese officers played to protect women and children has been glossed over by most historians in the Netherlands. The Japanese did everything in their power to protect the former internees. Bing Siong cites Dutch Lieutenant-Governor General H. J. van Mook, who as early as 1945 reported on the changed attitude of ex-internees, from "aversion" to "a certain gratitude and admiration. . . . Typically, [Van Mook's] telling report was cited *by no Dutch source until 1995.*"[13]

In Gubeng, a tree-lined neighborhood in southern Surabaya, the women and children were given shelter in homes where Japanese soldiers had lived. The few remaining officers who were still there were removed by the pemuda. (Possibly, these "protected" areas had been the kind of women's neighborhoods where the Japanese had interned Dutch women and children before they were moved inland to camps.) Bing Siong confirms that the RAPWI plan was to house the women and children in Darmo and Gubeng, where Japanese soldiers were living—this also meant that the Japanese had to live in unprotected neighborhoods all over the city, where they were exposed to "intimidation, plunder, kidnap or worse."[14] Nieuwenhuys-Lindner, who had regained consciousness, remembers that upon arrival in Gubeng, some twenty pemuda, who had accompanied and protected them during the transport, barged into the houses where the women and children were to stay and dragged out everything that was inside: "They threw everything onto a few empty trucks, so there we were in an empty house, without beds, cupboards, chairs, tables, you name it." Not exactly a warm welcome, but it could have been worse—if not for the intervention of the pemuda at the railway station, these women and children might have met with the same fate as the Japanese soldiers.

What they did not know was that until October 2 the RAPWI had worked with the Red Cross and the Japanese resident to look after the ex-internees who were arriving in the city and were already housed in the Darmo and Gubeng quarters. After the Indonesians captured the city, the Red Cross became the sole organization to look after some 1,850 ex-internees.[15] As time went by, the Indonesians became increasingly hostile to the RAPWI and later the Red Cross, both of whom they associated with the Dutch, Dutch control, and at their most paranoid, with Dutch undercover agents.[16] The ultimate low point in relief care came when Indonesian rebels began kidnapping RAPWI and Red Cross workers and attacking ambulances, and even hospitals. Something had snapped—the PRI and the BKR/TKR had underestimated, and had little control over, the power of the masses from the *kampung*. Frederick writes that after October 2 there was a "wild, unleashed fury of untargeted and exceptionally violent rioting. . . . The looting of warehouses and unoccupied Dutch homes by bands of Indonesians was common at the time as was the phenomenon of whole *kampung* erupting when Japanese or Europeans passed by."[17]

Shortly after the Indonesians seized power in the city, the PRI moved into the Simpang Club, Surabaya's exclusive Dutch club, which was associated with the white elite, racism, and Dutch nationalism. Indonesian spy hysteria went up a notch when, on October 10, the BKR searched the offices of the Red Cross as well as the Oranje Hotel, where, according to Indonesian sources, they found British invasion plans. Because of these discoveries all remaining RAPWI staff members were imprisoned on October 10 and 11.[18] The disastrous arms transfer discussed in the last chapter had already taken place.

October 10 was also Harry's eighth birthday. On October 10, 2006, I wrote Harry an e-mail for his birthday, telling him that I had just realized that he must have "celebrated" his birthday in Gubeng in 1945. He told me in an emotional e-mail response that he had completely forgotten about this birthday but that my reminder had triggered a repressed memory of his sisters, who had gone out of their way to make him two presents: "It was so special, the fact that they had gone to such lengths to make me something and show me that they loved me. . . . I had forgotten, completely forgotten until you wrote me yesterday's e-mail, and I consider this recovered memory the greatest gift anyone has given me for my birthday."

Fré and the children still received watery soup once a day, brought by Red Cross workers until most of them were imprisoned or kidnapped, too. This meant that gradually the ex-internees were cut off from food, water, and electricity altogether. Touwen-Bouwsma writes: "The violence in Java against Dutch and Indo-Europeans, which erupted mid-October, was impossible to turn around. There was a food boycott for all Europeans. Water and electricity, already in the hands of the Indonesians, were cut off, and the situation in the camps, which housed thousands of internees, became untenable. The first kidnappings of Dutch people and Indo-Europeans took place and street fights broke out. In all the big cities European and Indo-European men and boys were rounded up and imprisoned." By October 17 all RAPWI representatives in middle and eastern Java were behind bars.[19]

Nieuwenhuys-Lindner describes the lack of food and water and the power outage(s) simply as "teasing" by the Indonesians, which seems to indicate that most of the ex-internees did not quite realize the gravity of the hazardous situation they were in. "No water," she writes, "means the end in the tropics." But lack of water may not have been the worst of their troubles, compared to the unrest and violence in the streets. Dutch, Chinese, Japanese, Indo-Europeans, and Arabs who went outdoors were the victims of street riots and fights. It was important to stay inside even if you did not have any water or food.

Van Doorn, who helped out in a Bandung hospital during the bersiap, writes: "Aside from the gruesomely maimed adults, the rebels did not spare the defenseless children! Every day they brought in Chinese babies with hacked-off hands and feet, children with cut-off noses and ears, demasculated (castrated) bigger boys and raped girls with cut-off breasts . . . and the stream of victims never stopped! The blood thirst of the pemudas seemed infinite."[20]

Earlier, on or around October 6, a large kampung population gathered in front of Bubutan Prison, where Japanese survivors were held and protected by the PRI. The prison was stormed as if it were the French Bastille, and the Japanese were dragged outside and butchered until a reinforcement of the PRI arrived and intervened.

One can only imagine the rising suspense among the ex-internees in the dark, desolate, empty houses in Darmo and Gubeng. The mounting noise of violence and gunshots outside would become louder and more threatening as the days went by. Shibata also writes about the ominous and continuous beating of wooden drums.[21]

In mid-October Dutch men and boys were rounded up. Harry remembers the searches and calls them "razzias" (a term also used for Nazi house searches and arrests). One day Harry was picked up, too. Due to the intervention of a courageous housemate and former fellow internee named Ms. Van Wiekeren, the Indonesians left after she told them that Harry was a boy rather than a man and therefore needed to be left alone. Although Harry did not know it then, he had escaped a very uncertain fate, because all over town truckloads of white males were driven to the Kalisosok (or Werfstraat) Prison. Awaiting them was a "smoldering *kampung* population. Crowds streamed from central city *kampung,* shouting: 'Kill the NICA dogs!' and 'Filthy Dutch!' as they followed the vehicles to their destinations."[22] At the prison, the men and boys were ordered to run the gauntlet, that is, run toward the entryway of the prison while an angry mob hacked at them with spears and axes.

Other men and boys who were arrested ended up at the Simpang Club on October 15, when one of Surabaya's bloodbaths, known as "Bloody Monday," took place. Dutch and Eurasian men and boys, as well as a few women, who arrived at the Simpang Club were told to undress themselves to appear before a tribunal. They would be interrogated, indicted, judged, and condemned, all in a matter of hours. I hereby enclose Frederick's shocking account in an as-yet unpublished article. I do this not to sensationalize matters but because I think it is new and compelling material that Dutch, Indonesian, and English sources have not published in this kind of detail before. Frederick writes:

> Prisoners were commonly told to strip to their underwear, after which they were subjected to a humiliating process which involved kicking, beating, and painting NICA (i.e., the enemy) on their bare backs, as

well as, for some, life-threatening wounds from blows to the head with clubs or rifle butts. They were then held in small rooms until called by a tribunal of top PRI leaders. A few survivors report having been allowed to go to the toilet or get a drink of water, during which times they saw scattered, bloody parts strewn on the floor, or dead bodies hung from ceilings or cast aside.[23]

Though less graphic than Frederick, Meelhuijsen writes that these toilets became so gory and slippery with blood and human limbs that they became known as "blood cells."

Frederick continues: "In small groups they were then brought out for an 'official' examination, in which their names and addresses were noted and they were asked absurd questions by a panel of three or four examiners. Did they know Van der Plas (the much-feared governor of east Java and head of NICA)? Why did they have 'NICA' written on their backs?" As the "hearings proceeded, the violence grew more excessive." Frederick quotes a survivor:

I saw to my left and right piles of human body parts that the murderous crowd had severed from the bodies of their innocent victims, and lying scattered among them were many wounded people. Here in this room I witnessed a drama that was more than just horrible, it has no equal in history. At one point a young European girl of about 18 came in with bandages and medicine with which the Indonesian authorities had given her permission to help her wounded father, who was in the room. But one of the fanatical guards, when he saw the girl come in, fell on her in a fit of bloodthirstiness, took out a cobbler's knife, and in a few seconds performed the following before my eyes. Ripping open her blouse with his left hand, he cut her breast off with a single swipe, and then with his free hand he ripped out what lay behind—heart and so on—and fortunately for her that brought instant death.[24]

The total number of victims during this turbulent time in Surabaya is not known, but Frederick thinks that the total number of Dutch and Eurasian deaths in the city between September 19 and November 10 is probably between four and six hundred—he hastens to say that if Chinese and Indonesians and other ethnic groups are included, the numbers are significantly higher.[25]

While these horrors were taking place at the Simpang Club and Kalisosok Prison, what was happening in the homes at Gubeng and Darmo? How did the women survive without food and water? Maria Nieuwenhuys-Lindner and her housemates discovered an old well in the back yard, which had foul standing water in it. By descending into this well and digging out the water, filth, and mud with a small cup (a job that took hours), the women reached the bottom, from which they hauled up trash: "broken buckets, empty cans, rusty tools, old toothbrushes, and even some old revolvers that were covered in dripping and stinking mud." Nieuwenhuys-Lindner notes: "And yet we persisted until the end (until we were dripping with sweat and were too dirty for words and resembled slippery green toads). We had to work more quickly at this point because all of a sudden the clean well water poured in. We were ecstatic. After a few hours, we could pull up a bucket full of clean water."

In the last few days of October, just before the British set foot in Surabaya, the Barisan Pemberontaka Rakyat Indonesia (BPRI) had emerged as a new and aggressive pemuda faction. Its leader, Sutomo, known as Bung (compatriot/brother) Tomo, was variously described as a madman and a romantic populist. More than any of the local leaders, he realized the power of the mass hysteria that had been unleashed among the kampung population. He incited Surabaya's mob mentality even more by broadcasting inflammatory speeches. "Surabaya Sue," a British American woman who jumped on the bandwagon of the revolution, joined these broadcasts of fury and hatred and thus paved the way for future massacres.

At long last, on October 25, 1945, the British landed in Surabaya with the 49th Indian Infantry Brigade (Mahratta) under the command of Brigadier A. W. S. Mallaby. The Indonesian government, seated in Jakarta, formerly Batavia, urged the Surabayan population to receive the British in peace. The authorities in Surabaya promised this, but according to Meelhuijsen, Bung Tomo incited the population to distrust any kind of Allied rhetoric and urged the Indonesians to join a revolution in which "we shall rip out the intestines of every living organism that will try to colonize us anew."[26]

British intelligence about Surabaya in particular and Java in general was very poor, and from the moment of landing the British underestimated the social unrest and incendiary atmosphere of the city. While Sutomo accused the British of not recognizing the Indonesian Republic, the British wanted to remain neutral and stay out of the political tug of war between the Dutch and Indonesians. Unfortunately, they found themselves in the difficult situation of having to negotiate with the rebel leaders for the protection and evacuation of the internees and the Japanese. Mallaby, who received a chilly reception from Mustopo, the military leader and representative of the governor of the people of eastern Java, had the added difficulty that "every step" his troops took to do their "duties of repatriating the Japanese and aiding European RAPWI officials and former prisoners was likely to be interpreted by Indonesians as an act against them and their independence."[27]

On October 26, 1945, Mallaby and Mustopo met and agreed that the British troops would help with the maintaining of law and order and the evacuation of Japanese forces. No agreement was made yet regarding the evacuation of the ex-internees. Those who had been imprisoned (mostly Dutch and Eurasian men and boys above the age of sixteen) were not to be released at all because Mustopo told Mallaby that they were guilty of "political offenses against the Indonesian Republic."[28] However, on the same day, the Mahratta freed Captain Huijer and some RAPWI members who had been captured earlier that month. Mustopo, who allowed the release because there were so many Mahratta at the prison, lost face because of this incident. Because he had already been criticized for being too cooperative, he allowed more radical leaders, like Sutomo, free rein in the days to follow. A. F. J. Doulton writes that there was a power struggle going on between moderates and extremists and that the extremists in Surabaya seized any excuse or opportunity to force the agenda of the revolution.[29]

The final straw for the extremists came when, on October 27, thousands of British pamphlets were strewn over the city. These pamphlets, which actually mentioned "occupation" and the necessity of disarming the Indonesians, outraged the people and inflamed an already combustible situation. Mallaby had never mentioned these pamphlets to Mustopo, nor had there been any agreement yet on the disarmament of the Indonesians by the British. Nonetheless, the British began stationing themselves all over town, not only in places approved by Mustopo, but also in places for which no permission was given. At the same time, they began disarming people in the streets. The British soldiers thus seemed to counter everything that had been stipulated in the October 26 agreement between the two military commanders.

That same day, Maria Nieuwenhuys-Lindner writes, sixteen big trucks entered the camp, guarded by British-Indian soldiers. She writes that they had been ordered to take the women and children to a safer place in the city. The plan was to take the ex-internees to the safer Darmo quarter, which also became known as the Red Cross quarter. Meelhuijsen confirms that on October 27 women and children began to be evacuated. Again, these transports had not been discussed with the Indonesians or Mustopo, and the British tried to accomplish them in secret. Meelhuijsen comments: "Enormous mutual distrust was the cause of the tragic fate of the Gubeng transport. The British did not trust the Indonesians and they wanted to transport the women and children to the Darmo quarter 'at their own risk.' If the English had let the Indonesians know, the Indonesians might have advised against the transport."[30] Even Harry confirms this: "Possibly the English had been alerted about an ambush, but the British seemed to believe that they could pull it off." Richard McMillan also wonders how sensible it was for Mallaby to give these evacuation orders: "There was a very real danger that the women and children would be attacked by Indonesian 'extremists.'"[31]

These events cumulatively triggered a point of no return. After the dropping of the British pamphlets, both Bung Tomo and Mustopo spoke of betrayal. Although Mustopo had been advised by the republican government in Jakarta to strive for and preserve diplomacy, the very opposite happened because of a failure of communication among the British and between the British and the Indonesians. That night an inflammatory message from Radio Surabaya incited all patriotic Indonesians to rise and "drive the British into the sea" while "Dutch women and children, a large number of whom were in the south of Surabaya, were threatened with 'rape, torture and butchery.'"[32]

Chapter 15

OCTOBER 28, 1945

The Forgotten October Revolution

> When I was in Surabaya in November of 1992, I took a
> picture of Embong Sonokembang, the location where the
> Gubeng transport got stranded. An old Indonesian (a re-
> tired TKR man) stood next to me. Without my prompting,
> he intuitively felt what I was thinking and he said: "Yes,
> that was really bad what happened to those women and
> children."
>
> Willy Meelhuijsen in a letter to Inez Hollander

Did Fré and her children notice anything or were they awakened
by any of the street noises on the night of October 27? According to
Frederick there was a constant flurry of vehicles driving all over
town, and maybe the occasional gunshot was heard in defiance of
the British intent to disarm the population. Meelhuijsen, who also
lived in the Gubeng quarter at the time, writes that there were riots
and street fights everywhere that night. The atmosphere of impending doom influenced his and older brother Piet's decision to join the
Allied evacuation transport the next day to the safer Darmo quarter,
for the situation in the city seemed so "critical [that] staying behind
was irresponsible."[1] Yet the next day the Meelhuijsens decided not to
split up the family and to stay behind with their ailing grandmother
and aunt, regardless of the danger.

October 28 began quietly. The heat was oppressive, even early
in the morning. Mallaby had approved three transports from the
Gubeng quarter that day, in spite of the fact that the Swiss consul,

who had been in the city much longer, had warned him that the tensions, street barricades, and increased violence against Westerners made it irresponsible to transport women and children. What Mallaby did not know was that leaders of the different *pemuda* organizations had met with Mustopo and had come to the conclusion that the battle for Surabaya had become inevitable: Mustopo had given orders to attack the British on October 28, 1945, at four o'clock in the afternoon. The final transport from Gubeng that day was that of Fré and her children and was planned at four as well.

It must have been agonizing for Willy, Joke, and Harry to wait for the last transport of the day. They may have had a sense that the end was in sight, that after Darmo, Singapore, and the boat ride to Holland everything would change for the better. They probably could not wait to begin their new lives in a part of the world they knew only from their parents' stories.

The final transport that day would depart at four o'clock from Lombok Square. Different accounts mention different numbers of trucks, but based on Meelhuijsen's most recent findings it seems likely that there were six open trucks with about two hundred passengers in total. Harry remembers stepping outside and seeing five to six trucks. The reason we do not know the exact number of passengers is that there were last-minute passengers who decided to go but who were not registered on the passenger list.[2] Others, like Willy Meelhuijsen and his brother, may have been on the list but would never show up and could later have been registered as "missing."

Harry got a privileged place in one of the trucks because he was placed between one of the drivers and one of his friends, a girl who had been in Banyubiru with him. Most of the other passengers would stand on the flatbeds of the trucks, which had mattresses on the sides for protection. It is still not clear how many Mahratta accompanied the transport, but it is likely that besides the drivers, there were two or three Mahratta per truck. Fré must have been on the truck with her three children, although it may be that the four of them were separated and transported on different trucks.

Once the trucks were full and ready to leave, Fré must have heaved a sigh of relief. At last they were leaving the house with its house searches and lack of water, food, furniture, and electricity. They were driving away from all that, driving away also from Banyubiru, Java, and the dead Peddy—soon they would be on a ship headed for Singapore, and from there back to Holland, where relatives could help them with a new existence, a new life. Although she must have been worried, feeling sad and dispossessed, Fré may also have felt a certain pride: had she not managed to survive the Japanese hell? Her husband was dead, but she still had all three children. These children now gave her hope for a future that would be so much better than the long, agonizing internment. As the trucks sped up in the quiet street, they were on their way to a new beginning, an unwritten page of an account that would be so much better than the story of the Indies she was about to close and put away forever.

While one of the Mahratta took off his turban to entertain the emaciated kids, Brigadier Mallaby drove by on a motorbike to make sure the transport had left. This military man and advisor of Mountbatten was known for his courage and English stiff upper lip— "Take care," he said and drove off in a different direction.

It was eerily quiet in the streets of Surabaya. Meelhuijsen, who, with his brother, decided not to be part of this transport, saw the trucks go by his house. He wrote in his journal that day:

> The *cemaras* have become silent. There is no wind, just a stifling heat. Some crows are circling above our house. It's about four o'clock and it still is uncannily quiet. The last transport with evacuees which left from Lombok Square drives across the bridge.... Guarded by British-Indian soldiers six trucks go through Embong Sonokembang in the direction of the Palmenlaan. We had almost been part of this transport.
>
> The trucks disappear behind the fence of the Brantas Hotel. Suddenly there are fierce bangs, heavy shooting, screaming, and more shooting.[3]

According to Itzig Heine's unpublished Gubeng report, the transport, under the supervision of Captain D. N. Chopra, passed the bridge at about half past five. Although Meelhuijsen and Itzig Heine do not mention this, Harry clearly remembers that the first shots rang out as they were passing over the bridge. The transport stopped and some of the Mahratta got out, but then the shooting stopped. The convoy resumed its journey.[4]

Moments past the intersection with the Palmenlaan, the convoy stopped again because of a light barricade that had been put up in the street. Captain Chopra jumped out of his jeep to remove the barricade, and almost immediately he was shot dead. Behind the last truck, some of the women and children heard footsteps and saw how another ready-made barricade was put up in the street so that the six trucks were trapped.[5]

Maybe "ambush" or "crossfire" are not even the right terms if one knows that at the time the convoy was passing through the Palmenlaan, the revolution had finally come to fruition and more than a hundred and fifty thousand heavily armed Indonesians poured out into the streets to fight the 49th Brigade, which had only four thousand men, who were dispersed all over town. Wehl writes that British and Indian officers who happened to be out in the streets when the attack began were butchered: "Men were dismembered and their limbs tossed about the streets. One wounded officer was spread-eagled on the ground and his arms and legs were cut off, and finally he was decapitated. British-Indian troops who were taken prisoner were often bayoneted to death. For many days [Surabaya's] Golden River [Kali Mas] was to give up its sacrifices to the God of Independence; mutilated corpses, heads, limbs, bodies of British-Indian men roped together, women and children."[6]

What was it like for the women and children inside the trucks, who, protected only by the mattresses, became the living targets of incessant gunfire, which would last for four hours? One survivor remembers in Itzig Heine's report: "Our truck, the third one, managed to drive around the roadblock but then had to stop. Thousands of Javanese were hiding in Kampung Keputeran and began a barrage of gunfire." Fré and her children had ended up in a deathtrap that night: not only were they unlucky in being ensnared inside a transport that left the very moment the revolution broke out, but their convoy got stranded on the periphery of one of the most hostile *kampungs* in all of Surabaya. Kampung Keputeran had been squeezed and exploited by the colonial government in 1929, territorially and tax-wise. While the Dutch had promised to improve the living conditions there, the opposite had happened and people had become disillusioned and displaced. "For this," Frederick writes, "the municipal government was never forgiven and [the people of] Kampung Keputeran became known for their sullen, recalcitrant attitude and their refusal to obey city laws and officials."[7] The seeds of the revolution had been sown in the Surabaya kampung and Fré and her children would pay for all the injustices of the Dutch municipal government years earlier, at a time when Fré had just started her life in Java.

As the trucks were being shot at, the drivers and Mahratta sought cover behind the wheels of the trucks, and thus, one survivor remembered, "we spent four hours counting down our lives minute by minute. . . . Our driver had already expired after fifteen minutes."

One group of evacuees decided to lie down underneath the mattresses: "We were trapped like sardines in a can. Now and then we moved because it was so hot and suffocating. We smelled the burn holes and our biggest fear was that we would be burned alive. My mother received a shallow shot on her thigh; the hair of the lady next to me was grazed by bullets and another woman got a fairly deep flesh wound in her elbow. In the kampung the Javanese roared: 'Death to the white dogs!'"

Some of the trucks caught fire before the women and children could jump out. When this happened a number of Mahratta ran along the convoy, while being fired at, and opened the backs of the trucks. Some of them also accompanied a few women and children to surrounding houses.

Meelhuijsen describes the scene as pandemonium: "Flames shoot out from the trucks. We cannot see the trucks themselves but see the columns of smoke and the ricocheting sparks of fire. . . . The firing between the British-Indian soldiers and the *pemuda* in the Brantas

Hotel goes on and on. Shrapnel is pelting the roof tiles, bullets bounce off the lampposts."

Holes were torn in roofs and walls, while the air became thick with smoke and the smell of gunpowder. As pemuda crawled on roofs, in the streets, and in the gardens, Meelhuijsen's family sought cover underneath beds and the tables. "A mortar shell hits a fat branch of our mango tree. With a loud, cracking noise it falls to the ground. In the front room there is the sound of breaking glass. Shots have smashed the front window. A mortar shell hits the façade of the house next to us."[8]

If the situation was already so frightening indoors, how did the women and children hold up in the trucks? What was it like to be in the line of fire with a mere mattress to hide behind? As I recorded all this and tried to imagine what it was like, I could not continue. I took a break but did not want to return. For a week my books and papers lay unused on my desk.

I returned to this story after I received a letter from Meelhuijsen, the historian I have quoted so much already. His family history goes back to a Japanese prison too. His father, a KNIL officer with the air force, was active in Surabaya's resistance. Like Peddy, he died in a Japanese prison cell and now lies buried at Kembang Kuning in Surabaya. "Every time I visit Surabaya," Meelhuijsen tells me, "I visit his grave. I have been there nine times already. I also visit the mass graves of the victims of the third Gubeng transport." It surprises him that up until the 2000 publication of his book, "there [had] not been a book in Holland that is a detailed study of the Surabaya revolution." His remark that "Indonesian sources in their historical accounts are completely silent about the tragic fate of the Gubeng transport" motivates me to write on.

In his letters to me Meelhuijsen returns to the issue of the number of trucks that were involved in these shootings. In total that day there must have been around four hundred passengers who were moved during three different transports. According to Meelhuijsen and Radio Surabaya, the last transport or convoy consisted of no more than six trucks: "I believe," Meelhuijsen writes, "that the British reports have made a mistake with the numbers, because of the three different transports from Gubeng to Darmo." Fré, Joke, Willy, and Harry were riding on one of those six trucks, but as Meelhuijsen also remarks in his letter, "Maybe the number is irrelevant when one thinks of what those women and children had to endure: there was fear, pain, shock, and later the horrible memories which they had to process. The children who were part of this bloodbath must have been left with ineradicable trauma."[9]

I felt my own hesitation and dread when writing about these events after all the eyewitness accounts I had seen in Itzig Heine's unpublished report. Maybe the Franckens were on the truck with the girl who tried to get off the truck but then climbed back on, only to get shot, saying, "They hit me in my heart—I am dying." Her parents pulled her inside and the other passengers heard her death rattle until it ceased and her blind father pronounced her dead. Or maybe they were on the truck with A.A.,[10] who was a girl at the time and who told Itzig Heine:

> All hell breaks loose. Sounds of popping guns, the rata-rataing of machine guns and the explosion of grenades and fire bombs on the asphalt light up the dark evening. The British-Indian soldiers are positioned behind the wheels and trees. I see a Javanese pop up from behind a low wall of an empty house and throw grenades at intervals in the direction of the convoy. The battle seems to last a long time. The women put the mattresses against the sides of the truck to buffer against shrapnel and flying bullets. They huddle way inside against the back of the cab except for me. I sit, holding [my adopted] dog Waldi [a dachshund] near the tailgate. Mother tells us to cover our eyes with our hands. I peek through . . . to see the action. When the battle is at its worst, Mother orders me to let Waldi go and come into the truck and crouch down. I obey and drop Waldi down into the exploding grenade-lit street. While I watch Waldi waddle out of sight, I get hit by a piece of exploding hand grenade. Blood gushes out of my left eye and temple and from my left fingers. I feel no pain except the wetness of dripping blood. I flee into Mother's arms, soaking her dress with my blood.

Survivor and eyewitness L.K. wrote Itzig Heine that they were shot at for four hours: "At a certain moment they stormed the trucks in front of and behind us and set them on fire. People who jumped out of the burning vehicles were slaughtered, and while we were watching all this, we were waiting for our own death. Six of the sixteen people in our truck died."

Due to the heroic actions of the Mahratta, some women and children were accompanied to the surrounding homes. Still others may have escaped on their own. Many, however, did not get the chance and were trapped inside the trucks, burning to death or being pulled off to be killed. Itzig Heine comments: "After a period of four hours most of the Gurkha [*sic;* Mahratta] were shot and the Indonesians launched an attack on the remaining victims. Some survivors tried to get away. When we were being pulled out of the trucks we saw, before we were being taken away to the Northern *kampong*, how my oldest brother was lying, bent over, about twenty meters from the truck. While my mother and I were taken away by Indonesians, we managed to pull along my youngest brother who was being beaten up by the side of the street."

One could argue that the attack on the women and children was morally incomprehensible, but if British intelligence had done its job and if Mallaby had listened to the warnings of the Swiss consul or had communicated with Mustopo, these transports might not have taken place. Meelhuijsen emphasizes in one of his letters that at the time of the departure of the Franckens' convoy, the British and the Indonesians had not agreed yet on the evacuation plans, but the British were trying to accomplish the evacuation without notifying the Indonesians.

What *was* planned on October 28 at 4 p.m. was an all-out assault on British posts in the city. At that hour, all traffic was stopped by Indonesians, including trams, whose passengers were ordered out and chased off the road. In the Palmenlaan much more than that happened and the fact that the convoy got stranded next to one of the most hostile kampungs did not help. Finally, if Captain Huijer had not staged the mock surrender with the Japanese, the Indonesians might not have had the use of the many weapons with which they struck back on that dark day. The mob hysteria could not be controlled. "Indonesian leaders," Frederick writes, "were taken aback by the storm they saw unleashed, but most could not help but see a certain justification in it. After a period of restraint in the face of provocation, they reasoned, the masses had finally lost their patience."[11]

Where were Harry, Fré, Joke, and Willy in all of this? Which truck or trucks were they in? As mentioned before, Harry was sitting between the driver and one of his friends from the camp. Standing near him, or over him, riding along on the truck, was a guard with a gun. "Well," Harry told me in an interview, "it was bang, bang, a lot of noise, a lot of chaos and blood everywhere." The Mahratta was shot in the head and Harry was covered in blood. The driver then left the truck to lie on his belly and shoot. While this must have lasted for four hours, as other eyewitness accounts have confirmed, it seems as if Harry was suffering from blackouts, which may have been caused by the shrapnel in his legs. His two sisters and mother may all have been in the back of Harry's truck, but contact with them would have been impossible from where he was sitting. When Harry came to, he looked around and marveled at the carnage. Then the firing stopped, and Harry remembers how the door was opened and his friend was pulled out by one leg. She hit the ground and was shot. Harry remembers thinking that he would leave on his own account and somehow crawled out of the truck on the other side. He could not get up because of his injured legs, so he kept crawling until he hit a fence.

"And then I lay there . . ." he explained, as if it had happened yesterday.

As Harry lay by the fence and looked around, he saw how people around him were assaulted with bayonets and rifle butts. He froze when he saw a *pelopor* come into his direction with his bayonet raised and ready for the kill.

"I tried to remember my Malay, the language I had spoken at the plantation," Harry remembered emotionally, but after two and a half years of the camp all that came out was Dutch.

"Jij moet mij bewaken!" (You have to guard me!), cried the eight-year-old. "And miracle of miracles. . . . that's what he did," Harry continued. The *pelopor* retracted his gun and stayed by Harry, as his guard.

"Every time another rebel approached, the man told him to go away: "Jangan, jangan" (Don't, don't).

"So then I just lay there," Harry said. "It was really rather uncomfortable," he admitted with understatement.

"The injuries did not bother me—granted, I could not walk but I just crawled."

Where were Fré and her daughters? According to Marjolein, Harry's cousin, who must have heard the story secondhand from her parents, Fré had lost sight of her children because of the chaos and the pitch-black night. To give themselves cover, the Mahratta had shot out the streetlights. Willy had called out to her mother, "Mom, I'm hit, I'm hit," but Fré could not find her. Later Fré would realize that these were the last words of her eldest daughter, as she was never seen or heard of again.

The fact that Fré agonized over not being able to find her daughters seems to indicate that her daughters were on other trucks. Or she could have lost consciousness, like Harry, and thus she would have been rather disoriented when she came to. I cannot imagine her walking and searching the trucks, as that would have been impossible with the nonstop shooting that was going on.

A friend of Fré's recalls that Fré told her one afternoon after the war: "Suddenly, I found myself under a tree and Harry was sitting next to me with gaping holes in his thigh. Then two women came by with a stretcher. Joke lay on it with big chunks ripped out of her body. She looked up at me and said, 'Mommy, I am dead already and I don't feel it.'" Then she died. When Harry remembers and retells this part of the story, he breaks down and cries. Fré also told her friend that she regretted that she had not taken the Yogya-silver bracelet from Joke's bloodied wrist: "If I had done that, I would still have had something to remember her by."

The English Lieutenant Colonel F. H. G. Eggleton, who wrote a RAPWI report on the incident, says that at about 9:30 p.m. the remaining trucks were set on fire while "heavy sniping" continued. As mentioned earlier, some women and children managed to escape to the surrounding houses, but most victims had died or were dying on the trucks, and as soon as the battle had died down, "the mob swarmed over the lorries, looting and flinging dead bodies of women and children into the road. Owing to the necessity of conserving ammunition the few Indian troops defending the women could not open fire. Wounded sepoys were seen to be dismembered with Jap swords. Two women and children were butchered with swords by the crowd."[12]

According to Frederick, "many of the victims were killed not as a result of the general fighting but later in scenes of grisly torture in which the mouths of surviving women were reportedly cut open and stuffed with the severed genitals of British-Indian soldiers, and more than a dozen youths paraded through the streets with the heads of Dutch and Eurasian women and British-Indian soldiers impaled on bamboo spears."[13]

Since World War II, the Western, or maybe I should say the American, perception has been that wars are fought between forces of good and evil. However, war is never entirely black and white, as the scenes of the Gubeng transport reveal. While Willy was never heard of again and may have been killed and maimed by the mob, Harry was saved by a member of that same mob. This also seems an accurate reflection of Indonesian alliances during the war: whereas some Indonesians stayed faithful to the colonial elite (there are stories of *babus* who followed Dutch women and children around as they were moved from camp to camp), others served the Kempeitai and collaborated with the Japanese.

Also, rather than condemning the mob violence straightaway, it is more important to examine what the motivation of the mob could have been to attack defenseless women and children. Aside from mob hysteria and feelings of revenge aimed at representatives of Dutch colonial power, contextual evidence seems to point to the Indonesians wanting to keep the women and children hostage to warrant their own safety. As Meelhuijsen writes, the people of Surabaya feared that if all European ex-internees were evacuated out of the city, British troops would launch an all-out assault and invasion.[14]

It is further important to realize that while stereotypical *bersiap* literature in the Netherlands focuses too often on the cowardly and vicious attacks of Indonesians on Dutch people, there were also plenty of incidents where Indonesians helped and protected their former colonizers and employers. Likewise, although the stranded Dutch on Java have been very critical of the English for the delayed evacuation and evacuation failures, the heroic feat of the Mahratta in defending the Gubeng transport, a defense in which most of them lost their lives, is important to remember. As Meelhuijsen has argued, the Mahratta might have been sympathetic, as Indians, to the independence cause of the Indonesians, yet they fought valiantly all over Surabaya. Yes, Willy and Joke were slaughtered by Indonesian rebels, but Harry and his mother were saved by an Indonesian and members of the British-Indian army.[15] In the end, there seems to have been only one Mahratta in their transport who traveled to Britain to be decorated. I have no knowledge whether he was recognized by the Netherlands as well. The same phenomenon applies to Jack Boer, who played a heroic role on November 10, 1945, by freeing (with a tank and no more than ten troops) 2,384 Dutch men, women, and children from Werfstraat/Kalisosok Prison before they were poisoned by the Indonesians. His widow died in 2005, and even though there were special pleas to decorate her husband posthumously while she was still alive, Jack Boer has, as of yet, still not been formally honored.

While Harry was lying by the fence, protected by the unknown Indonesian, he must have passed out a couple of times. As he told me, "at a certain moment we were lying on mattresses in a little hut somewhere. . . . It was messy, some mattresses, I don't know where I was."

I asked him whether it could have been the nearby kampung, but Harry can't remember.

"My mother was there too," he said, "and so was Joke. Joke died there."

When I asked about Willy, Harry's favorite sister, he said, "I never saw Willy again. Nobody saw her again. My mother was afraid that she was taken by the Japs and had been used as a prostitute in the kampung." (Note: Willy could not have been taken by the Japanese because they were just as much victims at this point.)

Could the injured Willy have escaped with some of the other Dutch victims who survived the transport? Was she in the group with U.B., who writes in the supplement to Itzig Heine's report:

> It was about nine o'clock in the evening when we heard the remaining Gurkha [Mahratta] walk away. It turned out they were accompanying some women and children to safety. We saw a wild herd of Indonesians storming toward us with *klewangs* [single-edged machetes], spears, and guns. That was the worst moment. It was terrible having to die that way, while we had not even been reunited as a family. We closed our eyes and surrendered.
>
> The mattress was being pulled away from us, and they shot three times, right next to our heads. It was a miracle no one got hurt. We were dragged out of the truck by people of the TKR. The TKR had the hardest time protecting us from the mob. People were shooting at us and pulling at us. We were dragged through the *kampung*. It was very dark and people were still hitting and kicking us with guns and other weapons. That night tens of women and children were murdered. It was a great tragedy. The Javanese brought us to a radio post, where we were put [with our faces] against the wall.

"We were not allowed to turn around," another eyewitness writes. "Mother does so anyway and says in Malay . . . that wars are not being fought against women and children and that the Americans and the English will take revenge if they kill us."[16]

U.B. continues:

> They were aiming at us with about twenty men, but at that point we would have been happy to be relieved of our suffering by a bullet.

Nothing happened, but we were then (the ten of us) brought to a small room of three by three [meters]. On occasion, a mad face looked in through the trellised window, telling us we were all going to die, but we were too paralyzed to be affected by this. An hour later we were searched in a rough way by a Javanese man. We then heard and were shocked by the wailing of a mother whose child had been bleeding to death in one of the trucks, while in the background the mob screamed if yet another wounded Javanese fighter was brought in. They also asked us the names and places where government people might be located, but we could not and would not answer.

This group of women and children survived, protected by the TKR. The next day they were brought to another house where there were other Dutch women, and although this house was assaulted by the mob too, again they made it out alive. If Willy had been alive, she would have surfaced, but she did not. It is far more likely that her dead body was brought to the hospital where someone other than her mother identified her, for both Willy and Joke can be found at Kembang Kuning Cemetery, in a mass grave with a marker that says, "W. J. L. Francken, 4/10/30–28/10/45; J. L. M. Francken, 24/5/32–28/10/45; 84 onbekenden [unknown]."

The tragedy here is that Willy had just turned fifteen, a young woman on her way to a new life in Holland. Like her father, she died alone, and not, like Joke, in her mother's arms. But there is consolation, too—at least Willy was not one of the eighty-four unknown people who could not be identified because they were slaughtered beyond recognition. At least Willy may have been in one piece when someone at the hospital, maybe a housemate from Gubeng or a fellow internee from Banyubiru, managed to identify her. For Fré and Harry this consolation was and is not enough: like Peddy's unknown whereabouts or cause of death, Willy's "missing" status would hamper the mourning and healing process of both Fré and Harry.

Because of the incomplete registration lists of these transports and because there were last-minute passengers who got on without being registered, we still do not know how many of the passengers died that evening. Itzig Heine's estimate is probably the most accurate: 112 people dead, about 150 survivors (which includes people from the earlier two transports) and about 40 whose fate we do not know. The number of Indonesians who died in this street battle must have exceeded one hundred.

What happened to the survivors of the Gubeng transport who found shelter in the surrounding houses and kampung?[17] The girl who lowered her dog into the street and was then hit in the eye was one of them: "When the angry mob starts spraying the trucks with gasoline, a few Mahratta accompany us to a house where they kick in the door. We enter a small room with pretty furniture, Persian rugs, and tall Chinese vases. This little room is already filled with about thirty women and children and three or five Gurkha [Mahratta]. We are there for about thirty-six hours. Our wounds cannot be taken care of and we suffer from gangrene. We spend all night in that little room and use the vases to pee in. Mother prevents one of the Mahratta from drinking out of these vases. The nurse who is with us hesitates to clean my face wound because my face is covered with holes and chunks of flesh that stick out. The Mahratta finally leave through the back door; they apologize and are dressed in sheets."

On October 30, this group of women and children was discovered by uniformed Indonesians, who brandished their bayonets when they entered the house but led the women and children to trucks and took them to a hospital where the wounded were treated.

Some of the women acted heroically. One of these, J.S., was on one of the two trucks that finally managed to drive away. She wrote in a letter to her husband:

We had mattresses with us, with which we surrounded ourselves, and we waited for four hours while we were being shot at with machine guns, hand grenades, and flammable material. Many of the trucks caught fire while the women and children were still on them. I was in the car with Mrs. C. She had two daughters and a boy of three years

old. I was very calm and only became afraid when I heard the screaming mass of natives that was coming closer and closer. Mrs. C.'s oldest
daughter was fatally wounded. Her other daughter was shot in the
arm, as was N. And then all of a sudden the remaining Gurkha
[Mahratta] jumped in the truck and drove right through the barricade
to Darmo and stopped near the Zaalbergschool. It was very dark and
eerily quiet. The driver refused to drive on, and the other Gurkha
[Mahratta] lay down on the ground to die.

What could we do? I left the children with Mrs. C and said I
would leave to find help. . . . I walked away and ended up on the
Reiniersboulevard. Suddenly three Indonesian soldiers discovered me.
They went after me. I threw myself down in a ditch and they walked
past me and then discovered our truck, which drove away immediately. I heard N. crying out for me, and then it was quiet. I was in a difficult position. I crawled away and two times an unarmed native came
after me but they were scared of me and abandoned their hunt.[18]

This woman would survive her ordeal, but for a number of days
she could not find her children, until she discovered they were safe
in a hospital in Singapore. Mrs. C., who lost her eldest daughter,
would die herself of a stomach wound.

Of the approximately forty people who were missing, some must
have been led away too, but they were never heard of again. How
did Harry and his mother get away? I tried to match what Harry
told me during the interview with the little bit of information I can
find in other sources. I ended up with the account of L. H. O. Pugh,
a colonel who served under Mallaby and would assume command
when Mallaby was assassinated two days later, on October 30.

Pugh was at the Darmo hospital and saw one of the Gubeng trucks
there. Hearing that there were a number of injured children and
women hiding somewhere in the area, he immediately left with some
soldiers and stretchers. In a little house nearby he found them: women
and children were lying on mattresses, taken care of by a British-
Indian soldier who was dressing their wounds and was sharing his food
with them. In this group were two dead children, a dead woman,

three injured women, and two wounded children.[19] It seems very likely that the group Pugh found was that of Harry and his mother.

Fighting continued the next day. "Troops of the 49th Indian Infantry Brigade defended positions until they ran out of ammunition, when they were overwhelmed and massacred."[20] When Pugh returned to the scene in the Palmenlaan, the burned-out trucks and bloody remains of the massacre shocked him: "That evening there were few of the Mahratta, sepoys, and RIASC chauffeurs left. They lay dead, surrounded by piles and piles of dead Indonesians, dressed in white. The women and children, who were killed in the assault, had been slaughtered, maimed, stabbed, and slashed by Indonesian swords. The bodies, dressed in green uniforms, of the British-Indian soldiers lay among them. Everywhere there were puddles of blood, blood that slowly trickled away in the gutters of the street."

This scene is reminiscent of the scene in *Max Havelaar* when Saïdjah returns to his village and finds, amid the burning huts, the corpse of Adinda's father with a *klewang* sticking out of his chest. Next to him are his three sons, children still, Multatuli writes, and further down, the naked and terribly mutilated corpse of Adinda. The Javanese had been through many battles with the Dutch and always, because of the better arms the Dutch had at their disposal, generations of Saïdjahs and Adindas had to admit defeat or be killed. In that bloody month of October, 1945, the roles had finally been reversed. Willy and Joke had become the new Saïdjah and Adinda—they paid with their lives for the sins of their ancestors.

Frederick uses the word "genocide," a word the Dutch, even the victims themselves, have never used. "Whatever the reasons for this might be, it may be time to reconsider," Frederick argues. "Leaving aside, for the present, knotty questions of how terms like ethnic cleansing, genocide, or crimes against humanity ought to be defined in numbers and scope . . . a great many of the killings were aimed specifically at ethnic groups: Dutch, Eurasians, and Chinese in particular but also Ambonese, Menadonese, Timorese, and others linked in the popular view with the colonial power."[21] Whatever one calls it, attention should be drawn to the fact that the Gubeng transport was one of the three worst massacres (the other two being the Simpang Club tribunal and the incident at Kalisosok Prison) in Surabaya. However, in terms of historical and academic attention in the Netherlands, the account of the Gubeng transport has been underexposed, and may even have been silenced, considering the good diplomatic relations Holland has with Indonesia.[22] Or maybe the Dutch government refuses to acknowledge these deaths because doing so would also open the door to the war crimes the Dutch army committed during the "police actions" of 1947 and 1948.[23] The Gubeng transport eventually received its first full Dutch account in print in Meelhuijsen's book on the revolution, which was published by a small publisher in 2000, somewhat overdue, considering it was fifty-five years after the event.

Sukarno, who finally arrived in Surabaya on October 29, tried to calm the people and prevent further bloodshed. He came to the governor's house to meet with the local and Allied leaders. Both Mallaby and Pugh were there; Pugh apparently was still distraught and pale from what he had witnessed in Gubeng and the Darmo hospital. Sitting down on the back porch of this house, which had a view on Surabaya's Kali Mas River, Sukarno cannot have failed to see the reddish hue of the water and the decapitated heads of the 49th Brigade that came bobbing by. The view symbolized the fact that the birth of the Indonesian Republic had been tainted with violence and horror.

Sukarno's intervention and subsequent speech in which he condemned the violence seemed to have had little effect. The riots continued, and the next day Mallaby was assassinated. This was a slap in the face of the British. Frederick writes that a British response could not be averted: "On October 31 General Philip Christison, Commander of the Allied Forces in South East Asia, threatened 'to bring the whole weight of [Allied] sea, land and air forces and all the weapons of modern war to bear on Surabaya' if the perpetrators of the 'foul murder' of the 49th Brigade commander were not turned over." This was bloated rhetoric, as archival sources confirm that the British were intent on taking Surabaya regardless.[24]

Where were Fré and Harry when Sukarno was meeting with Mallaby in the house overlooking the bloodstained river? After Pugh took Fré and the others to the Darmo hospital, better known as the CBZ (Centraal Burger Ziekenhuis), Harry could not be helped immediately because of the overwhelming chaos. There was a constant flow of injured and dying people coming through. The doctors and nurses worked around the clock but could not stem the number of incoming victims.

Pugh remembers that while outside the sky was lighting up with red flames, an old Dutch woman stumbled in with a hole in her back as big as a grapefruit. Harry was probably put down in one of the hallways, surrounded by screaming and dying people. An eyewitness writes in Itzig Heine's Gubeng report: "I was hospitalized for fifteen months because I was so traumatized by everything that had happened to me in the war. I could not have a 'normal' life anymore. One of the traumas was witnessing the victims being carried in from the 'Gubeng Transport.' It was pure hell."

The girl who was wounded with her brother and whose mother had gotten off the truck to find help writes the following about their arrival in the CBZ:

> We were put on a rolling stretcher, all three of us [children] and taken to a doctor where we were cleaned. . . . We were then put in a big room where there were other injured people from the transport. We got one bed for the three of us. It was a feather bed with a pillow that looked very dirty. . . . We managed even though it was a little small. We just lay there with our dirty and bloody dresses until I was able, walking at an angle because of my festering and stinking arm, to rinse our clothes a little bit and hang them out to dry in the sun."

Fré, who was sitting by Harry, still in shock over the loss of her daughters, was ordered to leave because she was not wounded. This was an impossible request: after losing her husband and two girls, they could not expect her to abandon her son. Harry himself must have floated in and out of consciousness because there are gaps in his story. He does remember that he tried to console his mother: "I will become an engineer, mommy," he had told her, "so I will always be able to take care of you." What the camp children had missed in terms of academic schooling they had gained in maturity and life experience, however traumatic.

Someone kept insisting that Fré should leave, but Mrs. Van Wiekeren, who had also intervened during one of the house searches when they tried to take away Harry, interceded once more. She had worked in the CBZ before the war and used her influence to make sure that Harry, with the shrapnel still in his legs, could leave with his mother. From the CBZ they were taken to the Darmo quarter, the last safe neighborhood in Surabaya.

From there (or later from the harbor) Fré sent a telegram to my grandfather. It must have been the first communication Jacques received after the intense correspondence with Peddy had stopped completely, five years earlier. Jacques immediately sent a telegram to his eldest son, Jack, who was on his way to the Indies as a war volunteer, telling Jack to try and find Fré and help her however possible. Jack did get special leave for this but never found her, because on November 3 Harry and Fré were loaded onto more open flatbed trucks to be taken to the harbor for the trip to Singapore. After the disastrous Gubeng transport, Fré must have felt fearful to be traveling once more, so exposed, through a city that was still seething with anger.

The Englishman Anthony Brett James, who saw these trucks drive by, was struck by the courage and dignity of the women as they were being sent off: "The women and children in the transports to the harbor managed to stay calm and quiet as they were being driven through a grim and riotous city while being exposed to the threats of the Indonesians who were standing by the side of the road."[25] It was a sobering moment—jeering crowds watching the former elite on display in the trucks, impoverished, emaciated, terrorized, and anxious.

For many this was the last farewell to the Indies, a place where they had experienced both the advantages of the establishment and the depths of the underclass. They had come as the privileged white rulers but left as personae non gratae, humiliated, harassed, and hungry. Meelhuijsen argues that the hostility of the people in the streets was not so much directed at the women and children as it was an expression of fear and anxiety, for they seemed to realize that once all these women and children were gone, the English would pounce. "That the English had come in the first place, not to invade, but to help with the aftermath of the war and the protection of the ex-internees, did not enter the heads of most Indonesians, who were confused because of many miscommunications," Meelhuijsen writes.[26]

Once the trucks arrived at the port, the women started crying and waving at the British-Indian troops who had done the utmost to protect them. The same soldiers carried the injured women and children on board landing ship tanks, which were used because the Surabaya harbor was full of mines. From there they were transferred to the English ship HMS *Glenroy,* where they received food and bedding from the British Royal Navy. Navy officers gave their cabins and beds to the women and children. The women were starving: the Darmo neighborhood had been deprived of food as well, and most of the people in Darmo depended on food drops. They barely had any clothes left on their bodies, and they were exhausted, both mentally and physically. Nonetheless, that first night there was music and dancing on deck to celebrate their liberation . . . at last.

On November 1 the British 5th Division, consisting of twenty-four thousand troops, departed from Jakarta to arrive in Surabaya on November 4 and 9. The British wanted to swoop down on the city as early as November 5, but there were many more evacuees, six thousand instead of the assumed number of fourteen hundred, so the attack was postponed to November 10. Much of the city was evacuated before then and Bung Tomo told the population that it was "independence or death," but by the end of November the British were in full control of a once-vibrant city that lay in ashes.[27]

Meelhuijsen, Frederick, and Ricklefs all believe that the Surabaya Revolution was pivotal in the independence struggle. Not only did it draw the world's attention to the Indonesian cause, it also "shocked [the Dutch] into facing reality. Many had quite genuinely believed that the Republic represented only a gang of collaborators without popular support. No longer could any serious observer defend such a view."[28]

Nonetheless, the Dutch would move back into Indonesia and start a war that became known as the "police actions." It was a lost cause. Pressured by the international community and the United States in particular, the Dutch finally conceded defeat and granted Indonesia its independence in 1949. For a long time, 1949 date was marked by the Dutch as Indonesia's year of independence. This changed in 2005, when Dutch Minister of Foreign Affairs, Bernard Bot, who was born in the Indies himself, traveled to Indonesia and officially announced that the Netherlands would recognize Sukarno's Proklamasi of Independence on August 17, 1945, as the official date when the Indies ceased to be a Dutch colony. It was a proud and humbling moment that may, one hopes, stimulate Indonesia's own acknowledgment and examination of some of the darker aspects of the bersiap and the bloody revolution that have long overshadowed Indonesia's struggle for independence.

EPILOGUE

I live here in an apartment, small and comfortable. I often think: what a good camp this is; you can walk in and out freely, there is no hunger and you don't have to be afraid of being beaten up. I perceive everything in terms of my former camp life. . . . I am a *tjittjak* [i.e., *cicak,* lizard] whose tail they have cut off, but a new tail grew on, uglier, but it works. It's an Indies symbol that I cherish.

Paula Gomes, "To Live with an Ugly Tail"[1]

Just like the war veterans [of the police actions], the civilian victims of the war in the Indies did not have their "lieux de mémoire." After much difficulty, the Foundation National Indies Monument finally received a monument in 1988 in The Hague. It is located on a lawn by a pond, which is not at a typical monument location like a town square. The location seems to say: okay, dump it over there. And yet this monument distinguishes itself from all other World War II monuments in The Hague in that it is covered with flowers throughout the year.

E. J. Dommering, "De Nederlandse publieke discussie en de politionele akties in Indonesië"[2]

When Harry and Fré arrived in Singapore, they had to wait for a large group from Batavia (Jakarta) before they could be repatriated to Holland. For many families Singapore became the ultimate spot of family reunions, but for Fré and Harry these reunions were but sad reminders of what they had lost. Although NICA had hoped that many Dutch people would stay in Indonesia and pick up their lives where they had left off, this was for many a preposterous proposition. Their houses ransacked and looted, there was nothing to return to. The future novelist Jeroen Brouwers did return with his family, but the plundered house gave rise to a feeling of a paradise lost, which Brouwers seems to reexamine and mourn in book upon book.

During their layover in Singapore, Harry and his mother were added to the passenger list of the *New Amsterdam,* but they had to wait for two weeks on the hot ship before the group from Batavia arrived. Harry told me in the interview: "Those folks finally came with their refrigerators and suitcases but because the ship was already so packed, all these goods had to be dumped into the sea. These people were crying—so we showed them our possessions: one toothbrush and a wash cloth." Harry and his mother had lost all their material things, but these were irrelevant compared to that other, bigger loss which would be a gaping hole in the rest of their lives, a hole that could never be filled by another person, thing, or emotion.

Willy Meelhuijsen wrote me how he remembered his repatriation to Holland: at least the people in Holland, he says, had been able to stay in their homes, and most of them, except for the Jews, still had their families intact. Aside from the German occupation, their lives had gone on. This had not been the case for the people who had been hurt by the war in the Indies: many had lost all their possessions, and many more had lost family members. Fré did not even have a picture of her two lost daughters (see figs. 16.1 and 16.2).[3]

What had happened to Kali Jompo? In 1943 the Japanese had appointed an administrator who had only harvested coffee. In 1945 102 hectares were cleared to grow food crops for the local population. I see it almost as a way of Kali Jompo paying something back to the locals for what the Franckens had taken out, and I cannot mourn the loss of the coffee and rubber trees that are mentioned in the annual report of June 26, 1948, summarizing 1940 and 1941. Besides, Kali Jompo's damage was not excessive. Jaap van der Zwaag writes that some former plantation administrators could not even find their buildings or gardens, which had been completely demolished and

Figure 16.1 (*above*): Joke and
Willy as young children
Figure 16.2 (*left*): Joke and
Willy, just before the war
Fré had sent these pictures to
relatives in Holland during
happier times, and these relatives must have returned the
pictures to her after she arrived
in Holland with Harry.
Source: Harry Francken

overgrown by the jungle. After the first police action, one administrator discovered an entire factory that the Japanese had built near
Sukabumi; it was a hodgepodge of buildings and materials assem-
bled from more than half the sugar and tea estates in the area. Fifty
percent of Java's rubber capacity was lost during the war, and 30
percent of the coffee plants were destroyed. In 1948 the total damage
of the private plantations was estimated at between six and seven million guilders. For recovery more than a billion guilders was needed.[4]

On April 1, 1948, ownership of the plantation was restored to the
Franckens, but the land was damaged and the administrator's house
had been destroyed by Indonesian attacks after the first police action. The political instability was such that many plantations were
plundered on a regular basis by *rampokkers*. In 1947 Kali Jompo's administrator M. C. Lambert hit a mine with his car but survived.

In 1948 Mannes Francken died at age sixty, predeceased by his
older brother Henri, who died at fifty-one in 1937, and his older sister Laurine, who died at fifty-seven in 1942. When one reads of the
heavy financial losses and woes because of the rampokkers and frequent thefts of crops, cash, and tools, it is easy to believe that Kali
Jompo seemed doomed after Peddy left. At the same time, this situation was not exceptional; most private plantations were struggling
with the same security and burglary issues. In 1948 the Chinese con-
tractor who was hired to rebuild the administrator's house had to
abandon his work because of the plunderers. In that same year administrator Lambert resigned because of stress on the job.

In 1949 my grandfather took his two youngest children, Enny and
André, to a movie. My grandmother took André home on her bike,
while my grandfather ran to catch the tram. Enny remembers it well:
it took the wind out of him, and a week later he was dead at age
fifty-six. Enny still wonders whether running for the tram caused
his premature demise. According to Enny he had prayed all his life
for a death without a long sickbed; his wish was fulfilled, albeit much
too early.

My initial judgmental opinion of Jacques mellowed somewhat as
I neared the end of this book, and even more when my father died in

August of 2006. My father's ashes were lowered into the Francken grave in Bloemendaal in November, a ceremony I could not attend. My sisters gave me lurid accounts of peeping inside the deep grave and seeing the coffin of Jacques Francken. The graveyard attendant had covered it with some branches because the coffin had decayed so much, and one sister told me, "Yes, of course, the guy died in 1949— what do you expect?" For me, the "guy" is no longer a black-and-white picture on my mother's desk, because through writing this book I have come to feel a connection my sisters may not have felt when seeing the remains of their long-dead grandfather. For this connection I am grateful, even though it is a family tie that is both ambiguous and tragic.

And so the tragedy continues, because in 1949 when my great-grandmother Coba Kervel-Francken, who had survived all her children, heard the news of my grandfather's sudden death, she started sobbing, "Jacqui, Jacqui . . ." After outliving all her children it seemed pointless to live on, so she died at age eighty-six, on the very day of Jacques's funeral. As a relic of the old Indies society she had hung on to the very end but died in the year that the first Dutch troops were coming home, having lost the colony she had known so intimately. With her death Kali Jompo seemed doomed, even though the next generation was there to take over managing it: my uncle Jack Francken on location in Jember and Mannes's eldest, another Peddy Francken, taking hold of the reins as the director in Holland.

In spite of the robberies, which were often dangerous for the people who worked at the plantation, Kali Jompo managed to make slight profits of about fifty-five thousand guilders annually in the early 1950s. However, that could not cover the increasing cultivation costs plus what the family had to invest in the gardens to make them operable again. Dividend payments up until 1956, when the gardens were sold, leveled off at 10 percent. While the security situation improved slightly in the 1950s, most plantations were plagued by a constant lack of money, laborers, and materials.

Ironically, while Coba's father, the sugar baron Koos Kervel, may have extracted and exploited without giving anything back, Jack and

Figure 16.3: Kali Jompo after the war (1950). *Source: Jack Francken*

Peddy Francken Jr. made no significant profits but invested in plantation housing for their Indonesian workers. They also built a "prayer house" and a school for the children of the Indonesians who lived on the plantation. Notwithstanding the goodwill that this may have created in the local community and at the plantation, the thefts continued as never before, and in 1952 one of the Indonesian workers was killed by a fellow Indonesian who apparently had looted Kali Jompo several times before.

Somehow, Peddy's spirit seemed to watch over all of this, or rather the rubber trees that he had planted in 1936. Amidst all the bad news of the annual reports of the 1950s, the one positive development seems to have been that Peddy's trees produced the most rubber, a fact that is mentioned at least three times over the years. But even Peddy's trees could not stop the turning tide.

In 1952 the annual report opens with the announcement that in view of the land lease, which would expire in the late 1950s, the company had asked for an extension but the Indonesian authorities had not given any indication whether the leases could be assured for the future. It almost seems as if the family wanted to preserve Kali Jompo against all odds. But why hold onto something that seemed destined to decline further and fail? The staff was terrorized by the repeated robberies, and that same year, 1952, there was another 53 percent loss of the coffee harvest. After the murder, Kali Jompo finally obtained a permanent police guard, but the gardens received another hit when a storm in December of 1955 uprooted and damaged more than 170 rubber trees.

This event and the continuing rising costs and heavy losses may well have stimulated the decision to sell, and with the consent of the other shareholders this was accomplished. In 1956 the company was sold for half a million *rupiahs* to an Indonesian-Japanese company. It was the right decision; due to pressure building up around Holland's refusal to hand over Dutch-owned New Guinea, the Indonesian government nationalized all remaining plantations and forced the remaining Dutch nationals to leave in 1957. The worsening relationship between the Netherlands and Indonesia ultimately impacted Indonesia more adversely than the Netherlands. Jaap van der Zwaag writes that after 1957 Indonesian exports decreased sharply and agricultural proceeds, formerly in Dutch hands, went down dramatically. The former colonizers had been leaders in cultivation practices and research in tropical agriculture. As the last Dutch people left, they took most of that knowledge with them.[5]

Kali Jompo was a big financial loss for the family that year. The bigger, personal loss was never revisited and became a hidden source of grief in my family. However, I would like to believe that the spirits of Peddy and his daughters live on as threads of fog, reunited on a mountain ridge overlooking the gardens.

After I finished this manuscript, I sent it to Harry. The book that had started with my grandfather had become his story, and I needed his permission to publish it. Within forty-eight hours, he e-mailed me: "Hello Inez, I have had three guardian angels in my life: my sister Willy who always looked after me, the Indonesian who rescued me, and you because you *see* me. . . . It is as if I have been living inside a bunker all my life and you have been the only one who has hit a hole in that bunker through which love and light now come pouring in. That love consists of interest, compassion, and contact like I have never experienced in my life."

When I told Winnie Rinzema-Admiraal about Harry's response, she wrote me in an e-mail: "You have not only opened the bunker, you have been on a journey with an imprisoned man and you have acknowledged him fully. He has had the desire to be seen and acknowledged his entire life but never really was. It is called recognition, but it is so much more. He has become more centered in his own life because of this. This is something that no one has been able to understand in Holland of the people who had been through the war in the Indies. One did not know what it was."

Dutch Indies people and Eurasians who repatriated to the Netherlands in the fifties were not being heard, and worse, were discriminated against because of their accent or skin color. Andrew Goss writes that the Eurasians especially were exposed to comments like "You blacks, go back to Sukarno," whereupon it

> became exasperating to explain that you were against Sukarno and that you weren't an Indonesian but *Indisch*. You stopped explaining and gathered only with other *Indisch* people, who understood you. You didn't talk about the sadness: not about the camps, not about the police actions, not about the many dead that you had seen, not about the Indonesian citizens whom you had to shoot as a colonial soldier, not about the friends whom you had seen bayoneted by the Japanese. You came from a culture of shyness." For most of the 1950s then, any public recollection of the former Dutch colonial society was frowned upon. Indonesia was a hated subject, avoided by all.[6]

Rather than speaking their minds and sharing their stories, people like Harry and Fré stopped talking altogether. After the war Fré and Harry never spoke about the trauma, the memories, the flashbacks, the nightmares, and the demons. I hope I have shown with this book that we need to abandon the indifference, face the facts, and say to people like Harry: "I am listening, I hear you, I see you, and I love you."

The Second World War had many theaters of violence and carnage—the war in Asia, instigated by the Japanese, was as great in dimension and casualties as the war in Europe. Although Holland, through its colonial possession of the East Indies, found itself faced with the Germans *and* the Japanese, the German occupation of Holland has always loomed much larger in the public memory and imagination than the Japanese occupation of the Indies.

As I have shown in this book, after the Japanese landed, Dutch residents were forcefully interned in camps, and while these camps contained no gas chambers, many people died as a result of torture, forced labor, starvation, long train rides in boarded-up wagons without food or water, and through it all, a chronic lack of medical care and medicine. Many returned to their home country after the war, having lost relatives, their home, jobs, and most of their capital. They had to start from scratch, yet the majority of their fellow citizens looked the other way and felt disinclined to reach out or help them get back on their feet.

For ex-KNIL officers and Indo-Europeans who had stayed loyal to the Dutch and were therefore no longer welcome in their own country, there was even less understanding. The Dutch ultimately housed this particular group (mostly from the Moluccas) in a remote and depressed part of the country. Exiled, with views of peat fields instead of palm trees, these people did not complain; complaining was not part of their cultural identity. The Dutch (who, incidentally, love to grumble) misinterpreted their silence as contentment and even called them a "model minority."

However, the second generation of Ambonese and Moluccans, young men who felt neither Dutch nor Indonesian—a crisis of identity shared by some members of the second generation of Moroccans in Holland today—rebelled and took revenge for the feelings of betrayal their parents had suffered in silence. (This sense of betrayal was also rooted in the Dutch promise of a free Ambon, which never materialized.) Radicalized men hijacked a public school and a train in the 1970s, with fatal consequences.

With the new waves of terrorism and murders of Pim Fortuyn and Theo van Gogh, the Dutch are finally waking up to their essential xenophobia, which for a long time had been hidden under the veneer of "Dutch tolerance," which had been proverbial since the seventeenth century, when Dutch burghers opened their borders to religious refugees such as Portuguese and Spanish Jews and English Puritans. Today that tolerance has turned into a myth, as Eurasians, and later the Surinamese, Dutch Antillian, Turkish, and Moroccan immigrants to the Netherlands, can confirm. Yet Ian Buruma has insisted in both a *New Yorker* article and his book on the murder of Theo van Gogh that Dutch multiculturalism had not failed until recently. Strictly speaking, it was already failing when Dutch Eurasians settling in Holland were told to go back to Sukarno.

Soul searching about immigrant and national identity has given rise to a reassessment of Dutch tolerance, but it has also encouraged a revisiting of our national history regarding the Jews during the Second World War. A few years ago the Netherlands Railway System broke its silence regarding its dubious collaboration with the Nazis. Posters on all the major train station platforms with shocking texts such as "From this platform so many Jews were deported to the death camps" were received with mixed feelings.[7] Many Dutch people have identified with the Anne Frank story, when Anne was in fact helped out by an Austrian national (Miep Gies) and betrayed by a Dutchman. While some Dutch people helped with the hiding of Jews, the majority refused to take the brave stand the Danes took. Many refused to hide Jews, or worse, betrayed Jews for money. Even within my own family I have examples of two extremes: while my paternal grandfather offered shelter to Jewish friends who came to say good-bye on the eve of their deportation, my maternal grandmother hid non-Jews but refused to do the same for Jews, for fear of being deported or executed, and jeopardizing the fate of her children.

More than sixty years after the war, there are many untold stories left. The biggest of them all is the colonial one and Holland's reluctance to have a nuanced debate on what happened in colonial times, during the war, the *bersiap,* the independence struggle, and the police actions. Why does there seem to be a code of silence?

I started this manuscript in my mother tongue. In the early stages of my writing I sent one of my sisters some chapters in progress. After all, I was finding intriguing material about a grandfather whom neither one of us knew. Without having read the chapters, my sister's boyfriend brought up the evil acts my ancestors must have committed for the simple reason that they were members of the colonial class.

This sparked a heated argument between the two, even though both of them were born after Indonesia had become independent.

My own apprehension regarding this topic grew when I realized how problematic it was to find information on my great-uncle Peddy Francken. All the information about his arrest, subsequent torture, and death was hidden in restricted archives, which still have not been declassified or opened to the public. It is not clear to me why this kind of information cannot be given out to the public when most of those mentioned in the documents are no longer alive. These are not state secrets, and while the archivists have assured me that they are not intentionally trying to cover things up but are simply plagued by understaffing and a lack of financial means to go digital, the reality is that only a few researchers can get to the material they want and need.

The average Dutch person is barred from finding essential information because of restricted access, permissions, and bureaucratic procedures. For some, like Fré and Harry, this information, which is hanging, unread, in folders at NIOD and the Ministerie van Buitenlandse Zaken (Ministry of Foreign Affairs), was what they needed to process their grief and find healing. Instead, they had to make do with a letter by Queen Wilhelmina (dated January 6, 1947), or rather, her secretary, who wrote: "Bereft of his freedom, and possibly subjected to the most cruel abuse, your husband Ferdinand, whom you now mourn, sacrificed his life on March 15, 1945, in Sukamiskin Prison." Might the queen or her staff have had more detailed information regarding Peddy's fate, and if so, why were these facts not shared with the family?[8]

Because the Japanese accused Peddy of Dutch resistance efforts in the Indies, Fré would have been eligible for a pension. She never received any pension, most of all because she did not know what had happened to Peddy after his second arrest. Ultimately, I think that the money was the least of her concerns. Recognition by the public at large of what Dutch Indies people had sacrificed during and after the war has, as of yet, not been forthcoming.

Aside from common misperceptions and lack of crucial information about colonial times and the war period in Asia, there has been a blatant failure of education with regard to the colonial period in the Netherlands. Dutch children will learn all the facts about William of Orange and Holland's rapid rise to power from being oppressed by the Spanish in the seventeenth century to becoming a major empire, but colonial history beyond Jan Pieterszoon Coen, or the war in the Indies and its terrible aftermath, is hardly addressed at all. Anne Frank and the Holocaust figure prominently in the World War II record of school curricula, but Holland's history in the Indies is shrouded in silence. When Holland's highly educated Prime Minister Jan Peter Balkenende recently connected the need for Dutch globalism with a certain pride in the accomplishments of the often ruthless Netherlands East India Company (VOC) of the seventeenth century, he was the living proof of what W. H. Blok and R. C. Seriese have identified: "little to no nineteenth-century and twentieth-century Dutch history is being taught in the high schools," and in teacher-trainings and university history programs, students are not required to study the history of the East Indies at all.[9]

Since postcolonial studies have become a defined discipline in the academy, there has been a tendency to associate colonizers and colonialism with tales of exploitation and indigenous suffering. While I hope I have not been an apologist for the Franckens and their colonial pursuits, I also hope that scholars in the Western world are truly free and thus objective enough to be equally interested in the experiences of the colonizers and the colonized.

Violence is violence and murder is murder, whether committed by a Dutch plantation overseer, a Javanese plantation worker, a Japanese soldier, an Indonesian rebel fighter, or a Dutch soldier. For the sake of history, justice, and a complete record, we need to register everything, so that maybe after a hundred years the distant descendants of Peddy, Willy, and Joke will appreciate that Dutch society is not complicit in the silencing of their Indies relatives' voices. To aim for truth and a complete, uncensored record is not always to aim for beauty, but to be receptive to the truth should be a moral objective in a country as free as the Netherlands—only then can it, as a country and a former colonial power, move on.

Appendix

THE STUCKY FAMILY AND
THE DIEST-LORGIONS

The Stucky Family

When Laurine Francken returned to the Indies in 1914, she visited with her Aunt Adrienne (Coba's older sister) and Uncle Ferdinand Stucky. The Stuckys had a history of their own; family rumor has it that Ferdinand was a bastard son of William III, king of the Netherlands from 1849 to 1890. William was married to Sophie von Württemberg, and they had three sons who all predeceased him. The king would finally marry a second time, to the much younger Emma, who gave him a daughter, Wilhelmina. Wilhelmina would save the monarchy and would be the mother of Juliana and the grandmother of the current Queen Beatrix of the Netherlands.

William III was a renowned philanderer, and before he met Emma he sneaked into bed with Sophie de Quay, who was serving at the court. She became pregnant with a son, Ferdinand Maximiliaan. To cover up the pregnancy and a possible scandal, Sophie was married to the Swiss Colonel Louis Stucky, who also served the king. After Ferdinand, they would have a daughter together.

Ferdinand grew up at the Court in the Hague but when he became older he started resembling the king so much that the royal family became nervous. Thus (so the story goes), the king recommended that Ferdinand leave for the Indies. Black sheep in upper-class families, or people who had caused scandals, as Ferdinand may have, were often shipped off to the Indies. After receiving a lump sum to keep him quiet, Ferdinand left for Batavia and like my great-grandfather, made a good match by marrying into the wealth of the Kervels.

I managed to retrace part of this story in the *mémoires* of Charles Henri Felix Dumonceau, who was a private secretary to the king.[1] On May 29, 1881, Dumonceau writes, the king showed him a letter in which Stucky asked to be promoted to be one of the king's equerries or else given permission to resign. Stucky was already serving the king as one of the royal secretaries but since this meant having to stand for hours in the king's presence, this was, according to Dumonceau, difficult for the restless Stucky. The king decided to let Stucky go without a pension.

Dumonceau felt sorry for Stucky and put in a good word, which resulted in the payment of a pension of eighteen hundred guilders plus a letter of recommendation to the governor-general of the Indies. "I don't think that he used the letter," Dumonceau was to note, "because Mr. d'Echaussé placed Stucky on one of his sugar or rice plantations where he became an administrator and married Miss X., daughter of the Belgian Consul in Surabaya."[2]

Miss X. must have been Adrienne, but all in all, I was not quite sure what to make of this story, even though it is well-known fact that William III was a womanizer who liked to visit brothels and had numerous bastard children. While Ferdinand and Adrienne would have two sons with the very regal names Maximiliaan Willem and Willem Alexander Paul Frederick Lodewyck, I had no proof of Stucky's royal descent. Marjolein Francken, daughter of Mannes, tells me in a letter that Mannes was one of the favorite nephews of Aunt Adrienne, which is why she gave him a piece of jewelry with William III's initials on it.

After reviewing some genealogical material that I happened to locate on the Internet, I found the marriage between Sophie de Quay and Louis Stucky. This marriage produced, as mentioned earlier, one daughter by the name of Henriette Jeanne Josephine Stucky. However, Ferdinand, her older half-brother, is nowhere to be found—either Ferdinand was a fraud or his descent was successfully covered up. Or Ferdinand was not mentioned as a Stucky descendant because, strictly speaking, he was no Stucky but Ferdinand of Orange. When I Googled "Stucky" and "Willem III," I found what might be the final proof. A page of an antiquarian bookseller in Holland showed up, selling an old photograph of "two ladies de Quay." The text on the back of the photo identifies the ladies and adds that one of them is to be seen with "Stucky (*son of William III*) in Malang."

The Diest-Lorgion Family

Mannes Francken was married to Catharina (Kitty) Diest-Lorgion (1895–1967), who was a Eurasian. Kitty's family was of Huguenot descent. Kitty's great-grandfather was Evert Jan Diest Lorgion (1812–76), a well-known and prolific theology and church history professor at the University of Groningen. His son (Kitty's grandfather) was Johannus Jan Diest Lorgion (1838–69), who was also a doctor of theology. After his dissertation on Regnerus Praedinius and his marriage to Catharina Valter, he left for Buitenzorg to serve as a Dutch Reformed preacher.

According to Marjolein Francken, Johannus had a romantic liaison with the wife of Governor-General Mijer, after which he was demoted to a position in Padang. At this point Catharina Valter must have been out of the picture completely, because Johannus also had an affair with another woman in Buitenzorg, who gave birth to Evert-Jan in 1867. Johannus, who already looks rather sickly in the one brownish copy of a picture I have of him, died in Padang two years later. Kitty's father, Evert-Jan, was a handsome navigation officer in the Dutch steamer service. He was married to an Indonesian woman and died in 1910 after he tried to save a man from drowning at the beach in Tjilatjap. The drowning man held onto Evert-Jan's neck so tightly that the latter collapsed on the beach and died.

Kitty, who had seven siblings, was not there to witness her father's dramatic and heroic death. As early as 1898, at the age of three, she had been sent to The Hague to stay with an aunt and uncle, Aletta Diest Lorgion and Cornelis Arnoldus Bletz, to receive a good education. Bletz's own son would marry the daughter of a *nyai* (who was involved with her boss, the administrator Regnerus Tjaarda Mees).

Kitty's uncle, Cornelis Bletz, died in 1915, and one year later Kitty left her widowed aunt to return to the Indies to become a school-teacher.[3] She married Mannes instead and would teach her own children in the schoolroom at Kali Jompo.

Notes

All translations, in the text and in the notes, from sources not published in English are by the author.

Introduction

1. The police actions (1945–49) were the Dutch military attempts to recolonize the Indies after the Japanese surrendered at the end of the Second World War. This caused a guerrilla war, and the Dutch finally had to retreat in 1949 when Indonesia became independent.

2. If they do mention it, they do so in passing and inaccurately. For instance, Elly Touwen-Bouwsma writes, "A transport of women and children from the Gubeng quarter was attacked by Indonesian extremists on October 28[, 1945]. A number of trucks got away but the passengers of one truck were savagely massacred together with the British-Indian soldiers who accompanied the transport." "De Opvang van de burgergeïnterneerden" [The Relief Care of Civilian Internees], in *Tussen Banzai en Bersiap: De afwikkeling van de tweede wereldoorlog in Nederlands-Indië,* ed. Elly Touwen-Bouwsma and P. M. H . Groen (The Hague: SDU, 1996). In reality, the transport consisted of six trucks, of which only one got away, so five were brutally attacked, leading to about two hundred casualties.

3. As I was putting the finishing touches on this book, I heard about an Indies Film Festival that was held in the Netherlands in October of 2006. The festival opened with Peter Hoogendijk's *Soerabaja, Surabaya,* a documentary about the revolution in Surabaya. The last generation of Indies people is beginning to talk, and their descendants seem especially curious about the colonial period. Hopefully this marks a changing trend. In the meantime I have seen the movie. Hoogendijk's mother was holed up in a house in Surabaya during the outbreak of the revolution. She admits in the movie that she did not hear about the ill-fated Gubeng transport and bloodshed in Surabaya until much later, when her son was researching it for his movie.

4. Freek Colombijn, "Explaining the Violent Solution in Indonesia," *Brown Journal of World Affairs* 9, no. 1 (2002): 49–56. For the full text see

http://www.prevent.conflict.org. See also Elizabeth Fuller Collins, "Indonesia: A Violent Culture?" *Asian Survey* 42, no. 4 (2002): 582–604; and Freek Colombijn and J. Thomas Lindblad, eds., *Roots of Violence in Indonesia: Contemporary Violence in Historical Perspective* (Amsterdam: Royal Netherlands Institute of Southeast Asian and Caribbean Studies, 2002).

5. E. M. Beekman, *Troubled Pleasures: Dutch Colonial Literature from the East Indies, 1600–1950* (Oxford: Oxford University Press, 1996), 601.

6. Nationaal Archief is the National Archive, http://www.nationaalarchief.nl. Koninklijke Bibliotheek is the Royal Library, http://www.kb.nl. Koninklijk Instituut van de Tropen, the Royal Institute of the Tropics, can be found at http://www.kit.nl, and the Nederlands Instituut voor Oorlogsdocumentatie (NIOD) can be found at www.niod.nl. Also helpful is http://www.kitlv.nl (Royal Netherlands Institute of Southeast Asian and Caribbean Studies). Other useful The Hague resources are the Oorlogsgravenstichting (Foundation for War Graves), http://www.ogs.nl; the Dutch Red Cross, http://oorlogsnazorg@redcross.nl; and the *Ministerie van Buitenlandse Zaken* (Ministry of Foreign Affairs), http://ddi-bi@minbuza.nl. All of the above Web sites can be accessed in English. Finally, for potential business records or annual reports of plantations, it may be worthwhile to check the Internationaal Instituut voor Sociale Geschiedenis (International Institute for Social History) in Amsterdam, http://www.iisg.nl.

7. *Archieven in de Etalage* [Archives in the Shopwindow] (Zoetermeer: Ministerie van Onderwijs, Cultuur en Wetenschappen, 2000).

Chapter 1

1. William Z. Shetter, *The Netherlands in Perspective: The Dutch Way of Organizing a Society and Its Setting* (Utrecht: Nederlands Centrum Buitenlanders, 2002), 35.

2. Mike Dash, *Batavia's Graveyard: The True Story of the Mad Heretic Who Led History's Bloodiest Mutiny* (New York: Crown, 2002), 3.

3. Jack Turner, *Spice: The History of a Temptation* (New York: Knopf, 2004), 40–41.

4. Russell Shorto, *The Island at the Center of the World: The Epic Story of Dutch Manhattan, the Forgotten Colony That Shaped America* (New York: Doubleday, 2004).

5. Felipe Fernández-Armesto, *Civilizations: Culture, Ambition, and the Transformation of Nature* (New York: Free Press, 2001), 317.

6. Charles Boxer, *The Dutch Seaborne Empire, 1600–1800* (London: Hutchinson, 1965), 4.

7. Dash, *Batavia's Graveyard,* 47.

8. M. C. Ricklefs, *A History of Modern Indonesia since circa 1300,* 2nd ed. (Stanford: Stanford University Press, 1993), 15.

9. Ibid., 27.

10. Fernández-Armesto, *Civilizations,* 317.

11. Svetlana Alpers devotes *The Art of Describing: Dutch Art in the Seventeenth Century* (London: John Murray, 1983) to this very theme.

12. Giles Milton, *Nathaniel's Nutmeg, or, The True and Incredible Adventures of the Spice Trader Who Changed the Course of History* (New York: Farrar, Straus and Giroux, 1999).

13. Conrad Busken Huet, "François Valentyn," in *Litterarische fantasiën en kritieken* [Literary Fantasies and Criticisms], vol. 11 (1881), http://www .dbnl.org.

14. Batavia, named after one of the first tribes who settled in Holland's swamps, is now Jakarta.

15. Milton, *Nathaniel's Nutmeg,* 317.

16. Dash, *Batavia's Graveyard,* 154.

17. "Sir John Darrow Visits Dutch Batavia, 1792," in *Java: A Traveller's Anthology,* ed. James R. Rush (Oxford: Oxford University Press, 1999), 25.

18. Turner, *Spice,* 290.

19. Ricklefs, *History of Modern Indonesia,* 27.

20. Milton writes: "As the factories in the Spice Islands fell into decay, new ones sprang up on the Indian coastline and when Surat officially replaced Bantam as the eastern headquarters of the East India Company it was clear to all that its horizons had changed forever" (*Nathaniel's Nutmeg,* 354).

21. Turner, *Spice,* 291, 297.

22. Jonathan Israel, *The Dutch Republic: Its Rise, Greatness, and Fall, 1477–1806* (Oxford: Oxford University Press, 1989), 323–24.

23. Jean Gelman Taylor, *The Social World of Batavia: European and Eurasian in Dutch Asia* (Madison: University of Wisconsin Press, 1983), xix.

24. Ibid., 8.

25. Ibid., 9.

26. Dash, *Batavia's Graveyard,* 155.

27. Taylor, *Social World of Batavia,* 11, 14, 15, 17.

28. Rob Nieuwenhuys, ed., *Van roddelpraat en literatuur: Een keuze uit het werk van Nederlandse schrijvers uit het voormalig Nederlands-Indië* [Of Gossip and Literature: A Selection from the Work of Dutch Authors from the Former Netherlands Indies] (Amsterdam: Querido, 1965), 13–15.

29. Ibid., 52–53.

30. Otto Knaap, cited in *Tussen twee vaderlanden* [Between Two Father-lands], by Rob Nieuwenhuys (Amsterdam: G.A. van Oorschot, 1959), 39.

31. Nieuwenhuys, *Tussen twee vaderlanden,* 13.

Chapter 2

1. Lyndall Gordon, *A Private Life of Henry James: Two Women and His Art* (London: Random House, 1999), 41.

2. C. M. Vissering, *Een reis door Oost-Java* [A Trip through Eastern Java] (Haarlem: F. Bohn, 1912), 18.

3. Aletta H. Jacobs, *Reisbrieven uit Afrika en Azië, benevens eenige brieven uit Zweden en Noorwegen* [Travel Letters from Africa and Asia, together with Some Letters from Sweden and Norway], 2 vols. (Almelo: W. Hilar-ius, 1913), 2:494–95.

4. Ibid.

5. Louis Couperus, *Oostwaarts: Java en Bali* [Eastward: Java and Bali], in *Verzamelde werken,* 12 vols. (Amsterdam: G. A. van Oorschot, 1975), 12:443.

6. D. C. M. Bauduin, *Het indische leven* [The Indies Life] (The Hague: H. P. Leopold, 1927), 173.

7. Beekman, *Troubled Pleasures,* 49.

8. Rather than defining *adat* as "custom, usage, or tradition," I would like to use Upik Djalins's definition in her forthcoming article "The Adat Argument as a Site for the Exercise of Power: Reconstructing Adat in the Struggle for Rights of Ownership to Land in Pesisir, Krui, West Lam-pung": "Adat is a heavily loaded concept. In its most general sense, adat refers to the customs and practices of Indonesia's various ethnic groups. It includes customary law (hukum adat), ritual conventions, marriage rules, kinship system, methods of conflict resolution, rules for resource owner-ship and utilization and other formally articulated norms and ideas. Adat was one of the most debated issues in the East Indies colonial politics, espe-cially after Van Vollenhoven, a noted Dutch legal scholar, published an extensive work on indigenous adat law in the Dutch East Indies in 1906."

9. Jaap van der Zwaag, *Verloren tropische zaken: De opkomst en onder-gang van de Nederlandse handel- en cultuurmaatschappijen in het voormalige Nederlands-Indië* [Lost Tropical Matters: The Rise and Fall of the Dutch Trading and Cultivation Companies in the Former Netherlands Indies] (Meppel: De Feniks Pers, 1991), 24.

10. C. L. M. Penders, ed. and trans., *Indonesia: Selected Documents on Colo-nialism and Nationalism, 1830–1942* (Brisbane: University of Queensland Press, 1977), 14.

11. Paul Johnson, *The Birth of the Modern: World Society, 1815–1830* (New York: HarperCollins, 1991), 800.

12. Ibid.

13. L. Vitalis, as quoted in Penders, *Indonesia,* 24.

14. The Javanese middle class consisted mostly of Chinese shopkeepers and money lenders.

15. Edgar du Perron, *Country of Origin* (North Clarendon: Periplus, 1999), 424.

16. H. W. Dick, *Surabaya, City of Work: A Socioeconomic History, 1900–2000* (Athens: Ohio University Press, 2002), 41.

17. Harry G. M. Prick, *In de zekerheid van eigen heerlijkheid: Het leven van Lodewijk van Deyssel tot 1890* [In the Certainty of One's Own Magnificence: The Life of Lodewijk van Deijssel until 1890] (Amsterdam: Athenaeum Polak and Van Gennep, 1997), 129.

18. Lodewijk van Deyssel, *De kleine republiek* [The Small Republic], vol. 2 (1888; repr., Den Haag: Bert Bakker, 1975), 1–13.

19. A. Alberts, *Per mailboot naar de Oost* [By Mailboat to the East] (Bussum: Unieboek, 1979), 17.

20. Ricklefs, *History of Modern Indonesia,* 123.

21. Ibid.

22. Ibid., 124.

23. While in Dutch *babus* most often refers to as nursemaids, the term *babu* is much more generic and was also used for other help in the household, like *babu cuci* (maid for the wash), *babu koki* (cook), etc. *Babu anak* is the official term for nursemaid.

24. Eliza Ruhamah Scidmore, *Java, the Garden of the East* (New York: Century, 1897), 17.

25. David Fairchild, "David Fairchild Remembers the Java of His Youth, 1896," in Rush, *Java,* 96.

26. Jacobs, *Reisbrieven uit Afrika en Azië,* 415.

27. K. W. Woltering, e-mail to Inez Hollander, July 12, 2006.

28. Albert S. Bickmore, "Albert S. Bickmore Visits a Sugar Plantation, 1868," in Rush, *Java,* 64.

29. Bernard H. M. Vlekke, *The Story of the Dutch East Indies* (Cambridge, MA: Harvard University Press, 1946), 104.

30. There are stories that Coba, after her husband's death, made scoffing comments in the direction of her husband's portrait. Their match may have been a marriage of convenience rather than a torrid love relationship. Times were different, and it is not up to me to make judgments either way.

31. Taylor, *Social World of Batavia,* 68.

32. Ibid., 78.

33. Johannes Olivier, "De levenswijze der Europeanen" [The Lifestyle of Europeans], cited in Nieuwenhuys, *Tussen twee vaderlanden,* 59.

34. Nieuwenhuys, *Tussen twee vaderlanden,* 167.

35. Ibid., 135.

36. Couperus, *Oostwaarts,* 341. The Indonesian *rijsttafel* (rice table) is a Dutch colonial adaptation of the Indonesian *makan besar* and consists of rice and a wide variety of side dishes, served buffet style.

37. Nieuwenhuys, *Tussen twee vaderlanden,* 113.

38. The Southern novelist Hamilton Basso called this Southern Shinto-ism. "We are like the Japanese," one of his characters is heard saying in *The View from Pompey's Head* (1954): "we eat rice and worship our ancestors."

39. Conrad Busken Huet, letter to E. J. Potgieter, June 3, 1869, in Nieuwenhuys, *Tussen twee vaderlanden,* 112.

40. Willem Walraven, *Brieven aan familie en vrienden, 1919–1941* [Letters to Family and Friends, 1919–1941] (Amsterdam: Van Oorschot, 1966), 233.

41. Kees Snoek, *Edgar du Perron: Het leven van een smalle mens* [Edgar du Perron: The Life of a Narrow Person] (Amsterdam: Nijgh and Van Ditmar, 2005), 28.

42. Taylor, *Social World of Batavia,* 138.

43. Frank Okker, *Dirklands tussen de doerians: Een biografie van Willem Walraven* [Dirklands among the Durians: A Biography of Willem Walraven] (Amsterdam: Bas Lubberhuizen, 2000), 90.

Chapter 3

1. "John C. Van Dyke Admires Malang, 1929," in Rush, *Java,* 143.

2. Van der Zwaag, *Verloren tropische zaken,* 86–89.

3. Sumber Aju never made it into a full-fledged Cultuuronderneming, whereas Kali Jompo did, its shares being bought and sold at the Amsterdam stock exchange

4. T. A. Tengwall, "History of Rubber Cultivation and Research in the Netherlands Indies," in *Science and Scientists in the Netherlands Indies,* ed. Pieter Honig and Frans Verdoorn (Cambridge: Riverside Press, 1945), 344.

5. Van der Zwaag, *Verloren tropische zaken,* 116. One hectare equals about 2.5 acres.

6. Ricklefs, *History of Modern Indonesia,* 153.

7. Louis Couperus, *Kleine Zielen* [Petty Souls], in *Verzamelde Werken* (Amsterdam: G. A. van Oorschot, 1975), 5:16.

8. Willem Walraven, cited in Okker, *Dirklands tussen de doerians,* 112.

9. Van der Zwaag, *Verloren tropische zaken,* 78.

10. Jacobs, *Reisbrieven uit Afrika en Azië,* 500.

11. Vissering, *Een reis door Oost-Java,* 181.

12. Scidmore, *Java,* 265–66.

13. French: a world in which one amuses oneself.

14. Jacobs, *Reisbrieven uit Afrika en Azië,* 504.

15. Couperus talks about these bushes in *Oostwaarts,* 469–70.

16. Bauduin, *Het indische leven,* 119.

17. I. P. C. Graafland, "The Indies Maligned and Avenged," in *Mirror of the Indies: A History of Dutch Colonial Literature,* by Rob Niewenhuys, ed. E. M. Beekman, trans. Frans van Rosevelt (Amherst: University of Massachusetts Press, 1982), 142–43; originally published as *Oost-Indische Spiegel* (Amsterdam: Querido, 1972).

Chapter 4

1. Jeroen Brouwers, *De zondvloed* [The Deluge] (Amsterdam: Arbeiderspers, 1988), 520–21.

2. Hella Haasse, *Heren van de thee* [Tea Lords] (Amsterdam: Querido, 1997), 152.

3. Willy Meelhuijsen, letter to Inez Hollander, 2004.

4. Penders, *Indonesia,* 33–34.

5. Ricklefs, *History of Modern Indonesia,* 151, 154–155.

6. Ibid., 156, 158.

7. Malcolm Bradbury, *Dangerous Pilgrimages: Trans-Atlantic Mythologies and the Novel* (Harmondsworth: Penguin, 1995), 251.

8. Henry Hobhouse, *Seeds of Wealth: Five Plants That Made Men Rich* (Emeryville, CA: Shoemaker and Hoard, 2005), 134.

9. Van der Zwaag, *Verloren tropische zaken,* 37.

10. I have not been able to find who Kali Jompo's shareholders were. Jack Francken believes that the lion's share of the company was kept within the family, but unfortunately I have been unable to verify this. The few annual reports I have do not mention any shareholders by name.

11. P. Brooshooft, "The Ethical Direction in Colonial Policy" (1901), cited in Penders, *Indonesia,* 71.

12. *NRC Handelsblad* of June 24, 1917, states under Economic and Financial News that at the shareholder meeting of Cultuurmaatschappij Kali Jompo "the dividend was determined at twenty percent" and that J. W. E. T. M. Francken took over the scepter from his father, as the director of the company.

13. Ricklefs, *History of Modern Indonesia,* 167.

14. Vissering, *Een reis door Oost-Java,* 236.

15. The Stuckys have an intriguing family history. See the appendix.

16. Ann Laura Stoler, *Carnal Knowledge and Imperial Power: Race and the Intimate in Colonial Rule* (Berkeley: University of California Press, 2002), 67.

17. Ibid., 48–49.

18. Nieuwenhuys, *Tussen twee vaderlanden,* 148.

Chapter 5

1. Couperus, *Oostwaarts,* 243.

2. Tengwall, *History of Rubber Cultivation,* 349.

3. J. H. Boeke, "Budget Studies in Various Parts of Java," in Penders, *Indonesia,* 97–113.

4. Financial news from the various newspapers that the Koninklijke Bibliotheek has scanned and made available online. See http://www.kb.nl/krantencatalogus/krantencatalogus.html.

5. Van der Zwaag, *Verloren tropische zaken,* 79.

6. Note that small planters like the Franckens were not in the same league as Koos Kervel or cultivation system practitioners. Nonetheless, there has been a tendency to malign all Dutch plantations and their profits. Yet, as Van der Zwaag has argued, "Dutch plantations of the nineteenth century laid the foundation for the current Indonesian economy. That aspect of our colonial past ought not be denied" (Van der Zwaag, *Verloren tropische zaken,* 7).

7. Madelon H. Lulofs, *Rubber: A Romance of the Dutch East Indies* (London: Cassell, 1931), 145.

8. Stoler, *Carnal Knowledge and Imperial Power,* 57.

9. Willem Walraven, cited in Okker, *Dirklands tussen de doerians,* 94.

10. Stoler, *Carnal Knowledge and Imperial Power,* 51, 69.

11. Nieuwenhuys, *Tussen twee vaderlanden,* 22.

12. Ibid., 26.

13. Walraven, *Brieven,* 143.

14. Stoler, *Carnal Knowledge and Imperial Power,* 48.

15. Elsbeth Locher-Scholten, "Familie en liefde, Europese mannen en Indonesische vrouwen," in Esther Captain, Marieke Hellevoort, and Marian van der Klein, *Vertrouwd en vreemd* [Familiar and Foreign] (Hilversum: Verloren, 2000), 47.

16. Lulofs, *Rubber,* 129.

17. Ibid., 175–77.

18. Letter from Marjolein Francken to Inez Hollander, July 10, 2006.

19. It was common in Indies family companies to have one administrator (the boss of the plantation) locally, like Mannes and later his younger brother Peddy, and one director who managed the business from Holland.

20. Lulofs, *Rubber,* 103–4.

21. Couperus, *Oostwaarts,* 345.

22. Walraven, *Brieven,* 233.

23. Vissering, *Een reis door Oost-Java,* 229.

24. Nieuwenhuys, *Tussen twee vaderlanden,* 42.

25. Lulofs, *Rubber,* 106.

26. Ibid., 121.

Chapter 6

1. Lulofs, *Rubber,* 187.

2. Edgar du Perron, *Indies Memorandum* (Amsterdam: De Bezige Bij, 1946), 215.

3. Stoler, *Carnal Knowledge and Imperial Power,* 67.

4. Nieuwenhuys, *Tussen twee vaderlanden,* 57–59.

5. Ibid., 61.

6. The boat from Holland was not too bad, either. On this boat already the servants were Javanese boys (*djongoses*) and chefs (*mandurs*). The kitchen was French and the dinners were very formal, with passengers wearing tuxedoes and gowns.

7. Couperus, *Oostwaarts,* 233–34.

8. Ibid., 241.

9. A. Alberts, *Per mailboot naar de oost: Reizen met de Lloyd en de Nederlandse PakketvaartMaatschappij tussen 1920–1940* [By Mailboat to the East: Travels with the Lloyd and the Dutch KPM from 1920–1940] (Bussum: Uniebook, 1979).

10. Bas Veth, *Het leven in Nederlandsch-Indië* [Life in the Dutch East Indies] (The Hague: Thomas and Eras, 1977), 26.

11. Couperus, *Oostwaarts,* 243.

12. Veth, *Het leven in Nederlandsch-Indië,* 43.

13. Du Perron, *Indies Memorandum,* 7.

14. Veth, *Het leven in Nederlandsch-Indië,* 46.

15. Ibid., 8.

16. Ibid., 144, 145, 148.

17. Ibid., 52.

18. The Simpang Club apparently had a sign that said "No natives or dogs allowed."

19. Hobhouse, *Seeds of Wealth,* 175.

20. See http://www.indonesiaphoto.com/content/view186/44.

21. Dirk A. Buiskool, "Medan: A Plantation City on the East Coast of Sumatra, 1870–1942," in *Proceedings of the First International Urban Conference Surabaya, August 23–25, 2004.* This file can be found online under het NIOD: www.indie-indonesie.nl

22. Fré's family history remains very vague. Her son Harry told me in an e-mail that he does not know anything about her except that her father had a dairy factory in Wolvega (Friesland; Fré's last name, Zuidstra, is a Frisian name) and that she had one sister (Joke) who was married to a businessman (Harry Heynen) in Haarlem. He thinks his mother was never happy again in Holland after the war. Harry writes: "There was a great deal of distance between me and my parents. My father was distant because I was too young to remember him, and my mother was loving and caring but after the war she lived like she had drawn up a shield around herself."

23. Veth, *Het leven in Nederlandsch-Indië*, 43.

Chapter 7

1. Van der Zwaag, *Verloren tropische zaken*, 41–43.

2. A few annual reports of Kali Jompo surfaced after a search at the Internationaal Instituut voor Sociale geschiedenis: http://www.iisg.nl.

3. Humphrey de la Croix, *Indië herinnerd en beschouwd: Sociale geschiedenis van een kolonie (1930–1957)* [The Indies Remembered and Considered: Social History of a Colony, 1930–1957] (Amsterdam: KJBB, 1997), 46.

4. Stoler, *Carnal Knowledge and Imperial Power*, 36.

5. Walraven, *Brieven*, 180.

6. Robert Cribb, *Historical Dictionary of Indonesia* (London: Scarecrow Press, 1992), 196. Interestingly, Cribb also writes that the claim that without the Indies, the Netherlands' world and trading power would be reduced to that of Denmark was overblown: "Recent scholars have shown that Dutch investment at the close of the colonial period (40 percent of the country's external investments) was lower in proportion than that of Britain in her empire (50 percent) and that returns on that investment were modest (3.9 percent in 1938)."

7. Couperus, *Oostwaarts*, 245.

8. Du Perron, in Snoek, *Edgar du Perron*, 885.

9. Walraven, *Brieven*, 572.

10. Roel de Neve and Vincent Houben, "Heren op het land: Indische cultuurondernemers" [Lords of the Land: Indies Plantation Owners], in *Uit Indië geboren: Vier eeuwen familiegeschiedenis*, ed. Wim Willems et al. (Zwolle: Waanders, 1997).

11. *Awirran,* spelled "awiran" in Malay, was and is still used in eastern Java: according to Sylvia Tiwon it is an indigenous irrigation system that was known to be less destructive of the environment (and the humus layer) and more protective of the soil in case of floods.

12. P. A. Daum, *Ups and Downs in the Indies,* ed. E. M. Beekman (Amherst: University of Massachusetts Press, 1987).

13. Vlekke, *Story of the Dutch East Indies,* 191.

14. Hobhouse, *Seeds of Wealth,* 176.

Chapter 8

1. During my grandfather's childhood in the Indies it was quite normal not to wear shoes at all. In Harry's day, however, mothers preferred shoes for their children because of hookworm, which could enter the body through the soles of one's feet. It is nonetheless quite likely that the Francken children ran around barefoot most of the time.

2. Walraven, *Brieven,* 157.

3. Pamela Pattynama, "Beweging op het achtererf: dagelijks leven in de jaren twintig" [Activity in the Backyard: Daily Life in the 1920s], in Willems et al., eds., *Uit Indië geboren,* 124. Note that the Dutch Dutchified Malay words, both in spelling and semantically. Pattynama probably means *tukang kebun* (gardener), as *kebun* by itself means "garden" or "yard."

4. Hobhouse, *Seeds of Wealth,* 252, 296.

5. Ibid., 251.

6. Ibid., 275–76, 285.

7. Bauduin writes in 1927: "The association with natives endangers the mental health and physical well-being of our children and the sad proof of that has been given countless of times." Bauduin, *Het Indische leven,* 59. I am not sure what Bauduin means, but the fact that many Dutch children would have fond memories of their *babus* and *kokis* proves the opposite.

8. Lulofs, *Rubber,* 117, 119.

9. Couperus, *Oostwaarts,* 286–87.

10. Hobhouse, *Seeds of Wealth,* 181.

11. Lou de Jong, cited in Hella Haasse's memoir, *Het dieptelood van de herinnering* (Amsterdam: Querido, 2004), 402–3.

12. Ricklefs, *History of Modern Indonesia,* 187.

13. Walraven, *Brieven,* 92.

Chapter 9

1. Ian Buruma, *Inventing Japan, 1853–1964* (New York: Modern Library, 2004), 15–16.

2. Ken'ichi Goto, *Tensions of Empire: Japan and Southeast Asia in the Colonial and Postcolonial World* (Athens: Ohio University Press, 2003), 7, 16.

3. Ibid., 15.

4. Ibid., 20–21.

5. Ibid., 82.

6. Laurence Rees, *Horror in the East: Japan and the Atrocities of World War II* (London: BBC Books, 2001), 26.

7. Ibid., 28.

8. Ibid., 50.

9. Niall Ferguson, *The War of the World: Twentieth-Century Conflict and the Descent of the West* (Harmondsworth: Penguin, 2006), 607.

10. Buruma, *Inventing Japan,* 116.

11. Van der Zwaag, *Verloren tropische zaken,* 241. There was also a Tanks for Churchill Fund. Willy Meelhuijsen makes this point in *Revolutie in Soerabaja, 17 augustus–1 december 1945* [Revolution in Surabaya, August 17–December 1, 1945] (Zutphen: Walburg, 2000).

12. Jacob Zwaan, "The Netherlands Indies during the Japanese Occupation (1942–1945)," in *Oorlog en verzet in Nederlands-Indië, 1941–1949, en de voorlichting aan de na-oorlogse generaties* [War and Resistance in the Dutch East Indies, 1941–1949, and the Information Stream to the Postwar Generations] (Amsterdam: De Bataafsche Leeuw, 1989), 10.

13. Nicholas Tarling, *A Sudden Rampage: The Japanese Occupation of Southeast Asia, 1941–1945* (Honolulu: University of Hawaii Press, 2001), 79.

14. Likewise, after Nazi Germany invaded the Netherlands, German nationals living in the Indies were advised to leave for Japan or Germany. Some Germans were also interned.

15. Jack Francken believes that all communication between Peddy and his father Jacques Francken had already stopped in 1940, after the Germans occupied the Netherlands.

16. Rees, *Horror in the East,* 64.

17. Vlekke, *Story of the Dutch East Indies,* 213.

18. Elly Touwen-Bouwsma, "The Indonesian Nationalists and the Japanese 'Liberation' of Indonesia: Visions and Reactions," *Journal of Southeast Asia Studies* 27 (1996): 1–18. *Banzai* is a Japanese cheer meaning "a thousand years" and can best be translated "long life/hurrah!" While the Indonesians thought they would be liberated from the Dutch, the Japanese were in some ways more repressive than the Dutch, or, as Ken'ichi Goto has noted: "In contrast to the Dutch who recognized Islamic social and cultural values and followed a policy of noninterference, the Japanese tried to impose their values upon the Indonesian population" (*Tensions of Empire,* 235).

19. Jacob Zwaan, *Oorlog en verzet in Nederlands-Indië, 1941–1949, en de voorlichting aan de na-oorlogse generaties* (Amsterdam: De Bataafsche Leeuw, 1989).

20. Petra Groen, in Zwaan, *Oorlog en verzet,* 25–27. Zwaan also calls Sukarno a "traitor to his own people" for quietly supporting Japan's institution of Indonesian forced laborers (romusha) many of whom died in appalling circumstances. Goto seems to agree with Zwaan when quoting Sukarno, who said that the "sweat of the romusha" was "poison for the Allies." Goto also writes that Sukarno believed that his support of the romusha issue would persuade the Japanese to grant Indonesian independence (*Tensions of Empire,* 85).

21. Pamela Pattynama, "Herinnerd Indië: autobiografische teksten van Indische migrantenschrijvers" [The Indies Remembered: Autobiographical Texts of Indies Migrant Writers], *Tydskrif vir Nederlands en Afrikaans* 2 (December 2003): 6.

22. Remco Raben, *Representing the Japanese Occupation of Indonesia: Personal Testimonies and Public Images in Indonesia, Japan and the Netherlands* (Zwolle: Waanders, 1999).

23. Remco Raben, "War Memories: Battles in Perspective," *IIAS Newsletter Online,* no. 22, http://www.iias.nl/iiasn/22/theme/22T9.html.

24. Tarling, *Sudden Rampage,* 104. While Japan produced seventy thousand warplanes between 1941 and 1945, the United States produced three hundred thousand in the same period.

Chapter 10

1. Andrew van Dyke, in *The Defining Years of the Dutch East Indies, 1942–1949: Survivors' Accounts of Japanese Invasion and Enslavement of Europeans and the Revolution That Created Free Indonesia,* by Jan A. Krancher (Jefferson, NC: McFarland, 1996), 15.

2. Hein Matthijs, *Rennen voor je leven* [Run for Your Life] (Schoorl: Conserve, 1994), 18.

3. Ibid., 29–30. "BB office" refers to the Binnenlands Bestuur (Administrative Office of the Interior), the Dutch part of the dualistic colonial government structure. The other part was represented by the Javanese aristocracy. While this might raise the impression that the Dutch were very laissez faire in allowing the Javanese to govern their own people, the truth is, as Multatuli disclosed in his famous novel, that both the Dutch and the Javanese were guilty of exploiting the Javanese population.

4. Hobhouse, *Seeds of Wealth,* 177.

5. Willem Walraven, cited in Okker, *Dirklands tussen de doerians,* 208.

6. Pramoedya Ananta Toer, "Death in a Time of Change," in *The Mute's Soliloquy* (New York: Hyperion, 1999), 161.

7. Meelhuijsen, *Revolutie in Soerabaja*, 23.

8. *Verzet in Nederlands-Indië tegen de Japanse bezetting, 1942–1945* [Resistance in the Netherlands Indies against the Japanese Occupation, 1942–1945], ed. B. R. van Immerzeel and F. van Esch (The Hague: SDU, 1993), 20–21.

9. Only in 2006 were the first English-language books on the romusha question beginning to appear.

10. Rees, *Horror in the East,* 85–86.

11. Theo van Elzen, in Van Immerzeel and Van Esch, *Verzet in Nederlands-Indië,* 125.

12. Ibid., 33.

13. Jeroen Brouwers, *Het verzonkene* [The Sunken] (Amsterdam: Arbeiderspers, 1980), 33.

14. I. J. Brugmans et al., *Nederlandsch-Indië onder Japanse Bezetting: Gegevens en documenten over de jaren, 1942–1945* [The Dutch East Indies during the Japanese Occupations: Facts and Documents of the Years 1942–1945], 2nd ed. (Franeker: T. Wever, 1960), 323.

15. Winnie Rinzema-Admiraal, "De plantersaffaires in Oost-Java: Planters, Landwacht en Kempeitai in de Oosthoek" [The Planters' Conspiracies in Eastern Java: Planters, Dutch Militia, and the Kempeitai in the Oosthoek], in *Het einde van Indië: Indische Nederlanders tijdens de Japanse bezetting en de dekolonisatie*, ed. Wim Willems and Jaap de Moor (The Hague: SdU, 1995), 139–56.

16. Johan Fabricius, *Hoe ik Indië terugvond* [The Indies Revisited] (The Hague: H. P. Leopolds, 1947), 35.

17. Laurence Rees writes: "In a flawed and in many ways unjust series of trials held by the Allies at the end of the war, around 5000 Japanese were tried for war crimes. But this only served to highlight the immunity of the emperor and grow the fiction that he had been a puppet head of state unable to prevent the horrors that occurred—a fiction that carefully overlooked the truth that it had been this puppet, who by finally acting decisively, had brought the war to an end. Even if Hirohito had not stood trial he could have abdicated in favour of the young crown prince, thus preserving the institution of the emperor but still acknowledging his own responsibility. But it was not to be. The supreme commander of the Japanese armed forces, the man in whose name more than a million Japanese soldiers died, stayed on as an emperor. 'Why did the person at the top,' asks Hajime Kondo, that rarest of veterans in Japan—a man prepared to speak out about the past, 'why did the person who had the supreme responsibility, not take responsibility for

the war?' . . . Emperor Hirohito remained on the throne until his death in 1989. As a result, the majority of Japanese people had to learn to develop amnesia about events before August 15th, 1945. 'Veterans don't really talk about the war openly,' says Kondo. 'Don't talk about bad things,' they say, 'as it would shame Japan. Keep quiet'" (*Horror in the East*, 144–45).

18. For records of the Dutch Protestant/Reformed Church in colonial Indonesia one can check with the Geschiedenisbank in Oegsgeest: www.ga .oegsgeest.geschiedenisbank-zh.nl.

Chapter 11

1. Ministerie van Buitenlandse Zaken in The Hague, NEFIS, OM 10175/N, OM 10328/N, OM 10359/N, OM 10330/N, OM 10331/N. "NEFIS" stands for Netherlands Forces Intelligence Service. It was established in Melbourne soon after the fall of the Netherlands East Indies. All citations in this part of the text are from the above dossiers.

Chapter 12

1. Robert Cribb, *Gangsters and Revolutionaries: The Jakarta's People's Militia and the Indonesian Revolution, 1945–1949* (Honolulu: University of Hawaii Press, 1991), 1.

2. Ibid., 39. Harry remembers this was indeed the case: the plantation produced as usual to provide for the Japanese war industry.

3. *Rampok* "originally meant tiger-baiting, which had been, to modern minds at least, one of the less attractive spectator sports of old Java. The brigands themselves went by many names, by *perampok* (or the Dutch *rampokker*) and *garong* were common. . . . The central feature of the *rampok* gang was its boss, or *jago* (literally 'fighting cock')" (ibid., 18). In times of instability, the Chinese in particular, a group the Indonesians discriminated the most, also fell victim to these gangs.

4. Richard Voorneman, *Banjoe Biroe XI: Een vrouwenkamp op Java* [Banyubiru XI: A Women's Camp in Java] (Utrecht: Stichting ICODO, 1995), 11.

5. Ibid., 11.

6. At the end of the war, in August of 1945, the Netherlands Indies Civil Administration (NICA) estimated that one hundred and fifty-two thousand Dutch civilians had been interned, as well as sixty thousand POWs of the Colonial Army (KNIL) and the Dutch Royal Marine (ten thousand of whom were Indonesian). See Touwen-Bouwsma and Groen, *Tussen Banzai en Bersiap,* 125n30. In the 1950s the Dutch government fixed the number at one hundred thousand civilian internees, even though most historians now

believe that the number must have been more like two hundred thousand. See Winnie Rinzema-Admiraal, *Dit was uw Tjideng: Aspecten van de vertraagde afwikkeling van Japanse interneringskampen in Batavia met het Tjidengkamp als casus* [This Was Your Tjideng: Aspects of the Delayed Liquidation of the Japanese Internment Camps in Batavia with Tjideng as a Case Study] (Utrecht: Stichting ICODO, 2004), 20.

7. Elly Touwen-Bouwsma, "De opvang van de burgergeïnterneerden op Java en Sumatra" [The Relief Effort for the Civilian Internees in Java and Sumatra], in Bouwsma and Groen, *Tussen Banzai en Bersiap*. The Japanese effort to isolate the internees from the outside world was very successful in this respect: not only did the internees not know what was happening outside of the "bamboo curtains" of their camps, the Allies, while they knew the camps existed, did not know any details about them.

8. Voorneman, *Banjoe Biroe XI,* 18.

9. C. J. H. du Chattel, *Storm over Java* (Assen: Born, 1946), 36.

10. Esther Captain, "Golven van herinnering: Memoires van vrouwen over de internering in Ambarawa" [Waves of Memory: Memoirs of Women about the Internment in Ambarawa], in Willems and De Moor, *Het einde van Indië,* 111.

11. Ibid., 103.

12. Voorneman, *Banjoe Biroe XI,* 60.

13. David Wehl, *The Birth of Indonesia* (London: George Allen and Unwin, 1949), 5.

14. Alan Greenhalgh, cited in *Dit was uw Tjideng: Aspecten van de vertraagde afwikkeling van Japanse interneringskampen in Batavia met Tjideng als casus* [This Was Your Tjideng: Aspects of the Delayed Processing of the Japanese Internment Camps in Batavia with Tjideng as a Case Study], by Winnie Rinzema-Admiraal (Utrecht: Stichting ICODO, 2004), 48.

15. Rinzema-Admiraal, *Dit was uw Tjideng,* 49.

16. Voorneman, *Banjoe Biroe XI,* 40.

17. Ibid., 39–40.

18. Du Chattel, *Storm over Java,* 36.

19. Voorneman, *Banjoe Biroe XI,* 67–74.

20. Cribb, *Gangsters and Revolutionaries,* 42.

21. Rinzema-Admiraal, *Dit was uw Tjideng,* 26.

22. Brugmans et al., *Nederlandsch-Indië onder Japanse Bezetting,* 425.

23. Voorneman, *Banjoe Biroe XI,* 73.

24. Du Chattel, *Storm over Java,* 32.

25. Voorneman, *Banjoe Biroe XI,* 90.

26. Ibid., 86.

27. Ibid., 90.

28. Pieter H. Groenevelt, "The Bombs That Saved My Life," in Willems and De Moor, *Het einde van Indië,* 159.

29. Rinzema-Admiraal, *Dit was uw Tjideng,* 70.

30. Rees, *Horror in the East,* 79–80. N.B.: In March of 2007, the prime minister of Japan, Shinzo Abe, denied the use of *troostmeisjes,* comfort women, by Japanese soldiers in World War II.

31. Du Chattel, *Storm over Java,* 41.

32. Winnie Rinzema-Admiraal, "Wat de Atoombom voorkwam: Het Liquidatieplan van Japon voor de geïnterneerden van de Pacific" [What the Atomic Bomb Prevented: The Japanese Liquidation Plan for Pacific Internees] (Leeuwarden: KSB Repro BV, 2008.)

33. Henk Hovinga, "Einde van een vergeten drama: Opvang en repatriëring van *romusha* na de Japanse capitulatie" [The End of a Forgotten Drama: Relief and Repatriation of *Romusha* after the Japanese Surrender], cited in Touwen-Bouwsma and Groen, *Tussen Banzai en Bersiap,* 74. See also Shigeru Sato, *War, Nationalism and Peasants: Java under the Japanese Occupation, 1942–1945* (Armonk, NY: M. E. Sharpe, 1994).

Chapter 13

1. Harry also remembered that a later plane dropped a food package, which landed outside the camp: in it were cans. It also carried chewing gum, something Harry had never seen before. People warned him that he should not eat it because it would block his intestines and make him explode. "I also remember the milk powder," Harry writes in an e-mail of March 1, 2006, "I ate it for the first time and have loved it ever since."

2. Meelhuijsen, *Revolutie in Soerabaja,* 38.

3. William Frederick, *Visions and Heat: The Making of the Indonesian Revolution* (Athens: Ohio University Press, 1989), 183. Later, and for the Dutch in particular, the word *bersiap* became the synonym of the random killings of Dutch people by the Indonesians in the weeks leading up to, during, and after the revolution when a second *bersiap* took place.

4. Diet Kramer, *Thuisvaart* [Homeward Bound] (Amsterdam: Holland, 1948), 29.

5. Ibid., 32–33.

6. Rinzema-Admiraal, *Dit was uw Tjideng,* 18.

7. Han Bing Siong, "Captain Huyer and the Massive Japanese Arms Transfer in East Java in October 1945," *Bijdragen tot de Taal-, Land- en Volkenkunde* 159 (2003): 311.

8. Kramer, *Thuisvaart,* 33–34.

9. Voorneman, *Banjoe Biroe XI,* 104.

10. Lydia Chagoll, *Buigen in Jappenkampen* [Bowing in the Japanese Camps], (Mechelen: Bakermat, 1995), 164.

11. Richard McMillan, *The British Occupation of Indonesia, 1945–1946: Britain, the Netherlands and the Indonesian Revolution* (London: Routledge, 2005), 4.

12. Brugmans et al., *Nederlandsch-Indië onder Japanse Bezetting,* 612.

13. Frederick, *Visions and Heat,* 171.

14. Meelhuijsen, *Revolutie in Soerabaja,* 37.

15. Kramer, *Thuisvaart,* 36.

16. Rinzema-Admiraal, *Dit was uw Tjideng,* 105.

17. Iens van Doorn, *Geluk is als een vogel: Roman uit de nadagen van Nederlandsch-Indië* [Happiness Is Like a Bird: A Novel from the End of Days of the Dutch East Indies] (Franeker: T. Wever, 1981), 121.

18. "The RAPWI teams were deployed to give immediate relief and take care of evacuations. They were also expected to assess the number of internees and how much food and medicine was needed" (Touwen-Bouwsma and Groen, *Tussen Banzai en Bersiap,* 26). Unfortunately, because the RAPWI included so many Dutch people, the organization, and later the Red Cross, were seen as a Dutch cover for espionage and Dutch infiltration.

19. Ibid., 29. Richard McMillan confirms this and cites lack of proper sanitation and hygiene as a reason why the transports from Banyubiru were prioritized (*British Occupation of Indonesia,* 31).

20. McMillan, *British Occupation of Indonesia,* 31.

21. Frederick, *Visions and Heat,* 193–94.

22. Meelhuijsen, *Revolutie in Soerabaja,* 50.

23. Han Bing Siong, "The Indonesian Need of Arms after the Proclamation of Independence," *Bijdragen tot Taal-, Land- en Volkenkunde* 157 (2001): 811.

24. Bing Siong, "Captain Huyer," 328.

25. P. J. Drooglever, "SEAC in Indonesia: Voices from the Past?" paper presented at the International Association of Historians of Asia, Jakarta, Indonesia August 27–September 1, 1998, 8, 10.

26. Bing Siong, "Captain Huyer," 331.

27. McMillan, *British Occupation of Indonesia,* 32.

28. Yaichiro Shibata, "Surabaya after the Surrender," in *The Japanese Experience in Indonesia: Selected Memoirs of 1942–1945,* ed. Anthony Reid and Oki Akira (Athens: Ohio University Center for International Studies and Center for Southeast Asian Studies, 1986), 373.

29. Bing Siong, "Captain Huyer," 336.

30. Wehl, *Birth of Indonesia,* 48.

31. Cribb, *Gangsters and Revolutionaries,* 51.

32. Ibid., 17.

33. Ibid., 64.

34. Touwen-Bouwsma and Groen, *Tussen Banzai en Bersiap,* 25.

35. The Chinese, more than two million of whom lived in the Dutch East Indies, had always been an easy target for brigands. They were envied by the Indonesians because they were thrifty, prosperous, and successful. In times of political unrest, such as after the Dutch surrender in 1942 and the Japanese surrender in 1945, their shops were looted and burned while they themselves were the victims of kidnapping, mutilation, rape, and murder.

36. Van Doorn, *Geluk is als een vogel,* 146. Aside from the danger, it was not practical for the internees to leave the camps: they had no money or jobs and their houses were plundered or lived in by the Indonesians and Japanese.

37. Fabricius, *Hoe ik Indië terugvond* 19.

38. Ibid.

39. For the same reason, Dutchmen who had returned to town "were hauled off the street and strangled or hacked to pieces, their bodies being dumped in one of the canals. . . . The already colourful vocabulary of Indies Dutch acquired a new word, *getjintjangd,* meaning hacked to pieces. Family houses were also surrounded at night and their European inhabitants massacred, and every effort was made to terrify living Europeans by the painting up of threatening slogans or by unusual behaviour of young Indonesians near residences to suggest that they had been marked out for imminent doom" (Cribb, *Gangsters and Revolutionaries,* 65). Significantly, the assumption that the returning Dutchmen might claim their former jobs, lives, and the colony was not entirely unfounded, albeit unrealistic considering the malnutrition and poor health of most of the Dutch. Touwen-Bouwsma and Groen write that the Indies government was counting on the ex-internees to stay in the Indies because of a lack of manpower. Aside from the fact that they surmised that the Netherlands could not take in so many returning Dutch people, they believed that most of the Indies Dutchmen felt the Indies was their home to begin with. The colonial government expected (erroneously) that internees could recover in the mountains of Java and Sumatra. Those who were fit enough were expected to join the RAPWI, the military, or the civil service. Some of the really diseased people might recuperate in Australia or New Zealand, but the reality was that a large group wanted to repatriate. Touwen-Bouwsma and Groen, *Tussen Banzai en Bersiap,* 23.

40. Ibid., 30–31.

Chapter 14

1. Frederick, *Visions and Heat,* 195–201; Meelhuijsen, *Revolutie in Soerabaja,* 57.
2. Wehl, *Birth of Indonesia,* 51.
3. Meelhuijsen, *Revolutie in Soerabaja,* 54.
4. Cited in Reid and Akira, *Japanese Experience in Indonesia,* 351.
5. Frederick, *Visions and Heat,* 213–14.
6. Cited in Meelhuijsen, *Revolutie in Soerabaja,* 83–84.
7. Ibid., 214.
8. Cited in Reid and Akira, *Japanese Experience in Indonesia,* 354–56.
9. Meelhuijsen, *Revolutie in Soerabaja,* 84.
10. Cited in H. Itzig Heijne, "Een rapport over het Gubeng-Transport, Surabaya, 28 October 1945" [A Report on the Gubeng Transport] (1991) and "Aanvulling op het rapport van het Gubeng Transport" (1992) (Supplement), both unpublished and kept at NIOD in Amsterdam.
11. Heijne, "Een rapport over he Gubeng-Transport."
12. Both witnesses in the Gubeng report and Meelhuijsen confirm this bloody scene, reminiscent of the street scenes during the French Revolution.
13. Bing Siong, "Captain Huyer," 294 (emphasis added).
14. Ibid., 306.
15. Like so many numbers during this period, 1,850 may be too low—it is more likely that the number of former internees amounted to six thousand.
16. The same was true for the Netherlands Indies Civil Administration (NICA), which had an even worse reputation among the Indonesians than the RAPWI or the Red Cross because it had as one of its goals the restoration of Dutch power. At the same time, Frederick writes that the purpose of the NICA "was unclear even in Dutch circles" (*Visions and Heat,* 196). Meelhuijsen, on the other hand, claims that the NICA did represent the legal authority of the Indonesian archipelago, as was made clear in radio broadcasts from Singapore, Brisbane, and Melbourne. The NICA, according to Meelhuijsen, condemned Sukarno's and Hatta's republic, which it saw as a Japanese conspiracy (*Revolutie in Soerabaja,* 47–48).
17. Frederick, *Visions and Heat,* 234.
18. Meelhuijsen, *Revolutie in Soerabaja,* 95. Meelhuijsen believes that the Oranje Hotel documents were probably reports intended for the South East Asia Command and British headquarters in Jakarta.
19. Touwen-Bouwsma and Groen, *Tussen Banzai en Bersiap,* 33–34. Meelhuijsen writes that Dutch and Eurasian men and boys (above the age of sixteen) were seen as an unwanted fifth column in the city.

20. Van Doorn, *Geluk is als een vogel,* 173.

21. Cited in Reid and Akira, *Japanese Experience in Indonesia,* 361–62.

22. Frederick, *Visions and Heat,* 240.

23. William Frederick, "Blood Spilled in Darkness: Killings in the Early Indonesian Revolution (East Java, October 1945)," 18.

24. Ibid., 20–21.

25. Ibid., 22.

26. Meelhuijsen, *Revolutie in Soerabaja,* 140.

27. Frederick, *Visions and Heat,* 256.

28. Meelhuijsen, *Revolutie in Soerabaja,* 150–51.

29. A. F. J. Doulton, *The Fighting Cock: Being the History of the 23rd Indian Division, 1942–1947* (Aldershot: Gale and Polden, 1951), 250–52.

30. Meelhuijsen, *Revolutie in Soerabaja,* 212.

31. McMillan, *British Occupation of Indonesia,* 43.

32. Ibid., 41.

Chapter 15

1. Meelhuijsen, *Revolutie in Soerabaja,* 158.

2. Meelhuijsen is one of the first Dutch historians to write about the transport, and he has done so in more detail than anyone before him. See his account in *Revolutie in Soerabaja,* 171–81. Other facts about the transport I have gleaned from the different survivors' accounts in Itzig Heine's unpublished Gubeng report (NIOD).

3. Meelhuijsen, *Revolutie in Soerabaja,* 158.

4. Harry Francken, e-mail to Inez Hollander, March 2, 2006.

5. Heine, "Een rapport over he Gubeng-Transport."

6. Wehl, *Birth of Indonesia,* 56.

7. Frederick, *Visions and Heat,* 9.

8. Meelhuijsen, *Revolutie in Soerabaja,* 158–59.

9. Meelhuijsen, letter to Inez Hollander, 2004.

10. To protect the identity of the victims and the survivors, I use only their initials here.

11. Frederick, *Visions and Heat,* 260.

12. Lieutenant Colonel F. H. G. Eggleton, Report 16, RAPWHI Control Staff, Collection Maj. S. Gemma: IWM.

13. Frederick, "Blood Spilled in Darkness," 24.

14. Meelhuijsen, *Revolutie in Soerabaja,* 176.

15. It is not unlikely that Harry's protector was a member of the TKR, the protective army, but in the chaos it was impossible for the victims to determine who was who among the armed Indonesians.

16. H. V. Deight-van Witsen, "Tussen Banzai en Bersiap" [Between Banzai and Bersiap], *Kawatberichten* (July 1998): 25.

17. Even the figure of 150 survivors or so is misleading. Are they from the last (third) transport that day, or are they the people who were ferried across safely in the previous two transports? Meelhuijsen says there were most likely six trucks in that last transport, with up to twenty people in each, which would mean that the 118 and 40 were the numbers of the last transport, whereas the 150 must have been part of the two earlier ones. The number of trucks has been speculated on ever since, but Harry, too, thinks that Meelhuijsen is right: "I came out of the house [on October 28] and could see as far as the beginning and the end of the convoy, which means there would have been about six trucks." Harry Francken, e-mail to Inez Hollander, March 2, 2006.

18. Cited in Voorneman, *Banjoe Biroe XI,* 182.

19. Meelhuijsen, *Revolutie in Soerabaja,* 172.

20. McMillan, *British Occupation of Indonesia,* 45.

21. Frederick, *Visions and Heat,* 32.

22. By this I do not mean censorship but a reluctance by Dutch historians to pay attention to it as it might detract from the bigger picture and justifications for (and of) the revolution.

23. Andrew Goss, "From Tong-Tong to Tempo Doeloe: Eurasian Memory Work and the Bracketing of Dutch Colonial History, 1957–1961," *Indonesia* 70 (October 2000): 11. Goss further notes that although, since the 1960s, "the history of colonial society in the Netherlands East Indies has been a component of Dutch national history and identity, colonial history has not, however, entered the main narrative of the nation as an integral epoch or watershed, but rather as something put in brackets" (34).

24. Frederick, *Visions and Heat,* 262–63.

25. Meelhuijsen, *Revolutie in Soerabaja,* 210.

26. Ibid., 211.

27. Frederick, *Visions and Heat,* 278–79.

28. Ricklefs, *History of Modern Indonesia,* 205.

Epilogue

1. In Willems and De Moor, *Het einde van Indië.*

2. *NJB* (1994): 277.

3. When Fré arrived in Holland, my family gave her pictures of her daughters that Fré had sent them in the mail during happier times at Kali Jompo.

4. Van der Zwaag, *Verloren tropische zaken,* 282–83.

5. Ibid., 303.

6. Goss, "From Tong-Tong to Tempo Doeloe," 22.

7. Given that the Dutch railway system was built on the proceeds of the cultivation system, one could imagine a like-minded poster campaign with texts such as "These train platforms were built with money that was extracted from Java in the nineteenth century. As of yet, we still have not paid back the Javanese for their 'investment' in the Dutch economy."

8. Letter by Queen Wilhelmina, January 6, 1947. The Dutch text reads: "Van zijn vrijheid beroofd, en wellicht overgeleverd aan de meest wreede mishandelingen heeft Uw echtgenoot Ferdinand, dien U thans betreurt, op 15 Maart 1945 in de gevangenis van Soekamiskin het hooge offer van zijn leven gebracht. Bij dit voor U zo zware verlies kom Ik U Mijn hartelijke deelneming betuigen. Moge zijn offer ons land en in het bijzonder het Rijksgebied in het Verre Oosten, dat zozeer door de Japansche besetting heeft geleden, een betere toekomst geven."

9. W. H. Blok and R. C. Seriese, "Netherland Indies in History Education," in *Oorlog en Verzet in Nederlands-Indië, 1941–1949, en de voorlichting aan de na-oorlogse generaties,* ed. Jacob Zwaan (Amsterdam: De Bataafsche Leeuw, 1989), 73–74. Also, while some of the political history of the 1945–49 period is being covered, there is little to no attention toward "the bersiap and the fate of Indo-Europeans and Dutch Indies people."

Appendix

1. C. H. F. Dumonceau, *Sire . . . Herinnering aan Z.M. Koning Willem III en H.M Koningin Emma* [Sire—Memory of His Majesty King William III and Her Majesty, Queen Emma], trans. and ed. R. W. A. M. Cleverens, vol. 2 (Middelburg: Nobles, 1989).

2. Ibid., 55–56.

3. Bletz's death announcement, signed by Kitty and her aunt, can be found on the obituary page of *NRC Handelsblad* of June 21, 1915. See the historic newspaper archive of the Koninklijke Bibliotheek in The Hague.

Glossary of Dutch and Malay Words

Aside from the Dutch words and their meanings, I will give the Dutch spellings of the Malay words in brackets if the Dutch spelling varies from the Malay.

Alun alun (alo(e)n(g)-alo(e)n(g)): large central square in a city, used for sports; city square

Asia Raya (Japanese): Great(er) Asia

awiran (awirran): agricultural irrigation method to preserve the humus layer of the soil

babu (baboe): generic term for female house servant but often associated with the care of colonial children; like a nanny

bahmi (bahmie): Indonesian noodle dish

barang: things, luggage; burden

b(e)landa: white; Dutch

besar: big

be siap (bersiap): be alert; prepared

bini: wife

blijver (Dutch): permanent resident of the Indies

bolos (bollosser): truant, a Dutch-Malay hybrid of "bolos," to play truant

bung (boeng): comrade; brother

celeng (tjelleng): wild boar

cemaras (tjemaras): also known as cassuarina trees; mainly planted by the Dutch

gayung (gajong): dipper or small bucket used for bathing

gamelan: Indonesian orchestral music, sometimes to accompany a shadow puppet performance or to provide musical background for a special event, like a wedding

gedèg: bamboo fence or partitition, also used as walls in huts

gudang (goedang): pantry or warehouse where goods are stored

gula jawa (goela djawa): Javanese palm sugar, made from the liquid tapped from sugar palm and coconut palm flowers.

groenbemesting (Dutch): green fertilization

Gurkha: British-Indian soldier from Nepal

Indo (Dutch): Eurasian

jongos (djongos; possibly a derivative of Dutch *jongens*): houseboy

kabaya (kabaai; kebaja): Indonesian-style long-sleeved blouse

kain: a piece of batik cloth similar to a sarong but wider and in a more traditional style

kaki (kakkies): feet

kali: river

kampung (kampong): Javanese village or neighborhood

kantor (kantoor): office

kebun (kebon): gardener, although kebun is really just "garden"; correct term for gardener is *tukang kebun*

Kempeitai (KPT) (Japanese): Japanese military police

koki (kokkie): cook

kongsi (kongsie): firm, partnership

leestrommel (Dutch): container with Dutch magazines that was circulated among the colonials and the local nobility

luak (luwak): "coffee rat"; a civet; a common predator, especially of poultry, but also known to eat ripe coffee berries

Mahratta: British Indian soldier from North Deccan

mandi (mandiën): to wash/bathe

mandur (mandoer): chief; foreman on a plantation

mantri: indigenous, lower-class civil servant

merdeka: freedom/independence

mudah (moedah): easy, convenient

nakinderen (Dutch): the children of a European man with a European woman (after he had had children with his nyai)

nasi: cooked rice

nyai (njai): Javanese concubine

nona (nonna): Mrs.

orang: person; orang b(e)landa: white person

oudgasten (Dutch): long-time Indies residents

pacul (patjol): sharpened hoe

padas: rock

pedati: wooden cart to transport goods

pelopor (from Dutch *voorloper*): scout; during the revolution associated with rebels

pemuda: youth

pisang: banana

rampok: to plunder or rob

rijsttafel (Dutch): literally "rice table," but as part of an Indonesian menu it is rice served with sample sizes of various meat and fish dishes

romusha (romoesha): forced laborer

sado: small, two-wheeled, horse-drawn carriage

sapis: oxen

sarong: long skirt, worn by men and women and tied at the waist

sawa (sawah): rice field

siri (sirih): leaves of a peppery plant, which when combined with other ingredients can be chewed like tobacco; it will turn saliva bright red

selendang (slendang): long piece of cloth worn diagonally across shoulders and hips; sometimes used to carry babies; also used by women to cover the head

soos (short for Dutch *sociëteit* Dutch): social club of the colonial class

tempo dulu (tempo doeloe): the time before, usually having to do with colonial nostalgia

toko: shop

totok: European; literally meaning "pure," it could also refer to a Chinese who had not intermarried with a local

tukang (toean): Mister/sir

trekker (Dutch): European who would return to Europe for leave

udik (oedik): the country(side)

vendutie (Dutch): estate sale

verindischen: to become like the Indonesians

voorkinderen (Dutch): the children a European man would have with his nyai

wayang (wajang): shadow puppet

waringin: tall, imposing fig tree that produces many trunks and is believed to have magical powers

warung (waroeng): roadside eatery or a stall that sells all sorts of small items, such as cigarettes

Bibliography

Alberts, A. *Per mailboot naar de Oost* [By Mailboat to the East]. Bussum: Unieboek, 1979.

Alpers, Svetlana. *The Art of Describing: Dutch Art in the Seventeenth Century.* London: John Murray, 1983.

Bauduin, D. C. M. *Het indische leven* [The Indies Life]. The Hague: H. P. Leopold, 1927.

Beekman, E.M. *Troubled Pleasures: Dutch Colonial Literature from the East Indies, 1600–1950.* Oxford: Oxford University Press, 1996.

Bing Siong, Han. "Captain Huyer and the Massive Japanese Arms Transfer in East Java in October 1945." *Bijdragen tot Taal-, Land- en Volkenkunde* 159 (2003): 291–350.

———. "The Indonesian Need of Arms after the Proclamation of Independence." *Bijdragen tot Taal-, Land- en Volkenkunde* 157 (2001): 799–830.

Boxer, Charles. *The Dutch Seaborne Empire, 1600–1800.* London: Hutchinson, 1965.

Brouwers, Jeroen. *Bezonken rood.* Amsterdam: Arbeiderspers, 1981. Translated as *Sunken Red.* New York: New Amsterdam, 1988.

———. *Het verzonkene* [The Sunken]. Amsterdam: Arbeiderspers, 1980.

———. *De zondvloed* [The Deluge]. Amsterdam: Arbeiderspers, 1988.

Brugmans, I. J., et al. *Nederlandsch-Indië onder Japanse bezetting* (The Netherlands Indies under Japanese Occupation). 2nd ed. Franeker: T. Wever, 1960.

Buruma, Ian. *Inventing Japan, 1853–1964.* New York: Modern Library, 2004.

———. *Murder in Amsterdam: The Death of Theo van Gogh and the Limits of Tolerance.* Harmondsworth: Penguin, 2006.

Chagoll, Lydia. *Buigen in Jappenkampen* [Bowing in Japanese Camps]. Mechelen: Bakermat, 1995.

Chang, Iris. *The Rape of Nanking: The Forgotten Holocaust of World War II.* New York: Basic Books, 1997.

Couperus, Louis. *Verzamelde werken* [Collected Works]. 12 vols. Amsterdam: G. A. van Oorschot, 1975.

Cribb, Robert. *Gangsters and Revolutionaries: The Jakarta People's Militia and the Indonesian Revolution, 1945–49.* Honolulu: University of Hawaii Press, 1991.

———. *Historical Dictionary of Indonesia.* London: Scarecrow Press, 1992.

Croix, Humphrey de la. *Indië herinnerd en beschouwd: Sociale geschiedenis van een kolonie, 1930–1957* [The Indies Remembered and Considered: A Social History of a Colony, 1930–1957]. Amsterdam: KJJB, 1997.

Dash, Mike. 2002. *Batavia's Graveyard: The True Story of the Mad Heretic Who Led History's Bloodiest Mutiny.* New York: Crown, 2002.

Deyssel, Lodewijk van. *De kleine republiek* [The Small Republic]. The Hague: Bert Bakker, 1975.

Dick, H. W. *Surabaya, City of Work: A Socioeconomic History, 1900–2000.* Athens: Ohio University Press, 2002.

Dommering, E. J. *De Nederlandse publieke discussie en de politionele akties in Indonesië* [The Dutch Public Discussion and the Police Action in Indonesia]. Amsterdam: Universiteit van Amsterdam, Instituut voor Informatierecht Publicaties, 1994.

Du Chattel, C. J. H. *Storm over Java* [Storm over Java]. Assen: Born, 1946.

Du Perron, Edgar. *Indies Memorandum.* Amsterdam: De Bezige Bij, 1946.

———. *Het Land van Herkomst.* Amsterdam: G. A. van Oorschot, 1935. Translated as *Country of Origin.* North Clarendon: Periplus, 1999.

Fabricius, Johan. *Hoe ik Indië terugvond* [Revisiting the Indies]. The Hague: H. P. Leopolds, 1947.

Ferguson, Niall. *The War of the World: Twentieth-Century Conflict and the Descent of the West.* Harmondsworth: Penguin, 2006.

Fernández-Armesto, Felipe. *Civilizations: Culture, Ambition, and the Transformation of Nature.* New York: Free Press, 2002.

Frederick, William. "Blood Spilled in Darkness: Killings in the Early Indonesian Revolution." 2003.

———. *Visions and Heat: The Making of the Indonesian Revolution.* Athens: Ohio University Press, 1989.

Gordon, Lyndall. *A Private Life of Henry James: Two Women and His Art.* London: Random House, 1999.

Goss, Andrew. "From Tong-Tong to Tempo Doeloe: Eurasian Memory Work and the Bracketing of Dutch Colonial History, 1957–1961." *Indonesia* 70 (October 2000): 9–36.

Goto, Ken'ichi. *Tensions of Empire: Japan and Southeast Asia in the Colonial and Postcolonial World.* Athens: Ohio University Press, 2003.

Graaf, Hermanus Johannes de. *Nederlanders over de zeeën: 350 Jaar geschiedenis van Nederland Buitengaats* [The Dutch across the Oceans: 350 Years of the Netherlands Abroad]. Utrecht: W. de Haan, 1955.

Haasse, H. *Het dieptelood van de herinnering* [The Plumb Line of Memory]. Amsterdam: Querido, 2004.

———. *Heren van de thee* [Tea Lords]. Amsterdam: Querido, 1997.

Hillen, Ernest. *The Way of a Boy: A Memoir of Java.* Harmondsworth: Penguin, 1993.

Hobhouse, Henry. *Seeds of Wealth: Five Plants That Made Men Rich.* Emeryville, CA: Shoemaker and Hoard, 2005.

Honig, Pieter, and Frans Verdoorn, eds. *Science and Scientists in the Netherlands Indies.* Cambridge: Riverside Press, 1945.

Immerzeel, B. R. van, and F. van Esch, eds. *Verzet in Nederlands-Indië tegen de Japanse bezetting, 1942–45.* (Resistance in the Netherlands Indies against the Japanese Occupation, 1942–45) The Hague: SDU, 1993.

Israel, Jonathan. *The Dutch Republic: Its Rise, Greatness, and Fall, 1477–1806.* Oxford: Oxford University Press, 1989.

Itzig Heine, H. "Aanvulling op het rapport van het Goebeng-Transport" [Supplement to the Report of the Gubeng Transport]. 1992.

———. "Een rapport over het Goebeng-Transport, Soerabaja, 28 October 1945" [A Report on the Gubeng Transport, Surabaya, October 28, 1945]. 1991.

Jacobs, Aletta H. *Reisbrieven uit Afrika en Azië, benevens enige brieven uit Zweden en Noorwegen* [Travel Letters from Africa and Asia, together with Some Letters from Sweden and Norway]. 2 vols. Almelo: W. Hilarius, 1913.

Johnson, P. *The Birth of the Modern: World Society, 1815–1830.* New York: HarperCollins, 1991.

Kramer, Diet. *Thuisvaart* [Homeward Bound]. Amsterdam: Holland, 1948.

Krancher, Jane. *The Defining Years of the Dutch East Indies, 1942–1949: Survivors' Accounts of Japanese Invasion and Enslavement of Europeans and the Revolution That Created Free Indonesia.* Jefferson, NC: McFarland, 1996.

Lulofs, Madelon H. *Rubber: A Romance of the Dutch East Indies.* London: Cassell, 1931.

Matthijs, Hein. *Rennen voor je leven* [Run for Your Life]. Schoorl: Conserve, 1994.

McMillan, Richard. *The British Occupation of Indonesia, 1945–1946: Britain, the Netherlands and the Indonesian Revolution.* London: Routledge, 2005.

Meelhuijsen, Willy. *Revolutie in Soerabaja, 17 augustus–1 december 1945* [Revolution in Surabaya, August 17–December 1, 1945]. Zutphen: Walburg, 2000.

Milton, Giles. *Nathaniel's Nutmeg, or, The True and Incredible Adventures of the Spice Trader Who Changed the Course of History.* New York: Farrar, Straus and Giroux, 1999.

Multatuli [Edward Douwes Dekker]. *Max Havelaar of de koffieveilingen der Nederlandse Handelsmaatschappij* [Max Havelaar, or The Coffee Auctions of the Dutch Trading Company]. Amsterdam: J. de Ruyter, 1860.

Nieuwenhuys, Rob. *Mirror of the Indies: A History of Dutch Colonial Literature.* Edited by E. M. Beekman. Translated by Frans van Rosevelt. University of Massachusetts Press, 1982.

―――. *Tussen twee vaderlanden* [Between Two Fatherlands]. Amsterdam: G. A. van Oorschot, 1959.

―――, ed. *Van roddelpraat en literatuur: Een keuze uit het werk van Nederlandse schrijvers uit het voormalige Nederlands-Indië* [On Gossip and Literature: A Selection from the Oeuvre of Dutch Writers from the Former Netherlands Indies]. Amsterdam: Querido, 1965.

Nieuwenhuys-Lindner, Maria. "Een duik in de diepte: Herinnering aan de periode 1940–45." [A Dive into the Depths: A Remembrance of the Period 1940–45]. N.d.

Okker, F. *Dirklands tussem de doerians: Een biografie van Willem Walraven* [Dirklands among the Durians: A Biography of Willem Walraven]. Amsterdam: Bas Lubberhuizen, 2000.

Penders, C. L. M., ed. and trans. *Indonesia: Selected Documents on Colonialism and Nationalism, 1830–1942.* Brisbane: University of Queensland Press, 1977.

Pramoedya Ananta Toer. *All That Is Gone.* New York: Hyperion, 2004.

―――. *The Mute's Soliloquy.* New York: Hyperion, 1999.

Prick, Harry G. M. *In zekerheid van eigen heerlijkheid: Het leven van Lodewijk van Deyssel tot 1890* [In the Certainty of One's Own Magnificence: The Life of Lodewijk van Deyssel until 1890]. Amsterdam: Athenaeum-Polak and Van Gennep, 1997.

Raben, Remco. *Representing the Japanese Occupation of Indonesia: Personal Testimonies and Public Images in Indonesia, Japan and the Netherlands.* Zwolle: Waanders, 1999.

Rees, Laurence. *Horror in the East: Japan and the Atrocities of World War II.* London: BBC Books, 2001.

Reid, Anthony, and Oki Akira. *The Japanese Experience in Indonesia: Selected Memoirs of 1942–1945.* Athens: Ohio University Center for International Studies and Center for Southeast Asian Studies, 1986.

Ricklefs, M. C. 1993. *A History of Modern Indonesia since circa 1300,* 2nd ed. Stanford: Stanford University Press, 1993.

Rinzema-Admiraal, Winnie. *Dit was uw Tjideng: Aspecten van de vertraagde afwikkeling van Japanse interneringskampen in Batavia met Tjideng als casus* [This Was Your Tjideng: Aspects of the Delayed Processing of the Japanese Internment Camps in Batavia with Tjideng as a Case Study]. Utrecht: Stichting ICODO, 2004.

———. *Java, Het laatste front* [Java, the Last Front]. Zutphen: Walburg, 2000.

———. "De plantersaffaires in Oost-Java: Planters, Landwacht en Kempeitai in de Oosthoek" [The Planters' Conspiracies in Eastern Java: Planters, Landwacht and Kempeitai]. In *Het Einde van Indië: Indische Nederlanders tijdens de Japanse bezetting en de dekolonisatie,* edited by Wim Willems and Jaap de Moor, 139–56. The Hague: SDU, 1995.

———. "Wat de Atoombom voorkwam: Het Liquidatieplan van Japon voor de geïnterneerden van de Pacific" [What the Atomic Bomb Prevented: The Japanese Liquidation Plan for Pacific Internees]. Leeuwarden: KSB Repro BV, 2008.

Rush, James R., ed. *Java: A Traveller's Anthology.* Oxford: Oxford University Press, 1999.

Said, Edward. *Culture and Imperialism.* New York: Knopf, 1993.

———. *Orientalism.* New York: Vintage, 1978.

Sato, Shigeru. *War, Nationalism and Peasants: Java under the Japanese Occupation, 1942–1945.* Armonk, NY: M. E. Sharpe, 1994.

Schama, Simon. *The Embarrassment of Riches: An Interpretation of Dutch Culture in the Golden Age.* London: Collins, 1987.

Scidmore, Eliza Ruhamah. 1897. *Java: The Garden of the East.* New York: Century, 1897.

Shetter, William Z. *The Netherlands in Perspective: The Dutch Way of Organizing a Society and Its Setting.* Utrecht: Nederlands Centrum Buitenlanders, 2002.

Shorto, Russell. *The Island at the Center of the World: The Epic Story of Dutch Manhattan, the Forgotten Colony That Shaped America.* New York: Doubleday, 2004.

Snoek, Kees. *Edgar du Perron: Het leven van een smalle mens* [Edgar du Perron: The Life of a Narrow Person]. Amsterdam: Nijgh and Van Ditmar, 2005.

Stoler, Ann Laura. *Carnal Knowledge and Imperial Power: Race and the Intimate in Colonial Rule.* Berkeley and Los Angeles: University of California Press, 2002.

Tarling, Nicholas. *A Sudden Rampage: The Japanese Occupation of Southeast Asia, 1941–1945.* Honolulu: University of Hawaii Press, 2001.

Taylor, Jean Gelman. *The Social World of Batavia: European and Eurasian in Dutch Asia.* Madison: University of Wisconsin Press, 1983.

Touwen-Bouwsma, Elly. "The Indonesian Nationalists and the Japanese 'Liberation' of Indonesia: Visions and Reactions." *Journal of Southeast Asia Studies* 27 (1996): 1–18.

Touwen-Bouwsma, Elly, and P. M. H. Groen, eds. *Tussen Banzai en Bersiap: De afwikkeling van de tweede wereldoorlog in Nederlands-Indië* [Between Banzai and Bersiap: The Completion of the Second World War in the Netherlands Indies]. The Hague: SDU, 1996.

Turner, Jack. *Spice: The History of a Temptation.* New York: Knopf, 2004.

Van Doorn, Iens. *Geluk is als een vogel: Roman uit de nadagen van Nederlandsch-Indië* [Happiness Is Like a Bird: A Novel from the End of Days of the Dutch East Indies]. Franeker: T. Wever, 1981.

Veth, Bas. *Het leven in Nederlandsch-Indië* [Life in the Dutch East Indies]. Amsterdam: Thomas and Eras, 1977.

Vissering, C. M. *Een reis door Oost-Java* [A Trip through Eastern Java]. Haarlem: F. Bohn, 1912.

Vlekke, Bernard H. M. *The Story of the Dutch East Indies.* Cambridge, MA: Harvard University Press, 1946.

Voorneman, Richard. *Banjoe Biroe XI: Een vrouwenkamp op Java* [Banyubiru XI: A Women's Camp in Java]. Utrecht: Stichting ICODO, 1995.

Walraven, Willem. *Brieven aan familie en vrienden, 1919–1941* [Letters to Family and Friends, 1919–1941]. Amsterdam: G. A. van Oorschot, 1966.

Wehl, David. *The Birth of Indonesia.* London: George Allen and Unwin, 1949.

Willems, Wim, and Jap de Moor, eds. *Het einde van Indië: Indische Nederlanders tijdens de Japanse bezetting en dekolonisatie* [The End of the Indies: Indies Dutch People during the Japanese Occupation and the Decolonization]. The Hague: SDU, 1995.

Willems, Wim, et al., eds. 1997. *Uit Indië geboren: Vier eeuwen familiegeschiedenis* [Born in the Indies: Four Centuries of Family History]. Zwolle: Waanders, 1997.

Zwaag, Jaap van der. *Verloren tropische zaken: De opkomst en ondergang van de Nederlandse handel- en cultuurmaatschappijen in het voormalige Nederlands-Indië* [Lost Tropical Matters: The Rise and Fall of the Dutch Trading and Cultivation Companies in the Former Dutch East Indies]. Meppel: De Feniks Pers, 1991.

Zwaan, Jacob. *Oorlog en verzet in Nederlands-Indië, 1941–1949, en de voorlichting aan de na-oorlogse generaties* [War and Resistance in the Dutch East Indies, 1941–1949, and the Information Stream to the Postwar Generations]. Amsterdam: De Bataafsche Leeuw, 1989.

Index

Meelhuijsen, Willy, xiv, 46, 171, 175, 177,
180, 185, 193, 194, 196, 198, 199, 200, 201,
202–4, 205, 209, 215, 218, 221, 257n2,
258n17
Mees, Regnerus, 235
Merdeka committees, 120, 122
Mestizo, 10, 12, 13, 29, 34, 54
Mijer, Pieter (governor general), 235
Mil, J. G. van, 153
Mills, John, 64
Milton, Giles: *Nathaniel's Nutmeg,* 8, 239n12,
239n15
Mook, H. J. van, 182, 189
Mountbatten, Edwina, 176
Mountbatten, Louis, 172, 179, 200
Mulder, P. M., 149
Multatuli: *Max Havelaar,* xviii, xx, 19, 49,
214, 249n3
Muntinghe, Herman, 18
Mussert, Anton, 94
Mussolini, Benito, 90
Mustopo, 186, 195, 196, 199, 205
Mute's Soliloquy, The (Pramoedya Ananta
Toer), 46, 124, 130

NA, xxii, 238n6
Nagamatsu (nickname, Aurora), 150
Nagano, Yuichiro, 179
Nagasaki, 170. *See also* atomic bombs
nakinderen, 61
Nanking massacres, 116, 129, 135
Napoleon (emperor), 16
Nathaniel's Nutmeg (Milton), 8, 239n12,
239n15
Nationaal Archief (NA), xxii, 238n6
Nationaal-Socialistische Beweging. *See* NSB
nationalism (Indonesian), 47, 76, 93–94, 115,
120, 154, 170, 174, 178, 182, 187, 248n18.
See also independence (Indonesian);
Sukarno
Nederlandse Handelsmaatschappij. *See* NHM
Nederlands Instituut voor Oorlogsdocumen-
tatie. *See* NIOD
NEFIS, 147, 251n1
Netherlands Foreign Intelligence Service.
See NEFIS
Netherlands Indies Civil Administration.
See NICA
Netherlands Railway System, 229, 259n7
Neve, Roel de, 95
NHM, 16, 18, 19
NICA, 192, 193, 220, 256n16
Nieuwenhuys, Rob, 7, 12, 52, 67, 74, 100,
244n18

Nieuwenhuys-Lindner, Maria, xiii, 172, 173,
176, 187, 188, 189, 191, 194, 196
Nightingale, Florence, 14
Nijholt, Willem, 159
Nijk, Dr. H., 149
NIOD, xiv, xxii, 230, 238n6
NRC Handelsblad, xiv, 243n12
NSB, 93, 95
nyais, 52–54, 61, 62, 63, 74, 235. *See also* Indies
society

Okker, Frank, 34
Olivier, Johannes, 12, 29, 30
Olivier, Laurence, 78
Oorlogsgravenstichting, 238n6
Oostwaarts (Couperus), 15, 30, 57, 73, 78–80,
81, 85, 94, 95, 111, 138
opium (trade), 29, 61
Oranje Hotel, 82, 88, 184–86, 190, 256n18
orientalism, 121
Orientalism (Said), 7
oudgasten, 29, 76, 79
Out of Africa (Dinesen), 2

Paradise Road, 159, 160
Partai Nasional Indonesia. See PNI
Pattynama, Pamela, 106, 121
Pauls, Adriana (née Kervel), 31
Pearl Harbor, 116, 118, 119, 155
Pemuda Republik Indonesia. See PRI
People's Council, 50, 119
Per mailboot naar de Oost (Alberts), 23, 79
Perron, Edgar du: *Country of Origin,* 1, 20,
23, 74, 77; *Indies Memorandum,* 76, 80–81,
93, 94
Perserikatan Nasional Indonesia. See PNI
Planters' Conspiracy, 137, 138, 140, 143, 144,
146–54
Plas, Charles van der, 193
Ploeg, R. van der, xxii
Ploegman, V. W. C., 185
PNI, 75
Pol, Susanna van der, 31
police actions, xviii, 139, 215, 219, 220, 227,
229, 237n1
Potgieter, E. J., 77
Potsdam Conference, 171, 172
Pramoedya Ananta Toer: *The Mute's Solilo-
quy,* 46, 130–31
PRI, 186, 190, 191, 193
Prick, Harry G. M., 20–22
Proklamasi, 170–71, 219
prostitution, forced by Japanese, 129, 130,
135, 166. *See also* comfort women